'DON'T CALL ME CLYDE!'

- Jazz Journey of a Sixties Stomper -

PETER KERR

Oasis-WERP

Published by Oasis-WERP 2016

ISBN: 978-0-9576586-2-2

A catalogue record of this book is available from
the British Library

www.peter-kerr.co.uk

Cover design © Glen Kerr

Typeset by Ben Ottridge
www.benottridge.co.uk

ABOUT THE AUTHOR

Best-selling Scottish author Peter Kerr is a former jazz musician, record producer and farmer. His award-winning *Snowball Oranges* series of humorous travel books was inspired by his family's adventures while running a small orange farm on the Spanish island of Mallorca during the 1980s. Peter's books are sold worldwide and have been translated into several languages.

In the early 1960s he was clarinettist/leader of Scotland's premier jazz band, the Clyde Valley Stompers. The reason for the band's unlikely demise, at the height of its fame, is revealed for the first time in this enthralling book.

www.peter-kerr.co.uk

The author in 1960, age 19.

INTRODUCTION

THE CLYDE VALLEY STOMPERS were Scotland's premier jazz band and its first ever super group; Caledonian kings of the 'Trad Boom' that swept Britain during the late Fifties and early Sixties; creators of a phenomenon dubbed 'Stompermania' decades before most of the country's current pop and rock idols were even born. Yet in 1963, 'The Clydes', at the height of their commercial success, disappeared from the scene. Conspiracy theories were rife, but the true reason for this trailblazing band's untimely demise has never been revealed – until now.

Here is the story as told by clarinettist Peter 'Pete' Kerr who, in 1961 at just twenty years of age, inherited leadership of the Stompers after they'd moved their base from Glasgow to London. During what had become the most disruptive period in its already turbulent history, the band stormed the charts for the first time the following year with their recording of Prokofiev's *Peter and the Wolf*, produced by George Martin, soon to sign the Beatles.

A frenzy of incessant touring followed, punctuated by frequent network TV appearances in the company of big-star names of the day, like Shirley Bassey, Danny Williams, Brenda Lee, Morecambe and Wise, Dusty Springfield and the Beatles themselves. The Clydes also played the title music for Norman Wisdom's 1962 movie *On the Beat*, and appeared soon after in *It's All Happening* with Tommy Steele. Then, to the dismay and bewilderment of the Stompers' legions of fans, the curtain came down – literally.

But this is more than just a chronicle of the highlights and hardships, the bonhomie and back-stabbing, the generosity and greed that marked the rise and fall of one of the most iconic British bands of its time. It's also an affectionate recollection of family life in rural Scotland during the austerity-gripped years following the Second World War, and of how a young lad went all out to realise his dream of one day playing jazz for a living. It's an account of how friendships forged through a common love of music can develop into bonds sufficiently strong to survive fate's toughest trials. Well, provided you have a sense of humour to match (or temper!) an indefatigable faith in human nature, that is!

And a sense of humour is what carries Peter's childhood sweetheart Ellie through a seemingly ill-starred courtship into a marriage destined to withstand, not just the rigours of the unpredictable world of itinerant jazz musicians, but also the test of time. For this is a story that lays the foundations of a young couple's roller coaster ride through life which, in time, will introduce them to adventures and misadventures, to places, people and experiences that they could never have imagined. As such, *Don't Call Me Clyde!* is a precursor of Peter Kerr's bestselling *Snowball Oranges* series of humorous Mallorcan travelogues, and a companion to their set-in-Scotland prequel *Thistle Soup*.

So, whether or not you have an interest in or knowledge of jazz, this is a story that will entertain, surprise and amuse in equal measure – and will occasionally shock as well!

CONTENTS

"But pleasures are like poppies spread –
You seize the flow'r, its bloom is shed;
Or like the snow falls in the river –
A moment white – then melts forever."

(From *Tam o' Shanter* – Robert Burns, 1759–96)

CHAPTER ONE

'DOWN THE STAIRWAY TO THE STARS'

'THE CAVERN' – two white-painted words curving above a doorway in a Liverpool back street that struck me as one of the most drab and easily forgettable places I had ever laid eyes on. Yet this was the setting of what was to become an icon as far-famed and instantly associated with Britain as the tower of Big Ben itself. Pasted over the graffiti on a brick wall beside the doorway, a poster announced:

Tonight
THE CLYDE VALLEY STOMPERS
Scotland's No 1 Jazz Band!
(with Support Group)
8pm – Admission 6/-

'Where d'ya think you're goin', skin?' the bruiser guarding the door grunted.

I was the only other living soul in the street, so I knew he had to be talking to me. I nodded at the poster. 'I'm with the band.'

'Oh yeah? Wot one?

'The Clyde Valley Stompers.'

He glowered at me with a look that left me in no doubt that he considered himself king of the alley. However humble his domain, he was ready – itching even – to defend it.

'Honest, I'm the clarinet player,' I said with as much self-assurance as I could muster. 'And, ehm, the leader … as well, actually.'

His frown deepened. 'Yeah, and I'm 'er Majesty the bleedin' Queen!'

'Fair enough,' I came back, trying not to appear too cowed, 'you can check with the rest of the boys. They're in there, setting up.'

'Where *you* been, then?'

I hooked my thumb over my shoulder. 'Parking the bandwagon.'

'You the roadie, then?'

'Nah, we don't have one. I do the driving.'

'Thotcha sez ya was the bandleader.'

This conversation was going nowhere, and neither, apparently, was I.

The gorilla's brows lowered still further as his eyes wandered down my right arm. 'Worra ya gorrin yer 'andbag?'

I was sorely tempted to voice disapproval at having my faux snakeskin instrument case so unjustly demeaned, but my teeth were a vital part of my stock-in-trade, so I kept them clenched. I opened the case to reveal the matching pair of Selmer Paris clarinets nestling in velvet-lined luxury within. They'd been hard-earned and were my pride and joy.

A sneer tugged at the corner of the bouncer's mouth. 'See yerself as some kinda Jock version of Acker bleedin' Bilk, do ya?'

I thought it prudent to reply with a non-committal shrug.

A few tense moments ticked by. 'Awright then,' the bruiser finally growled. He shuffled aside from the door. 'Gerrin! An' next time ya come out, gerra fookin' pass! Awright?'

*

If the attitude of the doorman had seemed a mite chilly, the same most certainly could not be said for the reception afforded us by the jiving mass crammed into the club that night. The Sixties were now getting properly under way and the young folk of Liverpool were set to make them swing with a vengeance. The Cavern, originally a jazz club when it opened in 1957, had yielded to skiffle during the height of the washboard-and-tea-chest craze, but was enthusiastically promoting jazz once again. Now, whenever one of the top bands was on tour in the north-west of England, Sunday night at The Cavern had become an automatic fixture.

Although this policy was soon to be swept away by the biggest sea change ever in popular music, no-one could have foreseen that the reason would be a global eruption in the popularity of a bunch of young Liverpudlians who'd cut their musical teeth playing interval spots for jazz bands.

Many of these 'beat groups', as fledgling rockers like the Beatles were referred to at the time, had started out playing skiffle themselves. This two- and three-chord derivation of primitive American folk, gospel and blues was first popularised in Britain by splinter groups set up within, ironically, trad jazz outfits. The prime mover had been Lonnie Donegan, banjoist in the Chris Barber Band, who, switching to acoustic guitar, would lead his fellow rhythm section members in an interlude of novelty vocal ditties to give the band's horn players a breather.

But the skiffle craze soon passed. Accordingly, 'beat' was regarded by many music business experts as just another fad the fickle followers of pop would also discard before too long. Trad jazz was booming and jazz bands, with their customary line-up of trumpet, trombone, clarinet, bass, drums, banjo and (in some cases) piano, were, for the present at least, what young people flocked into clubs to dance to.

It has to be said, however, that a fair measure of creative licence would need to be applied to the word 'dance' by anyone attempting to describe what took place on the floor of The Cavern on a Sunday night.

This was a cellar of the low, vaulted variety, entered from street level by a narrow stairway which, as far as I could make out, would also serve as the only exit in the event of fire. It has been said, I think a tad unfairly, that when empty the Cavern had the appearance of a brick-lined sewer with alcoves off. My own first impressions were of a miniature underground station that had been blocked off at both ends, leaving enough room for maybe a hundred or so customers to strut their stuff in. But the reality was that well upwards of five times that number of determined clubbers would pack in there when a popular band was playing.

Dancing, therefore, was strictly of the stomp-on-the-spot kind; a technique more evocative of the grape-treading tub than the ballroom floor. Clearly, any hand movement above thigh level would risk inflicting injury on fellow dancers, so manual rhythmic expression was best limited to finger-popping – particularly in front of the bandstand. On a busy Sunday night, there was always the risk of a trombone player having his slide whipped away by the flailing arm of an over-enthusiastic jive monkey.

In such an enclosed and crowded venue, air conditioning would have been mandatory, had present-day regulations applied. Actually, ventilation of *any* kind would have been a godsend, but there was no evidence of even that back then. Not going by the Turkish-bath conditions prevailing on the tiny bandstand, at any rate. A one-night gig in The Cavern would inevitably result in even the leanest of musicians losing several pounds of body weight. It was a veritable sweat box, and the condensation glistening on the walls when the joint was jumping bore ample testament to that.

Conditions were no better in what passed for a band room. This was nothing more than a small recess at the side of the stage: a depository for outdoor clothes and instrument cases which had to be shared with the support group. When stumbling in there drenched with perspiration at cross-over time, you could cut the fug with a knife. The aroma of Old Spice mingling with cigarette smoke and the hum of b.o. would linger long in the nostrils.

There was a certain snobbery about jazz musicians when it came to guys who played pop music. It wasn't an openly declared attitude, nor even one discussed at any length in private. It was just assumed that we all agreed pop musicians to be in some way inferior, because ... well, because they didn't play jazz. That they may have been equal to or even better than ourselves as musicians didn't come into it. We saw them all as guitar-twanging posers, more interested in wearing tight-arsed jeans to titillate birds and looning about on stage to impress each other than actually ... well, playing jazz. And how about all their ear-splitting amplification? Take that away from your average two- and three-chord beat group, and what would be left? That's right – skiffle.

It may well be, of course, that similar derogatory thoughts about us jazzers were harboured by the beat boys. Given that each of our chosen brands of music stemmed from the same American roots, they could justifiably consider that we, although of the same generation as themselves, were stuck in a groove that hadn't changed all that much for decades, while they at least were attempting to take the music forward, albeit in an unashamedly brash form.

But musicians, no matter what their persuasion, are respectful towards their peers – in public at least. So, no discourteous words, or even looks, were exchanged as the four lads in The Cavern's interval group squeezed past us. A nod and a grunted 'Aye, aye!' or 'How's it goin'?' was the only communication; not that there would have been either time or space for anything more sociable, even if we'd felt so inclined. We were as relieved to get off that sweat-box stage as the beat group appeared keen to get on. And it immediately became apparent why.

Unbilled on the poster outside these boys may have been, but the audience were well aware of who they were, and they made their delight at seeing them amply obvious the moment they emerged from the band room. If the roof had had rafters, the cheering would have brought them down. But that was nothing compared to the noise that accompanied the intro to the group's first song and continued unabated right through to the end of their set.

Screaming! Screaming so loud it drowned out whatever sounds were blasting from all that amplification gear. Row upon row of girls were working themselves into hysterics in front of the stage. A peppering of boys too. Not dancing, not finger-popping, just screaming and shouting themselves into a frenzy over a band they couldn't even hear.

To a purveyor of acoustic music like myself, this was a disquieting new phenomenon indeed. Could this be the way things were heading? I mentioned my misgivings to our piano player Bert Murray when we were climbing the stairs at the end of the gig.

'Local band,' said Bert with patent disinterest. 'You get these over-the-top reactions. Probably a set-up as well. All stage-managed by the club. Like happened way back with Sinatra. Know what I mean?'

Bert was quite a bit older than me, and had been on the road a lot longer, so I respected his opinion – usually. But he must have noticed a look of doubt in my expression this time.

'Nah, don't worry about it, man,' he muttered. 'Ten-a-penny round here, these beat combos. Electric skiffle groups, I call them. Seven-day wonders. Here today, gone tomorrow.'

Who was I to argue? And why should I bother about possible competition from unbilled interval bands in a scruffy little back-street dungeon like this? In a few days we'd be playing London's Royal Albert Hall, in a festival featuring the foremost jazz bands in Britain. On top of that, our latest single, which we'd recorded for an up-and-coming producer called George Martin in EMI's Abbey Road Studios, was heading for the charts, and a string of promotional appearances on network TV had already been lined up. With our date sheet full to overflowing for months ahead, the future for the Clyde Valley Stompers could hardly have looked more rosy.

Banishing all thoughts of screaming teenagers and electric skiffle groups from my mind, I stepped from the depths of The Cavern into the Liverpool night. It was raining. In the glow of a solitary street light, puddles reflected the buildings rising dark and forbidding on either side of the alley. The scene reminded me of some ancient black-and-white movie, set in Al Capone's Chicago. Suddenly, the optimistic thoughts I'd been doing my best to nurture were replaced by the echo of words that had been spoken almost two years earlier and had haunted me ever since...

* * * * *

CHAPTER TWO

'IF THE WOMEN DON'T GET YOU, THE LIQUOR MUST!'

'He'll end up dead in the gutter!' The prediction was delivered with a matter-of-fact raising of the shoulders. 'Prostitutes and rotgut booze. Way of life in that game. The pox and cirrhosis of the liver … always ends the same … seen it all too often .'

My mother summoned up a weak smile, trying, no doubt, to give the impression that she took the words to have been spoken in jest, though unable to disguise the fact that she knew otherwise. She said nothing.

My father forced out one of his let's-lighten-things-up-a-bit laughs, as was his way when such conversational chasms opened before him. 'Aye, very good, Fergus,' he chuckled. 'Prostitutes and rotgut booze, eh? You have a grand sense of humour, right enough.' He took our guest's glass. 'Here,' he grinned, almost convincingly, 'have another drink!'

'Dope as well,' Fergus declared, warming to his theme. 'Marijuana and heroin.'

'Sorry,' said Dad, still grinning gamely, 'we're right out of them, so you'll have to make do with this.' He poured our guest a beer.

My mother was now busying herself re-washing washed dishes in the sink. She still said nothing, but her body language spoke volumes. I felt a sudden surge of remorse, quickly followed by one of sympathy. Remorse for having given my mother such deep cause for concern, and sympathy for the disappointment she was clearly now feeling. Yet she had shown no evidence of either emotion until now.

'What do you think about our Peter setting out as a professional jazz musician?' she'd asked Fergus, in some hope, I now realised, of having her mind put at ease by the opinion of this self-vaunted man of the world.

His cynical reply had been the last thing she'd wanted to hear. And the smug way he'd said it added anger to the confusion of feelings now flooding through me. I wanted to come right out and ask Fergus what the hell he knew about jazz musicians anyway. But I kept my lip firmly buttoned. I was nineteen, Fergus was in his fifties, and I had been brought up to show respect for my elders, even those I didn't think particularly worthy of it.

What made the situation even more awkward was that I'd always suspected that neither of my parents thought much of Fergus either. He was some sort of distant relation of my Dad's, who appeared unannounced on mercifully rare occasions when he 'just happened to be in the area'. He'd served in the Royal Navy during World War II, and my guess was that his clichéd concept of clap-ridden, junky musicians may have been influenced more by the habits of some of his own shipmates than by any exponents of jazz he'd bumped into on his travels. What's more, he had the swaggering air of someone trying very hard to give the impression he'd commanded vessels significantly more eminent than the clutch of rowing boats he now hired out in a down-at-heel holiday resort in the west of Scotland. Fergus was a braggart and a bore, and he had deliberately hurt my mother's feelings, as well as gratuitously predicting my descent into the gutter.

Nevertheless, here I was, obliged to be polite to him as we stood in the kitchen of our family home on the outskirts of Haddington, the hub of the agricultural county of East Lothian, seventeen miles east of Edinburgh, Scotland's capital city. It was 1960, and Britain was finally showing signs of making a real recovery from the long years of post-war austerity my parents' generation had had to weather. Yet I had just chosen to give up the securest of careers to embark upon one of the most precarious imaginable.

'Yeah,' Fergus smirked, without even a glance in my direction, 'dead in the gutter. That's where he'll end up.' He raised his glass and slapped Dad's shoulder. 'Happy days, mate!'

Now it was my father's turn to say nothing.

*

I could never have dreamt that learning to play the bagpipes as a ten-year-old would point me towards such an unexpected path through life, or would lead to such anguish for my parents. But that's the stamp that joining the Haddington Boys' Pipe Band had put on things.

It was barely six years after the end of the war, its lingering aftermath meaning that most families were obliged to live within fairly modest means. Food rationing was still in force, although there generally wasn't enough money about to buy anything but the bare essentials anyway. TV was years away from being within everyone's reach – both technically and financially – so home entertainment meant listening to the radio or gramophone, playing board games or cards, or, for those who could, making music.

My father, also called Peter, worked at the time as a clerk for a local road haulage company. He was a dapper little chap, with a neatly-trimmed Douglas Fairbanks Jr moustache and an impish twinkle in his eye. As an incorrigible, though strictly amateur, 'tickler of the ivories', he'd always made sure there was a piano in the house. And even if, as in 1951, his current instrument had seen better days, he never grudged paying to have it tuned. This, in my mother's opinion, was a shameful waste of money.

'It wouldn't be so bad if you could play the damned thing,' she would grouse, 'but your so-called honky-tonk is nothing but a hotchpotch of rubbish. My god, we had a cat back home that could play better – and he was only running up and down the keys trying to get at the mice inside!'

'Back home' for my mother was the northern Orkney island of Sanday, where her father, Tom Muir, farmed a 600-acre spread called Backaskaill. Her mother was the local school mistress. There had always been a piano in the Backaskaill front room, too, and my grandmother, herself an accomplished pianist, had taught my mother and two sisters to play 'properly'; which meant learning to read music.

This was a skill my father had never mastered, nor felt any need to. Playing by ear was his thing. Consequently, no matter what my mother said to the contrary, honky-tonk was what he heard when his fingers thumped the ivories on his old upright. And as if to substantiate this conviction, he'd then make a point of declaring that no bloody mice lived inside *his* joanna!

'They'd need to be tone-deaf if they did,' was Mum's standard reply.

To which Dad would blurt out, 'OK, let's see if you can do any better yourself, *Mrs* Fats Waller!'

But she never took the bait. While she hadn't kept up her piano practice beyond her teens, she could still sit down, when the mood took her, and play from the sheet music of any popular song that was put in front of her – yet quick to admit that she did so a lot more hesitantly than when a girl. The fact of the matter was, though, that Mum was neither

21

as keen on playing the piano as my father, nor did she have his natural 'ear'. In truth, if he had been subjected to the same musical discipline as a child, there's no doubting his piano playing prowess would have developed far beyond the enthusiastic mangling of Fats Waller favourites and the like that had become his trademark.

He may have been, in my mother's words, a poor imitation of a ham-fisted pub piano player of the most lowbrow kind, but he was happy to be just that. And he never missed an opportunity to prove it to anyone who happened to be around when there was a piano handy. Captive audiences at wedding receptions and funeral wakes were his favourite victims, their (and his) generous intake of alcohol contributing considerably to the raucous merriment that his brand of musical mayhem invariably generated. Many were the newly-weds and corpses sent cheerily on their way to his jangle-box accompaniment of *Somebody Stole My Gal* or *After You've Gone*. And if a bar or two of the melody had been missed or added here and there, by that stage in proceedings few of those singing along would notice – or care, even if they did.

Nor did the traditional music of his homeland escape Dad's attentions. He never failed to tune in to the weekly *Scottish Dance Music* programme on the BBC's Home Service. The volume of the radio would be screwed fully up, all the better to hear what the featured band was playing while he mercilessly pounded the piano in unison – or as near unison as his limited grasp of key signatures would permit. Mother always shut herself in the kitchen on these occasions.

But my sister Minnie and I usually braved it out in the front room, although for very different reasons. Minnie, fifteen months my senior, had already started piano lessons, so she would stand beside Dad, scrutinising his keyboard-thumping and yelling at him whenever she noticed a clanger being dropped. Not that this made any difference, other than adding a vocal element to the prevailing instrumental bedlam.

Meanwhile, I would sit with a finger in one ear, the other ear glued to the radio.

I suppose I had traditional Scottish music in my genes. My father always told us that his father, the first of a trio of Peter Kerrs, had been weaned on it in the little East Lothian mining town of Prestonpans, and by adolescence had become proficient at 'sook-blawin'' a fair-sized repertoire on the mouth organ. Then, while still in his teens, he escaped the grim darkness of the local colliery for the fresh-air life of a professional footballer. During a long career, which saw him play for each of the three top-division teams Scotland's capital boasted at the time, he was introduced to a wider social circle than might have been likely had he remained 'doon the pit'. One enduring friendship he formed was with a pioneer of Scottish accordion music called Peter Leatham, universally regarded as one of the most gifted players of the instrument in the years between the two World Wars.

It was probably exposure to Peter Leatham's talent that inspired my father to strap on a squeeze-box whenever he could get his hands on one, then attempt to get his fingers round a toe-tapping composition of Peter's called *Shufflin' Sammy*. In it's day, this had been regarded as a test piece for aspiring accordionists, and although my father did his best to negotiate the tricky nuances of the tune, he never quite cracked it. Still, his attempts had sounded pretty impressive to the untutored ears of a toddler like me.

So, too, had my maternal grandfather's belting out of Scottish Country Dance standards on his melodeon. This diminutive, button-keyed accordion operated on the same suck-blow principle as my other grandfather's mouth organ – except that, in the melodeon's case, the technique involved either pulling or pushing the instrument's bellows to obtain two different notes from the same button. Not a music machine for anyone but the most dexterous to grapple with.

For all that, old Tom Muir, his fingers like bananas from a lifetime of working with heavy horses, could still dazzle with the lightness of his touch. He and my grandmother had moved from their native Orkney to a farm near Haddington shortly before the Second World War. Some of my earliest memories are of visiting them every Sunday afternoon, and I recall that it never took long for my father to ask old Tom to fetch out his little ten-button Hohner melodeon for a 'swaree' after tea in the front room, where the piano just happened to be located.

So, without really noticing, I gradually became familiar with many of the old-favourite jigs, hornpipes, marches, strathspeys and reels that, only a few years later, were coming at me full-belt through the radio in our own front room. The difference now, of course, was that the same tunes were being played by the slickest Scottish Country Dance musicians in the land, and no group of them was slicker than the band led by ace button-key accordionist Jimmy Shand. Jimmy was already a worldwide legend, whose path, although I couldn't have imagined it back then, would eventually cross my own and have a considerable influence on my life.

As would joining the Haddington Boys' Pipe Band...

* * * * *

CHAPTER THREE

'FROM JIGS TO JAZZ'

'They teach ye to play the bagpipes and ye get a kilt for nothin'!'

I hadn't had reason to consider either of these opportunities before, but they'd been presented with such enthusiasm by my pal Derek Dewar that my curiosity was kindled.

'But how much does it cost for the lessons?' I checked. Kids born during the war like us were popularly known as 'Utility Babies', conditioned to food rationing, make-do-and-mend clothing and having to watch every penny. This mindset was still pertinent in the summer of 1951, even for ten-year-olds.

'Nothin'!' said Derek. 'Honest, ye just have to buy yer practice chanter. It's about thirty shillins, but they'll maybe let ye pay it up, if ye're skint.'

I *was* skint. All kids were skint in 1951, or so it seemed to me. My own weekly pocket money amounted to threepence, which was enough to buy a pocketful of hard little pears from an orchard near the school on Fridays. I did a quick calculation. Thirty shillings equalled three hundred and sixty pence. That's a lot of pears! It was immediately obvious that, even if I denied myself the pears, it would take an awfully long time to save up for a chanter. Too long. And I also knew that paying it up wouldn't be an option, as my parents would never entertain buying anything on the never-never.

'Where did *you* get the money to buy a chanter?' I asked Derek, curious as to how my equally skint chum had suddenly struck it rich.

'I haven't got the money,' he shrugged, '– yet. But they're lookin' for kids to pick berries on the wee fruit farms along the Pencaitland Road, so...'

*

So, we spent the rest of our summer holidays picking strawberries – and raspberries – and blackcurrants – and redcurrants – and gooseberries – and whatever else needed picking when the weather was right. By the time the pipe band was ready for its next intake of rookies in the autumn, Derek and I were there with enough money in our fruit-stained mitts to buy our chanters.

These little eight-hole instruments, a scaled-down version of the 'melody' pipe on a full set of bagpipes, look a bit like a cross between a snake-charmer's flute and a recorder. Made from African Blackwood with imitation ivory mountings, our MacPherson student models were regarded as being excellent value for money, and of proven quality too. Having a copy of *Logan's Bagpipe Tutor* included in the price made us even more pleased with our investment of all that berry-picking time as we joined a handful of other hopefuls for our first lesson.

One evening a week from then throughout the winter, we'd sit at little desks in a classroom of Haddington Primary School while Davie MacLeod, a veteran ex-army piper with the patience of Job, shepherded us through the rudiments of fingering, then on to playing scales and reading the related notation as written on the stave. Unlike the blood-curdling skirl of the full-blown Highland bagpipes, the little practice chanter has an altogether more gentle voice – akin, it could be said, to the buzz of bees with sinus problems.

As the weeks passed, the faltering efforts of the assembled novices progressed from what sounded more like the fight than the flight of the bumble bees to a stage at which we were able to wing our way through basic exercises in passable concert. By Christmas, we were ready to start on the embellishments that are essential for providing 'punctuation' in pipe music. First we learned to play simple grace notes, then tackled the more complex fingering of doublings, grips, throws, birls, shakes and finally the *taorluath*, a tricky manoeuvre separating two notes with a group of four others played rapidly in sequence. Once those techniques were mastered, the long-awaited step to actually playing tunes could be made.

The end of winter found us tiptoeing our way along such well-trodden paths of the piping repertoire as *Highland Laddie*, *Loudon's Bonnie Woods and Braes* and *The High Road to Linton*. And stumbling though our efforts were, they had become sufficiently developed for us to be actually reading the dots on the printed page, a skill none of us had had a clue about a few months earlier. We were as cock-a-hoop as old Davie MacLeod must have been exhausted.

What Davie didn't know, however, was that, while I had been practising legitimate exercises on my chanter at home, my father had encouraged me to play along with some of his honky-tonk piano favourites as well. My mother didn't just retreat to the kitchen on these occasions; she took the dog for a walk. And the dog was always out of the house first. For there's no denying that what they were escaping would have been torture to the ears of all but the two protagonists, oblivious as we were to the imperfections of our creative collaboration – or 'bloody racket', as Mother chose to put it. Even sister Minnie didn't hang around waiting for bum notes to pounce on.

The first musical hurdle we had to confront was that, unlike the piano, there are no half-notes on a chanter. However, I found that I could overcome this by blowing slightly harder whenever the melody demanded. The little double reed inside the chanter would respond by raising the note played by the required semitone, then returning to standard pitch as soon I reverted to normal blowing. It was crude, but it worked … well, sort of.

'Close enough for jazz,' Dad would reassure me if I ever showed the slightest sign of doubt.

Of course, what we were cooking up wasn't jazz, or anything even remotely approaching it. But it did involve an element of improvisation just to be able to follow each other, so maybe I actually was having the seeds of jazz planted in my subconscious.

The second hurdle presenting itself was that the chanter was pitched in the key of B-flat. Not one of Dad's favourites. Hence the proliferation of bum notes from which Minnie had elected to absent herself. The tactic Dad employed when ambushed by a particularly awkward chord in this key was to retreat to a key he was comfortable in and hammer out a free-form introduction to nothing in particular. Sometimes he'd manage to retrace his steps to whatever we happened to have been butchering in B-flat, sometimes he wouldn't. In any event, my ears were learning to follow musical lines that were anything but obvious, and this was something else that was to prove of value in the fullness of time.

*

With the arrival of the longer evenings of spring, the pipe band's practice sessions moved out of the classroom and into the school playground. While the older boys, who were already proficient in playing the bagpipes, rehearsed winter-learned tunes as they marched, wheeled and counter-marched with the drum corps in the main yard, we beginners were ushered away to a corner beside the boys' toilets. Here awaited the boss, Pipe Major Willie 'Pat' Paterson, an ex-army contemporary of Davie MacLeod's and an equally able teacher, though not entirely blessed with old Davie's gift of patience.

Pat Paterson's priority at this time of the year was to advance the progress of lads newly graduated from the novices' class. He would introduce us to a full set of bagpipes, explain the workings of the various component parts, show us how to secure the bag under the left arm, place the long bass drone and two shorter tenor drones over the left shoulder, grasp the blowpipe between the teeth and hold the full-size chanter in the 'strike-up' position.

In the Pipe Major's experienced hands, this demonstration looked like simplicity itself. In the hands of a young rookie, particularly one of modest stature, the exercise took on the appearance of a dwarf being mugged by a mutant octopus. And this was even before the beast had been given the kiss of life.

The Highland bagpipe's pigskin bag is about the same size as the body of a juvenile member of the donor species, and it takes a bit of inflating. Even for a burly adult with the knack, this undertaking presents quite a challenge for the lungs, cheek muscles and, though easily overlooked by the unwary, the sphincter. We soon appreciated the logic behind a location close to the boys' toilets being chosen for our first attempts at aerating an octopus.

'Castrating a pack of wildcats' would have been the term more likely used by immediate neighbours to describe the sound of our struggles to gain the upper hand over our new charges. Just as soon as Pat Paterson was satisfied we had grasped the rudiments, each of us had been presented with our own full set of pipes, and it was up to us to make whatever progress we were capable of in as little time as possible – but in our own time, not his. His priority had now moved on to furthering the piping skills of the older, more experienced boys. He'd give us our chance to join them in the band when we had earned it, and if that meant driving our neighbours insane in the meantime – tough. Haddington Boys' Pipe Band may not have been the regular army, but it was as near to it as our diehard Pipe Major was ever likely to return to.

*

It's surprising how much a young mind and body can cope with, if the opportunity and will are there. Although playing the pipes had become a passion for all the kids in my group, we had also just moved up to secondary school, with a daunting array of new subjects to learn from scratch. On top of that, we were now committed to playing rugby for our school team on Saturday mornings, which necessitated travelling to away games every other week. This all ate into valuable bagpipe-practising time. Or should have. But it didn't.

And it isn't as if those activities were all we were involved in. There was football to play in the cow field along the road after homework of an evening. We'd help our folks digging, planting and weeding the garden (big vegetable plots were the norm and cultivating them a necessity of life in rural areas back then). We went wandering along the riverside watching poachers 'guddle' trout from under the banks with their hands; the boys who knew the trick sometimes getting down on their bellies to do a bit of guddling themselves. We did evening and weekend drills with the school's contingent of the army cadets: map-reading in the hills, stripping and re-assembling Bren Guns and firing old Point-303 Lee-Enfields in the rifle range. But we still found time to read about the weekly adventures of *Dan Dare, Pilot of the Future* in *The Eagle* magazine, to follow the five-nights-a-week exploits of

Dick Barton, Special Agent on the radio, and to marvel (or laugh) at the serialised episodes of Sam Katzman's *Superman* during the local flea pit's Saturday matinees.

And then there was cycle speedway, a passion for some of us that matched even our zest for playing the pipes.

Motorcycle speedway racing had become a spectator sport to rival the popularity of football in Britain after the Second World War. Most cities had a team, and Edinburgh was no exception. Every Saturday evening during the summer months, thousands of fans would pack the terracing of Old Meadowbank Stadium to cheer on the Edinburgh Monarchs as they raced against such arch rivals as Glasgow Tigers, Newcastle Diamonds, Stoke Potters, Cradley Heathens, Fleetwood Flyers and Liverpool Chads on a shale oval surrounding the soccer pitch.

My father, a speedway enthusiast since his youth, had formed a Monarchs Supporters Club in Haddington, with a bus laid on to transport the members to every Meadowbank meeting. It didn't take long for a group of us kids to become totally addicted to the thrills. On arrival at the stadium, we'd press our way as close to the track's safety fence as we could, oblivious to the stinging showers of shale flung at us by the bikes as they were hurled broadside round the bends. The roar of the engines, the smell of burnt methanol fuel, the colours of the riders' racing jackets, the glint of their chrome-plated steeds under the floodlights, the bellowing of the crowds, and the latest hit records blaring out of the Tannoy system between heats created an atmosphere that was positively intoxicating. As impressionable boys, we couldn't wait to be speedway riders ourselves.

We were ten-, eleven- and twelve-year-olds, the bounds of whose imagination bore no relationship to reality. Nevertheless, the will was there, so we reckoned all we had to do was create a way. And we did – albeit with an inescapable measure of compromise. Even if we'd had the physique to handle a bucking, stripped-down 500cc motorbike with no brakes and the acceleration of a rocket, we didn't have anything like enough money to indulge the fantasy. The solution, then, was to adapt the motorised version of the sport to suit our pushbikes.

As so often happens, however, the solution to one problem was thwarted by the emergence of another. Our bikes may not have been brand-new, top-of-the-range models (in most cases just patched-up hand-me-downs), but they got us to school and back, and carried us on jaunts into the countryside with reasonable reliability. Under no circumstances would our parents allow us to remove the brakes and mudguards and whatever else we deemed surplus to requirements just to emulate the lean, mean look of our heroes' racing machines. Prudence, not to mention our own safety, was paramount.

Enter the mother of invention, in this instance dressed in her make-do-and-mend clothes...

The municipal rubbish dump was located on the farm of Barney Mains, a mile or so east of Haddington. We were tipped off by one of the boys whose father worked for the council that, from among the miscellaneous examples of household dross heaped there, recyclable bicycle parts could occasionally be gleaned. All it required was a keen eye and a blocked nose. So, any wheels, frames, pedals, forks or handlebars that peeped from beneath their blanket of smouldering ash and putrefying vegetable matter were keenly scavenged by us and stashed away until enough had been gathered for our needs.

What we didn't know about the assembly and maintenance of a cycle speedway bike was quickly learned. After an evening's racing round our makeshift track at Peffercraig Quarry on the outskirts of town, there would inevitably be damage to make good. The re-spoking and realigning of buckled wheels became second nature, as did fixing snapped chains, replacing bent pedal cranks and mending punctures. Broken bones we left to the experts.

Miraculously, though, those of us who also aspired to be pipers always managed to emerge from the quarry with our fingers intact. Just as well, too, because national service was still compulsory, so the pipe band was continually having to replace older lads when their time came to go off and do their two-year stint in the armed forces.

Cometh the hour, cometh the kilt for nothing?

*

As was inevitable, Derek and I did finally come to realise that, just as there is no such thing as a free lunch, neither was there a truly free kilt – not within a non-profit-making community institution like Haddington Boys' Pipe Band, at any rate.

By the summer of 1954 we had already spent a couple of years in the ranks of the band proper, our commitment to music having replaced our dreams of becoming speedway riders. Resplendent in our military-style tunics and Balmoral bonnets, our adolescent backsides would brazenly swing the pleats of those long-coveted kilts as we marched up and down the streets of Haddington every Saturday evening. How we enjoyed our moments in the limelight, proud to wear the tartan, chuffed to see the admiring faces of so many onlookers lining the pavements, and delighted to be playing with reasonable skill the band's modest but judiciously chosen repertoire of popular pipe tunes. Pipe Major Paterson was as acutely aware of the technical limitations of his young charges as he was conscious of the value of giving the listening public what they wanted to hear.

Still, all those expensive bagpipes, drums, tunics, bonnets *and* kilts had to be paid for, and if not by the pipers and drummers themselves, then through their 'entertaining' the local community. Public performances, therefore, doubled as experience for the boys and as fund-raising events for the band itself. Obviously, pubs were the most lucrative source of contributions on a Saturday evening. We'd stop outside a few of the most popular in turn, forming a circle and churning out our best selections for ten or fifteen minutes while the hat was passed round inside.

It was hard work, and could be uncomfortable, too, when the Scottish summer took a sudden wintry turn. Even so, I relished being part of a well-drilled band that seemed to give as much pleasure to those listening as we derived satisfaction from playing. Although blissfully unaware of it at the time, I had been bitten by a bug whose infection would prove to be incurable.

*

'Remember that Teresa Brewer record?' Derek asked me when we met for one of the pipe band's engagements during the summer of 1954. 'Ye know, the one they used to play all the time at Meadowbank Speedway a few years back?'

'*Put Another Nickel In?*'

'Aye, that's the one, but it was really called *Music, Music, Music.*'

'Fine, but it'll never make a good pipe tune, no matter what you call it.'

'Naw, I'm not talkin' about the pipes,' Derek bristled. 'I'm not even talkin' about *Music, Music, Music*. I'm talkin' about the B-side.'

'*Copenhagen?* Now you're talking! I even remember what the band was called. The Dixieland All-Stars, wasn't it?'

'That's right!' Derek's enthusiasm was showing again. 'And if ye liked that, ye've got to hear some of the music in the new flick that's on at the flea pit this week!'

'*The Glenn Miller Story?*' I shook my head. 'I'm not too keen on all that sugary *Moonlight Serenade* stuff.'

'Who's talkin' about *Moonlight Serenade?* I'm talkin' about jazz music, like the stuff on the B-side of that Teresa Brewer thing – but even better. I'm talking about Louis Armstrong's

All-Stars – the best! They've got a spot in the movie, and ye've *got* to see it!'

I sat spellbound in Haddington's County Cinema that very night, as the jazz club scene featuring Louis 'Satchmo' Armstrong and his seven-piece band brought the typically schmaltz-laden Hollywood film to life. *Basin Street Blues* was the tune they played; slow and easy at first, with a growled vocal from Satch, then a wild drum break from Gene Krupa that doubled up the tempo and set the band alight. Even the Haddington flea pit was swinging. I'd never heard or seen anything like it. From the moment Barney Bigard wailed out his clarinet solo, I was hooked – not just on this kind of music, but on that particular instrument too.

Up to now, the nearest thing to real jazz I'd heard (apart from the band on the B-side of Teresa Brewer's *Music, Music, Music*) came from my Dad's small collection of 78s featuring the let's-have-a-party toe-tappers of the Firehouse Five Plus Two and the musical mayhem of Spike Jones and his City Slickers. I now realised that, even if those guys had grafted what they played onto the same roots as Louis Armstrong, the branch they eventually swung on was on the other side of the tree.

A year or so after *The Glenn Miller Story*, Hollywood released *The Benny Goodman Story*. This chronicled the life and music of another star of the 1930s big band era, the 'King of Swing' himself, clarinettist Benny Goodman. If Barney Bigard's playing with Satchmo had hooked me on the instrument, Benny Goodman's stunning clarinet artistry had me hauled in, netted and – to borrow from the jargon of contemporary jazz musicians – gassed, sent and solid gone.

I'd *have* to get myself a clarinet!

* * * * *

CHAPTER FOUR

'A NAME WITHOUT A BAND'

It went without saying that no amount of raking about on the municipal rubbish tip would provide me with a potentially serviceable clarinet. These were delicate woodwind instruments, intricate pieces of craftsmanship that would only be thrown away if they had become damaged beyond repair. There was nothing else for it, then; I'd have to earn enough money to buy one. This was how it was in the days before obtaining credit became as easy as catching a cold. Youngsters from families bound to frugality either figured out a way of saving up for any extras they wanted, or did without.

I had no problem with that. It was how I'd bought my practice chanter. The difference now was that I'd have to earn a lot more to buy even a cheap, second-hand clarinet. As berry-picking was purely seasonal, I reckoned it would take forever to come by enough money that way. And I was in a hurry. The answer? Find work during other school holidays, and at weekends, too, if possible.

Farming was still a labour-intensive business, and, luckily for me, Lennoxlove Acredales Farm, just along the road from our house, could be relied upon as a source of casual employment for a fit young lad prepared to roll his sleeves up and muck in with the men. I became that lad, stooking and stacking sheaves during harvest, 'feeding' the mill at threshing time, lifting and clamping potatoes in the autumn, cutting hedges in the winter, mucking out cattle yards in the spring. And on occasions when there was no work on the farm, there were usually jobs to be had shifting timber about at the nearby sawmill, or thinning trees and planting saplings in the surrounding woods.

Busy times, and happy days. But it's a true saying that time flies when you're enjoying yourself. Before I knew it, I was preparing to sit my 'Highers', the Higher Leaving Certificate exams that finally determine your fitness for university entrance in Scotland. Although I had worked every bit as hard at my studies as I'd had fun engaging in all the spare-time activities that presented themselves along the way, I couldn't help feeling apprehensive about these tests. I would do my best and hope for the best, too, but without abandoning the sense of purpose induced by seeing *The Benny Goodman Story*. Obtaining a clarinet had become an obsession, and at last I'd saved up what I hoped would be enough money to buy one.

*

After trailing round most of the junk shops in Edinburgh's Old Town, where the few clarinets on offer looked like ex-military band instruments that had been discharged on health grounds during the First World War, I finally found what I was looking for ... well, almost what I was looking for. In a shopping arcade near the top of Cockburn Street, there was a 'bargain emporium', and nestled among the bric-a-brac in the window was a clarinet, which, although second-hand, had the appearance of having been well looked-after. The shop's elderly proprietor keenly affirmed this as he handed it over the counter for me to 'try out.' I didn't even know how to hold it properly, far less try it out. However, I had spent enough time reading about and looking at pictures of clarinets to be sure of a few important essentials.

'Springs all workin' fine too,' said the shopkeeper, tapping a couple of keys with his forefinger. 'Pads in good nick as well. Oh aye, best clarinet we've had in for a while. Good tone an' everything. A right bargain, son – complete wi' case.'

While unable to dispute any of that, and although the asking price just about matched my budget, I did have a couple of doubts.

The shopkeeper must have sensed this. 'Clean as a whistle too,' he gushed. 'Been disinfected wi' TCP an' everything.'

'No, it's not that,' I assured him. 'It's just that it doesn't have the right system.'

The shopkeeper raised a puzzled eyebrow, then lowered it, frowning. 'System? It's a bloody clarinet, son, no the *Rook-a-Bookie Handbook* or somethin'!'

I explained that I was talking about a clarinet's arrangement of keys. This one had the old Albert or so-called 'Simple' System, whereas the more technically advanced Boehm System was generally accepted as best nowadays.

The shopkeeper pulled a take-it-or-leave it shrug, thought for a bit, then said, 'OK, I'll knock a quid off for ye. How about that?'

Tempting. That pound would have amounted to more than a day's wages for my father. By the same token, it would have constituted a fair slice of my mother's weekly housekeeping allowance for the whole family. And I hadn't forgotten how many basketfuls of strawberries I'd had to pick or how many cartloads of cattle dung I'd had to fork before I could pocket the same twenty shillings. Like the cattle dung, a pound wasn't to be sniffed at. Yet I still wasn't sure about this clarinet.

'Covered holes,' I said to the shopkeeper. 'It's got covered holes, and that's not normal.'

He looked at me blankly.

I pointed out that, instead of having spring-loaded metal rings round each of the main finger holes, this particular clarinet had little covering discs. Which, I explained, would prevent the pads of the musician's fingers from 'being in touch' with the music he was playing, and would limit, therefore, the amount of expression he could put into it.

The shopkeeper's own expression degenerated into one of undisguised exasperation. 'Look, son,' he sighed, 'the only hole covers I've heard about are to do wi' drains, and this is a clarinet, no a bloody sewer.'

'Maybe it was adapted to suit a saxophone player,' I calmly suggested, hoping that I could convert the old chap's frustration into his knocking a bit more off the asking price. 'Saxes have covered holes, but clarinets don't … normally. So, I reckon this one would be best suited to a sax player doubling on clarinet, except that even sax players are going for Boehm System clarinets these days … without covered holes.'

'Listen,' the old boy snapped, 'I've got more to bother about than systems and holes!' He returned the instrument to its case. 'Do ye want the damned thing or not?'

I took another look at the clarinet, pondering, then raised my eyes to meet the shopkeeper's. 'Another quid off?'

He slammed the case shut. 'Go on, then! Take it away afore ye talk me into givin' ye it for nothin'!'

And so I became the grateful, if somewhat less than fulfilled, owner of my first clarinet, with enough money left over to buy myself a how-to-play manual and half-a-dozen spare reeds. I had to admit, though, that any elation I felt really was tempered by the fact that the instrument was both technically old-fashioned and bizarrely equipped with those covered holes. But then I recalled that I'd read even Benny Goodman had started out on an Albert System clarinet before switching to a Boehm. What's more, the older system had been and still was the one favoured by most of the legendary musicians from New Orleans, the city universally regarded as the cradle of jazz. This even went for Barney Bigard, the Louis Armstrong sideman whose appearance in *The Glenn Miller Story* first got me interested in taking up the 'liquorice stick'. And Monty Sunshine, star clarinettist with Chris Barber's Band, the English outfit currently scoring in the pop charts with their brand of commercial trad jazz, also championed the Albert System. So, I told myself, if it was good enough for those guys, it would be good enough for me – until, that is, I could save up enough money for a piece of proper Boehm kit.

*

As chance would have it, Kimber Buglass, my sister's new boyfriend, had also developed an interest in jazz and had recently bought himself a trumpet. I'd known Kimber, by sight at least, since my earliest days with the Haddington Boys' Pipe Band. He was some five years my senior and had been an established piper in the band long before I graduated from the novices' group. Somewhere along the line, our mutual interest in jazz helped bridge the age gap and we became firm friends. Now that he was visiting our house on a regular basis to see my sister, we were soon making our first tentative attempts at playing, if not jazz, then at least some simple jazzy tunes together.

As there were no teachers of clarinet or trumpet in the area, both of us had been obliged to teach ourselves from the pages of our respective tutor books. Get-togethers in the house were therefore useful progress-comparing sessions, as well as opportunities to 'have a blow'. While these intense tête-à-têtes between her boyfriend and me must have got right up my sister's nose, my father saw them as a wonderful chance to get in on an act that was right up his street. So, whenever Kimber and I indicated that we were ready, Dad would sit himself down at the piano and pound out an intro to *When You and*

I Were Young, Maggie, followed by *Little Brown Jug*, before segueing into the inevitable *When The Saints Go Marching In*. It was all fairly basic and, no doubt, corny-sounding stuff, but it was nonetheless a step in the right direction, and all the bum notes, squeaks and fluffs produced en route bothered us not a whit.

For the sake of our neighbours' comfort, Kimber always played with a mute stuffed up the bell of his instrument, a restriction not conducive to the cultivation of the full-blooded tone considered essential by bona fide jazz trumpeters. It followed that it was just a matter of time until our family's traditional Sunday visit to my grandparents' farm was hijacked for what I saw as a logical progression from the Scottish Dance Music 'swarees' of times past; except that the front room was no longer the location, nor were the featured instruments Grandfather's melodeon and my little practice chanter.

The cattle shed became the venue and its bemused occupants the audience for the un-muted blasts of Kimber's trumpet and ear-piercing wails of my clarinet as we gave no quarter to whatever jazz standard we'd decided to attack. It says much for the average bullock's indifference to musical quality that our efforts didn't trigger a stampede. Indeed, apart from a lethargic bellow or two from the line of cud-chewing beasts staring at us, the only reaction to our performance was the faint 'clap, clap, clap' of cowpats being produced when it ended. Apt applause, perhaps, but to us it was a standing ovation at the Newport Jazz Festival. We savoured every dung-dripping decibel.

'You know what this means?' I eventually said to Kimber, a hint of apprehension in my voice.

He stood expressionless for a moment or two, thinking. Then, as a knowing smile spread across his face, he canted his head and ventured, 'You mean a –?'

'That's right,' I cut in. 'A band. We'll *have* to form a band!'

Kimber thought a bit more. 'Hmm,' he nodded, 'and we could maybe call it something to do with the Hidden Town. That's Hidden Town, as in the old name for Haddington, if you see what I mean.'

I did see what he meant, and I liked the idea.

'Maybe something along the lines of the Hidden Town Jazzmen?' he suggested.

Not bad, I thought. But something was tugging at the strings of my memory. The name of the band on *Copenhagen*, the B-side of that old Teresa Brewer hit they used to play at Edinburgh Speedway. What were they called again? The Dixieland All-Stars, that was it!

'How about the Hidden Town Dixielanders?' I said.

An exchange of winks, grins and back-slaps clinched it.

'Done!'

The fact that we couldn't even play our instruments properly was only one of the realities we had to face up to when the euphoria of our cattle shed debut finally wore off. To put a jazz band together we'd need other jazz musicians: a trombone player, drummer, bass player and banjoist at least. And there were none of those readily available in a little country town like Haddington. On top of that, Kimber, his time as an apprentice joiner now served, was about to embark on a two-year stretch of national service. At a stroke, our proposed six-piece combo was reduced to a one-man band: me, a greenhorn clarinet player, still fumbling his way around a few simple licks in just one key.

But the will was there, so, yet again, it would be merely a matter of finding a way.

* * * * *

CHAPTER FIVE

'CRIME AND PUNISHMENT'

Also *in* the way for me, however, were those Higher Leaving Certificate exams. My maternal grandmother, once a teacher herself, had instilled in me the old Scottish ethic of 'sticking in and doing well at school'. The respect and affection I had for her had compelled me to do just that, particularly when it came to subjects I didn't have any particular aptitude for. Perhaps this is what prompted the teaching staff of Knox Academy, Haddington's venerated state secondary school, to appoint me head boys' prefect for my final year. It was a choice that surprised me. I certainly didn't have any claim to be the best scholar in my class; others easily outshone me in that respect. But I did always try to give everything my best shot, which was my way of accentuating the positive and thereby making the most of my lot.

Rebel Without a Cause, a film starring James Dean as a mixed-up young American, had recently attained cult status, spawning a whole generation of James Dean clones.

It had become the 'in' thing to be a brooding teenage martyr to nothing in particular – or maybe even to everything. Whatever, I couldn't see the point in deliberately making life difficult for yourself when there were other, more constructive, ways of coping with the 'injustices' of youth. And, with any luck, while having a bit of fun into the bargain.

'You have a commendably pragmatic disposition,' old Frank 'Spoof' Rayner, the head English teacher, told me at the time.

I took this as a compliment, although I wasn't all that sure what having a pragmatic disposition actually meant. One thing I was sure about, however, was that the sacrifices my parents had made to allow me to stay on at school wouldn't be taken for granted. I had been given an opportunity, and I wasn't about to waste it.

*

While enforcement of discipline may not have been about to vanish totally from the list of prefects' duties when I began my stint as lead enforcer, it could be said that an erosion of certain standards did begin to set in. This was certainly the view of Headmaster A.B. Anderson, an ex-Latin teacher of the old Victorian school and, ergo, a strict disciplinarian. He summoned me to his office to discuss the matter.

My mumbled reading of scripture lessons during school assembly in the mornings was, he said, unacceptable. It gave the impression that I neither understood nor was particularly interested in the message being conveyed. This sort of thing spread apathy, manifested by a general lowering of the attention threshold throughout the hall, but most notably expressed by a marked increase in chattering and sniggering among the older girls towards the rear. A tape recording would be made to demonstrate how drastically my diction and delivery needed to be improved.

There was also, A.B. judged, too much 'chumminess' developing between prefects and the more recalcitrant members of the school roll. He was referring particularly, he added, to known recidivists within the lower grades.

'Recidivists, sir?'

The beak observed me owlishly for a moment. 'A recidivist, Kerr, is a person, according to the Oxford English Dictionary, who constantly commits crimes and is not discouraged by being punished.'

'*Crimes*, sir? Here in the Knox Academy?'

'For example, it has been brought to my notice – for your actions *are* being observed by members my staff, you know – that a certain boy who is habitually late for school is not being dealt with severely enough when you are on door duty in the mornings.'

'A *certain* boy, sir?'

A.B. rummaged through some papers on his desk. 'McLatchie. Yes, uhm, McLatchie, I believe his name is.'

'There are several McLatchies in the school, sir. McLatchie's a fairly common name in Haddington. A big family – a clan, almost.'

The rector continued to rummage. 'Yes, I'm well aware of that,' he muttered, his glasses slipping down his nose. 'Scant regard for authority, most of them.'

'So, which particular McLatchie is the recidivist on this occasion, sir?'

'Ah, here we are!' A.B. pointed to a scribbled note. 'Patrick. Yes, Patrick McLatchie.' He adjusted his specs and glanced up at me. 'Class 3D, I believe?'

I thought for a bit, then shook my head. 'A Patrick McLatchie in 3D? Hmm, no, I don't think so, sir.'

The headmaster drew a slow, long-suffering breath. He indicated the scribbled note with a backwards flick of his hand. 'I checked this against the relevant page of the school register, and I can assure you, Kerr, that 3D is confirmed as the form class of McLatchie, whose given name is Patrick.' A.B. stared at me, waiting for a positive response. When none was forthcoming, he consulted the note again. 'A stocky, tousle-haired lad, the reporting teacher states here. Unkempt. Looks as though he's been hauled through a hedge backwards.' He shot me a chastening look. 'Hardly how we expect pupils of the Knox to turn up for studies, is it?'

At last, the penny dropped. 'Ah yes, sir, yes. Now I know who you're talking about. Never heard anybody call him Patrick before, though. No, *Patchy* McLatchie is what he's always called.' I couldn't help smiling. 'Yeah, Patchy – a real character. And right enough, he does usually look like he's been hauled through a hedge backwards. Although he's more likely to have *crawled* through – forwards!' The thought made me chuckle.

'I'm surprised you think it funny!' the beak snapped. 'You've been entrusted with a position of authority within the school, and in that capacity you are responsible, among other things, for ensuring that your subordinates abide by the rule of punctuality – as well as maintaining an acceptable degree of personal tidiness.'

Except for a hint of incredulity betrayed by an occasional narrowing of his eyes, the headmaster's expression remained inscrutable throughout my ensuing attempt to explain the enigma that was Patchy McLatchie. Even my optimistic suggestion that Patchy should be prized as the school's very own version of Huckleberry Finn failed to elicit the slightest sign of empathy.

Undaunted, I went on to speculate that aspects of Patchy's appearance might indicate that traces of Romany blood flowed through his veins. After all, it was well known that certain families in the old Nungate quarter of Haddington (on the other side of the river from the town's more 'affluent' parts) were descended directly from gypsies who had settled there many centuries earlier. Even the vocabulary they still used in everyday conversation contained words that had their roots in Sanskrit, the ancient language of northern India, from where the gypsies first set out on their wanderings a thousand years ago.

'For instance, *joogal*,' I said, 'is their word for a dog, and –'

A.B. stopped me there. 'All very interesting, Kerr, but totally irrelevant. School rules apply to all pupils, no matter what their background.' He thumped his desk to emphasise the point. 'The boy McLatchie *must* be made to toe the line.'

I was painfully aware that I could be putting my own neck in a noose by attempting to save Patchy's. But if I didn't, the relatively minor issue of his timekeeping was liable to develop into a situation of confrontational strife for the school. Any such turn of events would inevitably implicate me, and I didn't relish the prospect of being bushwhacked by a bunch of vengeful McLatchies.

'The thing is, sir, Patchy – the boy McLatchie – is a free spirit.'

The beak eyballed me over the top of his specs, sceptically this time. 'Free spirit?'

'Yes, sir. I mean...' I swallowed hard, bracing myself for the tongue-lashing I'd be in for if old A.B. didn't buy the premise I was about to put to him. 'I mean, you could actually call him a real nature boy.'

The rector arched his brows, then knotted them. '*Nature* boy?'

'That's right – it's in his blood, sir – that gypsy blood I mentioned.'

A.B. had clearly heard enough. He made to cut me off again, but I got in first:

'You see, to Patchy's way of thinking, it's the rest of us, the so-called *normal* pupils, who are the recidivists – turning up on time every day to sit cooped up in classrooms, when we could be out in the open air catching rabbits, or guddling trout.'

The headmaster continued to frown, but I detected the merest twitch of a smile. He motioned me to go on.

I did, and with no small sense of relief. 'What I'm saying, sir, is that poaching is a way of life for Patchy. It's in his genes. I mean, left to his own devices, he probably wouldn't come to school at all.' I had the bit between my teeth now, so I pressed on. 'In fact, it probably isn't an exaggeration to say that he doesn't actually see a classroom as a place of learning – just somewhere to have a quiet kip after being up all night checking his snares and stuff.'

The beak pulled at his nose, a little cough stifling what I suspected was the makings of a chortle.

I grabbed the chance to deliver what I hoped would be my coup de grâce. Telling Patchy to write out 'I must not be late for school' a hundred times, I explained, had been found to be a pointless exercise. While Patchy duly produced the scrawled lines on arrival at school next morning, his arrival was invariably late. The next step, logically, would be to march Patchy along to his form teacher's room for six of the best. But the damage inflicted upon his snare-making fingers by a licking from the twin tongues of a leather belt would only provoke Patchy into skipping school entirely. This in turn would necessitate calling upon the services of the truant officer, resulting in additonal cost to the school and the likelihood of the officer involving himself in a potentially suicidal difference of opinion with Patchy's kinfolk over in the Nungate. I summed up by submitting that, under the circumstances, sticking with the status quo would seem the more attractive option.

Clearing his throat, the beak resumed his air of authority. 'Pragmatism is commendable, Kerr, and does indeed have its place – at times. The enforcement of discipline is, however, mandatory – always. You'll do well to remember that.' He then dismissed me with a doorward jerk of his head. 'See to it that the boy McLatchie toes the line!'

Now that I knew better what old 'Spoof' had meant when he said I had a pragmatic disposition, I decided this would be as good a time as any to put it to the test.

Next morning, when Patchy turned up, late as usual, I recounted the gist of my conversation with the headmaster, and suggested that he should make an extra effort to be punctual. This, I reasoned, would save us both the bother of dishing out and writing lines, but, more crucially, would nullify any risk of the truant officer becoming involved. Patchy grunted one of his customary grunts, but didn't say a word. Nor did a scowl or smile give any clue to his thoughts. Indeed, when it came to being inscrutable, Patchy was in a higher league than even old poker-faced A.B. Anderson himself.

Predictably, Patchy continued to check in late when it suited him. Nothing changed, except that I jettisoned the futile gesture of giving him a hundred lines to scribble for his sins. Patchy McLatchie had his own set of values, and if upholding them in defiance of petty rules and regulations made him a recidivist, then so be it. He neither knew what the word meant nor was he interested in finding out. Likewise, not even the possibility of never learning how to spell 'snare' or 'guddle' would make him a bad poacher. Which is where Patchy's interest in the whole matter of school discipline began and ended.

I admired his determination to be free from the shackles of convention – even envied it, in a way. That old Scots ethic of sticking in and doing well at school was anathema to Patchy, and he seemed so content with the simple life he'd been born to that I admit having considered, both then and on many occasions since, that he might actually be right.

The headmaster never broached the 'problem' of Patchy McLatchie again, causing me to presume that he'd given the whistle-blowing members of his staff instructions to turn a blind eye to my turning a blind eye. This got me thinking that being able to accept things that can't be changed takes courage, while doing so in a way that isn't detrimental to your own position takes skill, with perhaps a generous measure of duplicity chucked in. Whatever, A.B. Anderson had clearly mastered the art. He was, in essence, an ace practitioner of pragmatism, whose handling of the Patchy McLatchie affair had taught me a lesson in how to deal astutely with fellow members of the human race – and even with some professional jazz musicians, too, as I'd find out in the fullness of time.

* * * * *

CHAPTER SIX

'SCHOOL'S OUT'

'Heh, you! The laddie wi' the eyes like a fuckin' googie-wog! Ye're marchin' like ye've got two hairs in yer arse tied thegither!'

So screamed the Royal Scots sergeant (we'll call him Jimmy) who came out from Edinburgh's Redford Army Barracks to drill the school's Combined Cadet Force contingent every Friday afternoon. Sergeant Jimmy always screamed those same words of abuse – sometimes at the laddie wi' the googie-wog eyes (whatever they were), sometimes at the laddie wi' the tumshie heid (turnip head), sometimes at the laddie wi' a face like a skelped erse (spanked backside), yet without ever identifying his current target by name. He knew, of course, that such outbursts were guaranteed to elicit a ripple of giggles from the ranks, thereby giving him an excuse to let rip with another blanket bollocking, which would duly add to his feeling of superiority over the 'horrible little men' in his charge.

Small and stocky, with a nose that looked as though it had routinely led his face the wrong way through a revolving door, Sergeant Jimmy could never claim to have been blessed with a commanding presence. He was in the poison-dwarf mould of Scottish soldiers, built like a brick shithouse (his own description), hard as nails and with an accompanying aura of alcohol fumes, stale cigarette smoke, b.o. and cheap aftershave – a distinctive redolence which would be brought back to me years later on entering the band room of Liverpool's Cavern Club for the first time.

Another particularly noticeable characteristic of the sergeant's was his guttural way of pronouncing the letter 'R'. This mannerism has a somewhat exotic quality when spoken softly by the French, but takes on an altogether less alluring resonance when rasped out in Scottish parade-ground observations such as, 'Ye're marchin' like ye've got two hairs in yer arse tied thegither'.

Sergeant Jimmy knew that finesse was never going to be his strongest suit. Crudeness was his speciality, and he flaunted it whenever the opportunity arose. Which it frequently did during his lessons on the dismantling and re-assembling of the Bren Gun. These demos were usually conducted in a corner of the playing field adjacent to the girls' hockey pitch. If a game happened to be in progress at the same time, our redoubtable Royal Scots veteran would make a particular point of stressing the importance of properly inserting the gun's body-locking pin, or, as he would refer to it while ogling the nearest hockey player, 'the ladies' delight'.

Even if a few prepubescent boys in the younger squads didn't quite get the relevance of arse hairs and body-locking pins, they never failed to be impressed by Sergeant Jimmy's spiel. And this went for everyone. His chosen method of exercising control over those in his command may have been less subtle than that of our esteemed headmaster, but it was no less effective for all that.

Initially, I hadn't any real interest in most of the soldierly baggage attached to the cadets. But being a member was compulsory, so, as was my wont, I got stuck in and made the most of the experience. And it paid off. By the time I reached my sixth and final year, I had become Company Sergeant Major, head honcho of the school's contingent. Although it wasn't really in my nature to be the one who yelled the commands during square-bashing exercises in the school quad, I had long since twigged that doing the yelling was preferable to being yelled at. By now, I had also recognised the logic behind such ostensibly trivial exercises as making a column of foot-sloggers count the required number of paces between being ordered to halt and actually halting, essentially in perfect unison. Here was the instillation of discipline in its most fundamental form, cunningly conceived to make an idiot of any individual who got out of step with the herd. As this was a ploy exploited by the military since time immemorial, it was fascinating to ponder that Sergeant Jimmy's arse-hair gibe may once have been screamed at rookie legionaries – in Latin.

Back in the 1950s, few of us thought twice about respecting our teachers and following a reasonable code of discipline. We just did it. It was how most of us had been brought up. We, like generations before us, had been taught to accept that, if we did something wrong at school, we'd feel the sting of a leather strap, the dreaded 'tawse', on our hands. And I doubt if it ever entered our parents' minds that some teachers might get a sadistic kick out of dispensing corporal punishment to the kids in their charge. Mind you, thinking back, I suspect that one or two probably did – though, to be fair, they may well have been driven to it! Whatever, the point is that the system worked. Respect and discipline prevailed – by and large, at any rate.

I grew to enjoy those Friday afternoons in the cadets, when we could escape the day-to-day routine of the classroom to be groomed – even if blissfully unaware of it – into reliable team players and, in some cases, leaders. Finding yourself in the latter category, while remaining keen to be 'one of the boys', placed a weight on young shoulders that could be as tricky to balance as walking any authoritarian tightrope of the Patchy McLatchie variety. But if you got it right, the resulting relationship with your so-called subordinates was likely to be a whole lot more productive than by adopting the domineering approach I'd seen employed by a few of my predecessors.

I had a hunch that playing the bagpipes could also be a useful means towards the same end.

There were only two other pipers attending Knox Academy at that time, but they were just as enthusiastic as I was about forming a school pipe band. And they cared no more than I did that it would doubtless be the smallest in all of the Combined Cadet Force contingents in the country. Rehearsing would give us an excuse to skip some of the more mundane Friday-afternoon exercises, while playing at the head of the entire school company on parade days would give us a real buzz, as well as helping inject an essential element of swagger into those marching behind. After all, our parent regiment was the Royal Scots, and no 'Jock squaddies' – even Friday-afternoon pretend ones – were worthy of the name without having a bit of wiggle-waggle in their gait.

Yes, a school pipe band would be just the ticket. And old A.B. Anderson agreed when I put the idea to him in his office:

'Excellent, Kerr! Precisely what we need – added kudos for our cadet corps.'

I allowed myself a smug little smile.

'And as Pipe Major,' the rector continued, 'you will represent Knox Academy in the massed pipes and drums of Scotland's schools at Edinburgh Castle this summer. I'll make the necessary arrangements.' The audience over, A.B. nodded doorwards. 'Carry on!'

Massed pipes and drums? Edinburgh Castle? Pipe Major? *Me*? That's when it struck home that announcing my idea to the beak had been a tad premature. I'd already been pushing it to call a trio of pipers a band. But what about drummers? None who'd played in Haddington Boys' Pipe Band were still at school, so I found myself leaving the headmaster's office decidedly less cocky than when I'd entered. What the hell had I talked myself into?

I was still worrying about it next morning, when I saw a bus from one of the outlying areas pulling up as I rode my bike through the school gates.

'Heh, wait a minute, daddy-o!' someone shouted. 'Ah need to talk to ye!'

Jim Douglas hailed from Gifford, a sleepy little village nestling in the lower folds of the Lammermuir Hills, about five miles south of Haddington. He was a couple of years younger than me, and I didn't know much about him, other than that he played guitar in a local skiffle group called The Tynesiders. Hence the hip 'daddy-o!' salutation.

Skinny and gangly, like a younger version of *The Goon Show*'s Spike Milligan, he loped towards me with a look of controlled exasperation on his face. It was the sort of look a doctor might give a patient who hadn't the common sense to take aspirin for a headache. He flashed me a quick smile. 'They tell me ye're lookin' for drummers.'

'Bad news travels fast,' I muttered.

'Aye, right enough. Anyway, Ah can solve yer problem for ye.'

I automatically thought of Jim's skiffle links. 'Well, thanks all the same, but it's drummers we need, not washboard players.'

He gave a short, staccato laugh. 'Nah, we've no even got *one* washboard player. Naw, it's me Ah'm talkin' about, man.'

'You – a drummer? But I thought you played guitar.'

Jim rolled his shoulders. 'Yeah, well, that'll be ma main instrument, right enough. Once Ah've mastered the rest o' the Bert Weedon *Play In A Day* book, like. But, nah, drummin's ma natural bag.'

'You've played in a pipe band, then?'

'Me? Naw, but ma old man did – in the army. Top man on the skins. Oh aye, taught me the lot. Marches, strathspeys and reels? Two-four, three-four, four-four, six-eight?' Jim hunched his shoulders. 'Nae bother. Ah've got paradiddles and flams in ma genes.'

I reckoned that, if his drumming was even half as sharp as his flair for self-promotion, he'd be able to do a reasonable enough job for us. Anyway, what was there to lose? 'OK,' I shrugged, 'bring your snare drum along to the practice on Friday afternoon, and we'll take it from there.'

'Yeah, far out,' Jim replied, in a way that suggested he'd taken what I'd just said as read, even before I'd said it. Clearly, he already had something else on his mind, which he proceeded to express with an air of reciprocal benevolence: 'But listen, man, talkin' about washboard players – we're needin' one for the group. So, ye know, if ye fancy havin' a go –'

A don't-even-think-about-it scowl stopped him right there. Having finally saved up enough to part-exchange my old Albert System clarinet for a Boehm, I felt that adapting to the change was asking enough of my fingers, without having their flesh torn to ribbons thrashing a washboard. Besides – and I'm sure it wasn't lost on Jim – I was a would-be jazz musician, in whose veins the seeds of anti-pop-music prejudice had already started to germinate. Stuff playing in a bloody skiffle group!

Meanwhile, any concerns I'd had about Jim's drumming were swiftly dispelled. His technique may have been a mite unorthodox, but he knew how to kick a piper up the kilt, rhythmically speaking, which is the hallmark of any good pipe-band drummer. Also, like the best of that rare breed of Scottish percussionists, he showed that he could really 'swing' – in the jazziest sense of the word.

This got me thinking ahead. 'Listen, Jim,' I said, adopting a confidential air as I drew him out of earshot of the two pipers, 'there's, ehm – there's maybe gonna be a jazz band starting up here in Haddington.'

'Oh, aye?' Jim's mien was distinctly guarded. 'And ye're lookin' for a drummer, are ye?'

'No – well, yes – but I was thinking more about you being a guitar player, and…'

Jim's expression grew more wary. 'And?'

'And I wondered if you'd be interested in switching to banjo?'

The scowl that darkened Jim's face mirrored the one I'd given in response to his washboard proposal a few days earlier. Banjo-playing, evidently, did not have a place in his natural bag, so I swiftly dropped the subject – for the present at least.

Returning to more immediate considerations, it proved fortunate that Jim had plenty of confidence in his own abilities, for he was destined to be the one and only member of our drum corps. There would be no 'second tippers' echoing his snare drum lead, no syncopated 'fills' from stick-twirling tenor drummers, no bass drummer thumping out the beat. Just Jim.

Yet, despite its dearth of personnel, our mini pipe band proved amply able to do what was required of it. We played the squads out of the quad after marching drill every Friday, led them deliberately through the billet lines of larger, more eminent educational establishments at cadet camp (manoeuvres that provoked the occasional inter-school confrontation after lights-out), and finally headed the entire company in its parade past the Scottish Division Brigadier who took the salute at the end of our school year.

In keeping with custom, A.B. Anderson stood on the dais beside the army brass, and though his expression remained as inscrutable as ever, an almost imperceptible tapping of a toecap beneath the hem of his headmaster's gown gave the game away. He was delighting in the increased kudos he'd predicted the addition of a pipe band would bring to his school. He had long taken pride in Knox Academy being the only non-fee-paying school in Scotland to boast a cadet corps, but unlike those of its more prestigious associates, the Knox contingent had never before had its very own pipe band to march to.

While referring to the four of us as a band stretched the meaning of the term to breaking point, this bothered the beak no more, apparently, than it did us. And if our goading some sniffy boarding-school boys into a scuffle or two at camp had met with his disapproval, he never let on. As I had already noted in his handling of the Patchy McLatchy affair, our headmaster was an ace practitioner of pragmatism – when it suited.

*

School taught me a few more lessons that were outside the set curriculum. Not least of those was the value of fully committing to whatever you undertake, whether by choice or of necessity. Then, if things don't work out as well as hoped, at least you could say it wasn't for want of trying. Little did I know at the end of that final school term, however, that I'd be putting this principle to the proof a lot sooner and much more crucially than I could ever have foreseen.

But prize-giving day was intended more for reflecting on what had already been achieved than anticipating what the future might hold. And, on the face of it, I had a fair bit more to celebrate than I'd have predicted just a year earlier. One way or another, I had scraped together more than enough qualifications to allow me to apply for a university place. The snag was, though, that the group of subjects on my Higher Leaving Certificate was, as the careers master put it, 'a wee bit quirky' – or, to my way of thinking, totally bloody useless.

Only now did I fully realise the importance of one thing that school had *not* taught me, which was to have the courage of your own convictions. Looking back three years from the ripe old age of seventeen, I could see how wrong I had been to ignore my natural inclinations in favour of following ill-suited advice, for all that it had been given with the best of intentions. But how many fourteen-year-olds possess the self-assurance, or confidence in their own foresight, to reject the guidance of their mentors?

In those days, the policy was for pupils starting fourth year at high school to specify which subjects they wanted to specialise in for their final three years. And, for reasons that presumably made sense to decision-making educationalists of the day, certain 'main' subjects could not be paired. For example, if you wanted to specialise in geography, you weren't permitted to study history as well. The same applied to science and art. My opting for science had earned me my first invitation to the rector's office.

Flanked at his desk by head art teacher Kathleen 'Granny' Weir, old A.B. Anderson wasted no time in telling me that choosing science as my primary subject was a glaring mistake: one that I'd regret for the rest of my life. I had a certain flair for art, a talent even, whereas my marks in exams over the previous three years had shown him that I wasn't endowed with the same gift for matters scientific. In short, I could lay the foundations of a career in art with relative ease, while following a science course would require an arduous regime of study, with no guarantee of success at the end of it.

Crestfallen, I explained that, for as long as I could remember, what I'd wanted more than anything was to be a farmer like my grandfather. But as I was one generation removed from being given the opportunity on his farm, the alternative was to gain a formal qualification in agriculture and find my own way in the industry from there. My attempt to assure the beak that I wouldn't mind working as hard as was necessary to achieve this goal was doused by an exasperated shake of his head and an 'it's all yours' gesture to the principal of his art department.

'Granny' Weir's nickname was a misnomer, in that she was, in appearance at any rate, the archetypal maiden aunt, and an extremely genial one, normally. Even on the greyest of days, she would cut a sunny figure sweeping jauntily along the corridors, exuding so much bonhomie and joie de vivre that it was easy to imagine bluebirds sitting on her shoulder and butterflies flitting round her head. Also, as befitted a woman whose life was framed in art, her face, akin to the Mona Lisa's, seemed to be lit by a permanent smile. But she wasn't smiling today...

How could I be so blinkered? How could I be so ungrateful? How could I even *think* of spurning the ability I had been blessed with? Couldn't I see the wonderful opportunities that lay before me, once the basic skills I possessed had been honed and polished at art college? Why, to contemplate doing anything else with my life would be nothing short of a crime!

What defence does an adolescent, with the complexities of an adult world crowding his head, have against such a put-down from a matronly madonna with butterflies circling hers? In my case, none.

Fast-forward, then, to prize-giving day, those three years later...

'You've decided *WHAT*?' Miss Weir wasn't smiling again. So much so that any bluebirds and butterflies lingering about her person would have been wise to wing it.

'I'm not going to art college,' I replied, feeling more regret for disappointing her than fear of the dressing-down I sensed would be coming my way.

She uttered a plaintive squeak, squinting. 'B-but you've been awarded this year's special prize for art, for heaven's sake!'

I was tempted to say that I'd also won the cadet medal and a special prize for English, but this didn't mean I was obliged to join the Foreign Legion or become a poet. But I held my tongue. Bad enough to have turned against the advice of a teacher who genuinely believed in me, without adding backchat to brush-off.

A smile returned to 'Granny' Weir's lips while she gathered her thoughts. It was a smile of the kind you'd expect to see on a dog-owner's face as she laid her late pooch to rest.

'Just think of the careers you could have chosen,' she murmured at length.

I could have told her I'd been trying *not* to do precisely that for the past three years, but judged it more appropriate to say nothing.

'After art college, you could have come into the teaching profession.'

Another wasted three years, I thought, just to qualify for a life of frustration trying to make silk purses out of sows' ears? I don't think so.

'Or, like one of my former pupils, you could have gone into industry. He's a designer in a leading ceramics factory in England now, you know.'

If the slightest doubt about the wisdom of turning my back on a career in art had been lurking in my mind, it had finally been given the boot. The idea of sitting at a drawing board in a Black Country plate factory painting flowers every day filled me with even more dread than the prospect of being an art teacher. I'd rather muck out cattle sheds for a living.

Miss Weir seemed to have read my thoughts. 'Are you still set on going into farming?' She was smiling again, but in a puzzled way. Clearly, design was more attractive to her than dung, and I could appreciate that. Still, no point in debating the matter.

'Yes,' I said, as firmly as I could, 'farming *is* really what I want to do.'

She sighed a resigned sigh and gave a little shake of her head. 'But, you know, the subjects you've got exam passes in – Highers in English, Latin, Geography and Art, Lowers in Maths and French – well, they won't give you access to a BSc course in agriculture at university.'

DON'T CALL ME CLYDE!

Which, I felt like reminding her, was precisely what I'd tried to get across to her and the beak three years earlier. But there was nothing to be gained by bringing that up again.

'So,' she continued, 'how *are* you going to get into farming?'

'I've no idea at present,' I shrugged, before adding somewhat lamely, 'but where there's a will, there's a way.'

Gentle soul that she was, instead of giving me the dressing-down I'd been expecting, 'Granny' patted my hand and smiled again. This time, however, the smile suggested she'd come to the conclusion that I was a misguided half-wit – a nice enough lad, but seriously, if not dangerously, deluded.

'Perhaps you're right about wills and ways,' she nodded. 'Though a more fitting proverb may be the one about leading a horse to water.'

* * * * *

CHAPTER SEVEN

'AND THAT'S JAZZ?'

Even if I felt the Fates had dealt me a bum hand academically, I had to admit they'd more than compensated by slipping me a couple of aces personally.

The first materialised in the shape of someone I'd first noticed when I was cycling home from school one afternoon. What made her stand out from the other kids swarming along the street was that she was vaulting a low wall onto the pavement, where she proceeded to knock six bells out of the school bully. But it wasn't the bizarre sight of a mere slip of a girl beating up a thug twice her size that really caught my eye. It was her face. The prettiest face I had ever set eyes on.

First thing next morning I made a point of finding out who she was. I was told her name was Ellie – German by birth, her war-widowed young mother having married a Haddington airman who was stationed near Cologne after hostilities ended. At fourteen, Ellie was two years younger than me. But since I was still fairly clueless about how to chat up girls, I decided I'd use my position as a prefect to give her a hundred lines for running in the corridor. She hadn't, but it was the best intro I could think of.

The look she gave me made it plain she was distinctly unimpressed. 'I wasn't running,' was all she said.

Up close, I could see she was even more beguiling than the little wildcat I'd spotted setting about the hard case the previous day. Her face wasn't just pretty; it had a delicate, even refined, quality to it. There was a shyness about her as well, but with a feisty, don't-meddle-with-me glint in her eyes. Those eyes! Not only drop-dead big and beautiful, but of different colours too. One a misty blue, the other green as an autumn leaf and flecked with amber.

I was mesmerised.

'I wasn't running,' she repeated, firmly but politely.

'A hundred lines,' I said. 'Delivered here, after assembly tomorrow morning.'

She didn't do the lines. I doubled the sentence, with the same negative results. This ritual was repeated daily, until Ellie eventually capitulated by accepting my offer to carry her books home from school – but only, she insisted, if one of her chums could walk along with us. A case of a boy chasing a girl until she catches him? I liked to think so, despite Ellie's eyes delivering the same message as when I'd first spoken to her: she didn't trust my motives, and what's more, thought I was a creep.

Yet this faint spark of high school romance kindled a flame that would burn, to paraphrase an old Gershwin lyric, for ever and a day. Truth to tell, though, if Ellie had had the slightest inkling of how many roller coaster rides she'd be subjected to along the way, she'd have grabbed a fire extinguisher right there and then.

The second of fate's trump cards had been dealt me in the form of Jim Douglas, whose involvement in skiffle soon led him, via the inspirational hits of Lonnie Donegan, to the toe-tapping trad of the full Chris Barber Band and an infatuation with jazz to match my own. Our shared musical leanings, which had quickly extended beyond the confines of the school pipe band, would eventually take us along life-changing paths that neither of us could have predicted. Paths that were to surprise us with more tricky switchbacks than we would have liked as well.

But for the present, we were content to enjoy our new hobby of trying to play jazz together whenever we got a chance. At first, this tended to be restricted to Saturday afternoon 'jam sessions' at my place, with Dad on piano. The repertoire was almost as limited as the choice of compatible keys. Predictably, the simpler of the current records featuring Chris Barber's star clarinettist Monty Sunshine were copied as near note-for-note as our techniques allowed. *The Old Rugged Cross* and *When You and I Were Young, Maggie* (yet again) took the most regular bashings.

Occasionally, I'd cycle the five miles up to Jim's home in Gifford, where we'd try out our stuff on his mother, his granny and their old collie dog Sheila. His mum and the dog always gave an encouraging response to our fledgeling jazz flights, but Jim's granny greeted the end of every duet with a request growled in the patois of her native Berwickshire.

'Geez Banonzie!' was her call for Jim to give a solo performance of the guitar-twanging title music of *Bonanza*, the hugely popular TV western series of the time. Jim was always happy to oblige, reminding me that guitar still took pride of place in his 'bag', and any entreaties to double on banjo would still fall on deaf ears.

*

In the meantime, my sister's boyfriend Kimber was doing his national service at an RAF base in Germany, where he had been drafted into the station dance band. This brought on his trumpet playing by leaps and bounds, and also exposed him to the influence of more experienced musicians with a kindred interest in and a wider knowledge of jazz. Whenever he came back on leave, he would get together with Jim and me for a blow. He would also introduce us to whatever jazz LPs he'd bought since his last visit home. As a national serviceman, he didn't earn much, but it still amounted to a lot more than the combined pocket money of two schoolboys, so we were always eager to soak up every note from the grooves of his latest purchases.

Those introduced us to some of the top American purveyors of Dixieland: the bands of Bob Scobey, Muggsy Spanier, Wingy Manone and Bob Crosby; musicians of the calibre of Bobby Hackett, Jack Teagarden and Matty Matlock. Having been weaned on the 'neat-and-jaunty' British trad records of Chris Barber and Humphrey Lyttelton, hearing this free-swinging music for the first time was both a revelation and an inspiration.

Of course, the so-called 'Jazz Revival' we were becoming absorbed in had been going on for over a decade, with Scotland producing some notable bands in that time. Those led by trumpeter Alex Welsh and clarinettist Sandy Brown, both originally from Edinburgh but based in London since the early Fifties, were already established as top exponents of their respective styles, and highly regarded by jazz pundits everywhere. Having listened to their radio broadcasts, I could understand why.

But now, in 1957, it was a band formed five years earlier in Glasgow, and still based there, which was making the biggest impact in Scotland, commercially at least. The Clyde Valley Stompers had been shaped in the Chris Barber mould by their leader Ian Menzies, who, like Barber, was a trombonist himself. Even the inclusion of a skiffle group within the Stompers' ranks was a Barber take-off, as was the featuring of a girl singer. Mary McGowan may not have had the authentic blues feel of the Barber band's Ottilie Patterson, but, petite as she was, she could belt out skiffle songs and traditional jazz standards in a gutsy style that had made her the darling of legions of Stompers' fans throughout Scotland.

The band had first come to prominence after winning the Scottish Jazz Band Championships in 1955. A spin-off was a deal with Decca Records, whereby some tracks recorded live in Glasgow's St Andrew's Halls were released the following year on the company's Scottish label, Beltona. Those sides, which included jazzed-up renditions of tartan evergreens like *The Uist Tramping Song* and *I Love a Lassie*, together with Mary McGowan's skiffle-style *Open Up Them Pearly Gates*, showed that, while the band probably had as many rough edges as most other amateur and semi-pro outfits around, it did have a certain 'something' that clicked with a youthful public ready to be carried along on the latest wave to engulf popular music.

And carry them along the Clyde Valley Stompers duly did. They turned professional and took to the road, playing to sell-out crowds in dance halls, town halls, village halls and ballrooms all over Scotland. While it could be claimed that the band's following comprised a fair proportion of young people more smitten by the atmosphere generated in these packed venues than gripped by any deep appreciation of jazz, the fact remained that 'The Clydes' were rapidly becoming a national sensation. 'Stompermania' was sweeping the land long before most members of Scottish pop/rock super groups like the Bay City Rollers, Wet Wet Wet and Simple Minds were even born.

And so what if there were more jive monkeys than jazz buffs queuing to get into Stompers gigs? Jazz started out as dance music in the cat houses and honky-tonks of early twentieth century New Orleans. It was good-time, easily digested fare, served up to make people happy, to help them boogie their cares away. By that definition, the Clyde Valley Stompers were a *jazz* band in the truest sense, and their fans couldn't have cared less if more 'discerning' students of the music thought otherwise.

In any case, the band was now more than capable of defending itself against those who eschewed boogieing in favour of analysing jazz through some kind of highbrow microscope. The Clydes had come a fair way musically since those enthusiastic though unrefined performances on Beltona. Changes of personnel, including the recruitment of Dean Kerr (no relation) on trumpet and Maurice Rose on soprano sax, had given the Stompers a sound sufficiently mature for Decca to have promoted them to their main label by 1957. A single, coupling *Milenburg Joys* with *Bill Bailey, Won't You Please Come Home?*, helped both cement the band's popularity on its native stomping ground and introduce it to a potentially much larger audience south of the border.

I remember hearing that single on the jukebox in Haddington's Mocca Cafe when I popped in after cadets one Friday evening. I'd just been tipped off about it by Jack Blair, an old cycle speedway chum, who had also been bitten by the jazz bug and, with the intention of joining our still-embryonic Hidden Town Dixielanders, had recently bought himself a trombone. Jack's assessment that the Stompers had developed a sound all their own proved to be absolutely right. I was impressed by the record, to such an extent that I scrounged three bob from my parents to go and hear the band when it was playing in town a few weeks later.

*

The local Corn Exchange, a huge barn of a place that served as a trading rendezvous for farmers and merchants on Fridays, morphed into a dance hall on Saturday nights. But the morphing didn't entail any change to the decor or the addition of creature comforts. It was a spartan barn on Fridays and was still a spartan barn on Saturdays. The only difference, apart from the presence of a band, was that a few dozen amiable agricultural folk were replaced by hundreds of young and not-so-young people bent on having a bloody good time, in many cases fuelled by a liberal intake of alcohol. The expansive floor of Haddington's 'Cornie' had become renowned as a Saturday night battlefield.

'As long as you keep clear of any trouble,' my mother said as I left the house.

'And leave before the end,' Dad added. 'It's when the fresh air hits them that the piss artists go doolally.'

Mum gave him a you-should-know look.

I had been to the Corn Exchange a few times with my grandfather many years before. The smells that lingered in my memory were rustic ones, of boot polish, moth balls, pipe tobacco and the mellow dustiness of grain samples being proffered and appraised in the little fold-out booths that lined either side of the hall. Those smells had now been ousted by the sweet aroma of Slipperine dance-floor lubricant, vying bravely with the tang of Jeyes Fluid wafting from the gents' toilets. It was a potpourri characteristic of such dual-purpose country venues that I was destined to become very familiar with.

Following the advice of seasoned Saturday night Cornie-goers, I arrived early, planning to claim a good spot for listening to the band before the pubs closed and the juiced-up mobs poured in.

'Gonna be a record crowd the night,' the old guy on the door said as he took my money. 'A thousand in there already. Aye, and it's a while yet afore chuckin'-oot time at the boozers.'

The sound of live music reverberating off the hall's high, open ceiling gave the impression of being inside a cave, the effect curiously undampened by the mass of human bodies milling inside. Not ideal acoustics for musical appreciation, perhaps, but plainly of no concern to the dancers, who appeared to be divided into three distinct camps. Nearest the entrance, there was enough space (just) for couples to be foxtrotting and quickstepping over the floor in flamboyant ballroom style.

Edging my way towards the bandstand at the far end of the hall, I noticed that the middle ground was occupied much more densely. The dancers, for want of a better word, were clearly of the shuffling persuasion, the female's hands draped over her partner's shoulders, his placed either side of her waist – or thereabouts – while both sets of feet paid only token homage to the Slipperine. They were doing what was graphically termed 'The Creep'.

A few couples, however, managed to stir even less. These were dancers of the 'vertical expression of horizontal intent' school: bodies frontally abutting, hands clamped to the other's buttocks, each face buried in its opposite number's neck. Only their fingers moved – apparently.

The area immediately in front of the bandstand was where the real action was happening. This was the domain of the jive-and-boogie brigade of Teddy Boys and their 'Judies'. There was certainly no lack of music-to-feet coordination here.

The stimulus was *Muskrat Ramble*, an upbeat Kid Ory number first recorded by Louis Armstrong's Hot Five way back in the 1920s, and covered by just about every other jazz band since. I had become familiar with the Bob Crosby Bobcats' version, having listened to it many times on one of the albums Kimber brought back from Germany. While the Clyde Valley Stompers, in common with most of their contemporaries on this side of the Atlantic, still lacked the subtleties of such legendary American outfits, they did have a distinctive sound – a sound characterised by Dean Kerr's punchy lead, which was a perfect foil for Maurice Rose's fluent yet economical soprano phrasing. This front-line partnership had a more tempered quality than others in the British trad mould I'd been listening to. That's not to say the Stompers weren't generating excitement. Their pint-size drummer Bobby Shannon was driving them along like a train, his rollicking style punctuated with bass drum 'bomb-drops' that had the Cornie's old skylights rattling.

I had expected to see a crowd of fans rubber-necking in front of the band, but only one had braved the Teds' flying brothel-creepers and the swirling petticoats of their chicks. My chum Jack Blair was standing at the corner of the apron stage nearest the trombone player. Jack was looking up at him, chewing gum and taking everything in. He acknowledged my arrival with the sort of wink that suggested there wasn't much about this trombone-playing lark that he couldn't get to grips with easily enough.

Jack was a bright, studious lad, of a modest disposition and not prone to blowing his own trumpet – or even trombone, for that matter – so I knew he wouldn't be giving off such a cocky vibe without first having weighed things up carefully. It didn't take me long to follow his line of thought.

Tall and gaunt, his hair swept back Chris Barber-style, Ian Menzies also favoured his role model's 'tailgate' approach to trombone playing. This is the no-frills method established by early New Orleans trombonists like Kid Ory himself. In its simplest form, it's little more than an 'oom-pah' statement of a tune's harmonic roots, decorated with growled swoops and smears, somewhat disparagingly described as 'barnyard glissandi', or even the death roars of a wounded elephant, by those inclined towards a more polished technique. The Stompers' leader had garnished the basic tailgate recipe with a little bowl of his favourite licks, which he dipped into freely. Essentially, though, his style was a straightforward one that would encourage rather than daunt any tyro trad trombonist. Hence my pal Jack's self-assured wink.

We stood watching the band for the remainder of the set. It had a front line of trumpet, trombone and soprano sax (in place of of the customary clarinet), with a conventional rhythm section comprising banjo, double bass, drums and piano. The musicians, who appeared to be in their late twenties to early thirties, cut a colourful dash in their tartan jackets. But what struck me most was that they didn't resort to flashy showmanship to grab the audience's attention. They just got on with playing their music, each soloist spurred on by occasional shouts of encouragement from the rhythm section, while his front-line colleagues helped the rhythm section out with some back-beat hand-clapping.

Least demonstrative of all was bandleader Menzies, who, when he wasn't playing, tended to survey the crowd in the manner of a school teacher watching unruly pupils cavorting in the playground. And when it came to announcements, he showed that he was as sparing with words as he was with musical statements. He didn't smile a lot either, but a droll sense of humour was hinted at by his use of an old enamel 'chantie', or chamber pot, as a plunger mute for his trombone. So, even if he did come across as being a bit aloof for a jazzman, he looked a likeable enough bloke to me – in a big-brotherly kind of way.

'And now,' he said, stooping over the mike, 'the skiffle group, with … Mary … McGowan!' His slow, Glasgow drawl exuded about as much stimulation as a bedtime mug of Horlicks. Yet those few words – or at least the final two – were enough to set a babble of anticipation rippling through the hall.

From where Jack and I were standing, it seemed all interest in dancing had ceased. Even the most adhesive of horizontal-intent couples were prising themselves apart to join a surge towards the stage, where a sea of beaming faces was gathering to gaze up at the wee Glasgow lassie in a party frock thrumming out a one-note intro to *Old Time Religion*. The other members of her group were the band's banjoist and drummer, plus leader Menzies, who, in further homage to his idol Chris Barber, had consigned his trombone to its case for the duration of the skiffle interlude and had turned his hand to plucking the string bass. It was his band, and if the girl singer was about to grab the limelight, he was making sure he'd be caught in its beam. That, at least, was how it struck me.

From a jazz enthusiast's point of view, it was ironic that the paying public's interest in the band had only been properly kindled once its principal exponents had left the stand. That's no reflection on Mary McGowan. She did what girl singers with dance bands had always done: she added the touch of 'glamour' that audiences find so irresistible. And the fact that she didn't contribute much in the way of actual *jazz* to the band's appeal was clearly of no consequence to the hundreds now idolising her from the floor of Haddington's Corn Exchange.

'Gawn yersel', Mary hen!' a well-oiled fan yelled in encouragement as he ricocheted his way stage-wards. 'Geez *Bill Bailey*, eh!' He then wheeled left and set an unsteady course for the toilets, while reaching for the half-bottle of whisky protruding from his hip pocket. Since the sale and consumption of alcohol on the premises was strictly prohibited, the gents' conveniences served as a clandestine drinking pit for those sufficiently bold, or drunk, to risk bringing their own 'cairry-oot'.

Just then, roared expletives and a woman's scream erupting from the direction of the entrance suggested that the first punch-up of the evening was kicking off.

'Pubs must've closed,' Jack observed.

'Yeah, let's fade, man,' I said, slipping effortlessly into musician-speak after just one hour of listening to live jazz for the very first time. 'It's when the fresh air hits them that the piss artists go doolally!'

* * * * *

73

CHAPTER EIGHT

'EVERY PATH HAS A PUDDLE'

It transpired that, with over thirteen hundred punters piling into Haddington's Corn Exchange, the Clyde Valley Stompers had smashed yet another attendance record. And even if bona fide jazz fans had been (to borrow from the vernacular of the Friday farmers) about as easy to find as lumps of unicorn shite on the Cornie's floor, most dedicated jazz clubs anywhere would have been delighted to pull in even half as many customers.

Yes, the Clydes were a potent commercial force, whose prospects appeared assured. Which was more than could be said for mine...

'You could always join the civil service,' Dad remarked after breakfast next morning. He didn't raise his eyes from his newspaper. If he had, he'd have seen the look of shocked disbelief on my face.

'An *office* job?'

'Hmm, says here they're starting some kind of scheme to fast-track recruits into the EO class.'

'E? ... O?'

'Executive Officer.'

'An *office* job?'

Now Dad did look up. 'But,' he winked, 'with a farming connection'

'An *office* job?' I glanced over at my mother. 'With a *farming* connection?'

Mother looked as confused as I felt. She motioned Dad to hand her the paper.

Dad chuckled. 'Seems we may have found a career for the boy.' He pointed to the relevant article. 'See what you think yourself.'

The puzzled frown on Mum's face was replaced by a little smile, which broadened as she read. 'I think you could well be right,' she nodded.

I shot her a look of utter dismay. 'An *office* job?'

'Well, up to a point, but even your grandfather has to attend to paperwork too, you know. All farmers do.'

'Yeah, but I wouldn't be farming at all in the civil service, would I? I'd be a pen-pusher, period!'

'No, no, you've got it wrong there,' Dad countered. 'OK, you wouldn't be farming, but EOs aren't pen-pushers either. They've got minions to do all that stuff for them.' He pulled a wry smile. 'I should know – I was one of those minions, once!'

He went on to explain that he and my mother had been in the civil service before the war. That was how they'd met: working in the same Ministry of Labour office in Edinburgh. They'd both been COs, Clerical Officers, and back then it could take years for a CO to be promoted to an EO, with special exams to pass as well.

He consulted the newspaper again. 'According to this, if you've got university-entrance qualifications, which you have, you can now become an EO right away. All you have to do is make it through an interview.'

I scratched the back of my head. 'CO... EO... EO... CO. Chuck in an EIO and we've got *Old MacDonald Had a Farm*. And even that would be more like the real thing than working for the Ministry of Labour.'

Mother gave a little laugh. 'But you wouldn't be applying to join the Ministry of Labour.'

'I wouldn't?'

'That's right,' said Dad. 'You'd go for the Ministry of Agriculture – or the Department of Agriculture, as it's called in Scotland.' He cocked his head and gave me another wink. 'See what we're getting at now?'

I did, but I still suspected I'd be committing myself to a life sentence of desk-jockeying. I looked Dad in the eye. 'So, what exactly do EOs *do* in the civil service?'

'Bugger all, as far as I saw. No, they just sit on their arses behind closed doors, drinking tea with their secretaries and dictating memos for the flunkeys. Believe me, boy, it's money for old rope being an EO. Oh aye, and they're pensioned to the eyeballs an' all, by the way!'

Mum noticed immediately that Dad's waggish reply hadn't had the effect he'd hoped for.

'Being an Executive Officer isn't like that at all,' she assured me. 'And I should know, because *I* was an EO's personal secretary.' She cast Dad one of her withering looks. 'The advice your father just gave you is like his piano playing – not to be taken seriously.' While Dad huffed and puffed, she proceeded to tell me that Executive Officers were administrators, managers, decision-makers, who, depending on their grade (for the entire civil service pecking order was clearly defined by grades) kept the wheels of government moving smoothly by seeing to it that –

'The minions,' Dad cut in, 'do the donkey work EOs dish out in all those bloody memos.' He flashed Mum one of his one-up-for-me looks, before addressing me directly again: 'Like I said – money for old rope!'

'Spoken by someone who was never likely to be considered executive material himself,' Mother came back. Ignoring Dad's muttered objections, she concluded her broad description of an EO's role in the civil service, then gave me her views on what a career in the Department of Agriculture might mean for me. Apart from the fact that I'd be in one of the most secure jobs imaginable, starting farther up the promotion ladder than had been possible for anyone of my age before now, I'd be making regular out-of-office visits to farms and I'd be –

'Pensioned to the eyeballs,' Dad reiterated, '– just like I said.'

'Your father is absolutely right on that score,' Mother swiftly conceded. 'Just think... when you're still a relatively young man – early sixties, maybe even late fifties – you'll be able to retire to a life of leisure, with no financial worries at all.'

I was still only seventeen, a schoolboy until a few days ago, so thoughts of what would be in store for me forty-odd years from now weren't exactly in the forefront of my mind. Pensions were for old folks, and I was just setting out in life, with a determination to make it a worthwhile and enjoyable one to boot.

Again, the will was there, but for once, and just when it mattered more than ever, there was no discernible way. I had missed out on taking an academic route into practical farming and I had rejected the opportunity to go to art college. All the future held for me at present was the usual casual job mucking out cattle sheds at Acredales Farm along the road. Hardly what my parents had hoped for when they gave me the chance to stay on at school.

'And there are loads of perks for EOs too,' Mother enthused. 'Discounts at the best shops and special rates for first-class travel and that sort of thing.'

'Aye, and plenty of free time,' Dad added. 'Nine-to-five, five-day week. Plenty of time for hobbies. You know, like your music and everything.'

'And the salary,' Mum chipped in. 'You'll be a really well-off young man, with guaranteed increments year after year.'

'Absolutely,' Dad concurred. 'And pensioned to the eyeballs as well, don't forget!'

Mother nodded again, while offering Dad a supportive little smile.

This was a sign I knew well. Although many of the conversational exchanges between my parents were ostensibly bristly, this really amounted to nothing more than a kind of good-natured jousting, not in any way symptomatic of the friction a casual observer might assume existed in their relationship. Verbal sparring was just their peculiar way of getting along, and I had never known it to be any different. Of course, they had their individual tastes and values too – as witness their conflicting estimations of Dad's piano playing. Even so, there were two characteristics common to them both: a keen sense of humour and an unfaltering commitment to seeing my sister and me make the best possible start in life. With Minnie already settled into a good job at one of the local banks, the onus was now firmly on me to get my future sorted out.

My folks had never put this to me in so many words, but Mother's allusive smile to Dad a moment ago said it all.

I took a deep breath, then declared with as much conviction as I could fake: 'You know, the way you've described it, I reckon the civil service could be just the thing for me, right enough. Yes, I'll send for an application form right away!'

*

Drumsheugh Gardens is a leafy terrace in the west end of Edinburgh's New Town; an area of the city that exudes architectural elegance and basks in the air of Victorian conservatism for which Scotland's capital is famous – or infamous, if you come from Glasgow. In the 1950s, it was the location of the Scottish Land Court, to whose austere offices I had been summoned just one month after applying to join the Department of Agriculture as a direct entrant Executive Officer.

The five grey suits sitting at the other side of the boardroom table looked depressingly identical, like ageing quintuplets who had been subjected to a life devoid of humour and, to add discomfort to their misery, now suffered from chronic constipation. Never mind, I told myself, it would soon be time for their long-incubated pensions to hatch, so that might cheer them up a bit. The centre suit dipped his head to indicate that I should sit down on a chair occupying an otherwise empty expanse of floor between the table and the door. All that was missing, I mused, was a naked light bulb dangling above my head and a shadowy figure standing arms-folded in the corner with a revolver in his hand.

I had been dreading this moment more and more as the appointed day approached. But now that I was actually in the dragons' den, a feeling of inevitability came over me, not just calming my nerves, but prompting me to regard the situation as slightly surreal, if not totally absurd. It was as if I had wandered into a time warp, caught in a twilight zone occupied by colourless old men whose outlook on life echoed that of generations of career civil servants before them. Theirs was a world I didn't belong in. I felt that in my bones. Yet I owed it to my parents to make an effort to comply. Like it or not, the circumstances that had brought me to this spot were now water under the bridge, so there was nothing else for it: I'd give this thing my best shot – and hope for the best too.

As the interview progressed, it became increasingly apparent that the panel of judges were no more comfortable about the situation than I was. They had made it clear at the outset that I was the very first applicant in the entire country to be considered as a potential direct entrant EO. It followed, to my way of thinking, that the grey suits were therefore totally unaccustomed to vetting someone who hadn't emerged from the ranks of their own subordinates. Consequently, they probably didn't feel free to grill me as severely as they would an existing civil servant desperate to improve his current grade. In other words, *I* had nothing to lose, *they* couldn't pull rank, and so the whole process was conducted in a somewhat benign and stilted atmosphere.

After half an hour, I was back in the sunshine of Drumsheugh Gardens, the smell of government carbon paper and pencil sharpenings still in my nostrils, and a sneaky hope in the back of my mind that the interview hadn't gone as well as it seemed to have done. That said, I had genuinely done my best to give a good account of myself, answering all questions in an honest and respectful way. That's how I'd been brought up. With regard to my inquisitors, my impression was that they had been chiefly trying to assess if I was the right 'sort' to wear the stereotypical civil servant's clothes, literally and metaphorically. They had asked for my views on leadership, teamwork, playing by the rules and respecting 'the establishment', which I took to mean conducting myself publicly in a manner befitting one of 'them'. At the end of the hearing, thin smiles all round gave the impression that the suits had been reasonably pleased with my performance. On the other hand, there was always the chance that they were simply glad to see the back of me.

The answer came in a brown OHMS envelope two weeks later. My parents and sister Minnie watched as I silently read the letter at the breakfast table, their expectant grins fading by the moment.

'You failed the interview, didn't you?' Minnie said in a big-sisterly way that contained about as much surprise as sympathy.

I frowned at the letter and shook my head. 'No, I passed the damned thing.'

'Well, why the glum face?' Dad breezed. 'First direct entrant EO in the country!' He leaned over the table and slapped my shoulder. 'Congratulations, boy!'

'That's right,' Mother chirped. 'Cheer up! You should be proud of yourself!'

I tried to smile, but my face muscles refused to follow orders.

'You've been posted to some far-away, God-forsaken place, haven't you?' said Minnie, a trace of big-sisterly hope in her voice. 'Like maybe St Kilda – to administer the gannets.'

'St Kilda would be a blessing,' I mumbled, still gazing cheerlessly at the letter. 'No, I've been posted to Edinburgh.'

A puzzled hush descended on the kitchen.

Mother was first to break the silence. 'Edinburgh? But that's wonderful. You'll be able to live at home here.'

'Dead right,' Dad beamed. 'Forty-five-minutes bus ride morning and night. Piece o' cake!'

Minnie prodded me with her finger. 'So, wee brother, what's your beef?'

I looked up and managed to simulate a smile. 'Well,' I sighed, 'it's not so much where I've been posted, but to what.' I surveyed the trio of confused faces staring at me for a few moments, then said, 'You see, I won't be working for the Department of Agriculture after all.'

'You … won't?' my family chorused.

'No,' I replied dryly. 'Believe it or not, but I've been posted to the Ministry of bloody Labour!'

* * * * *

81

CHAPTER NINE

'ONLY A MATTER OF TIME'

The only comfort I drew from the letter was that it stated I wouldn't take up my appointment as a civil servant until the beginning of January – a month after I reached eighteen, the minimum admissible age for becoming an Executive Officer. As it was now only mid-August, this meant I still had over four months to work along at the farm, and that suited me just fine.

Tractors had already replaced horses on most East Lothian farms, but farmer John Taylor, a devoted horseman, still retained a token presence of Clydesdales at Lennoxlove Acredales. These gentle giants were the charges of two old worthies called Johnny Rutherford and Joe Ward. Now well into their sixties, Johnny and Joe had worked with Clydesdales all of their lives. In their eyes, tractors were trespassers in a timeless world of which they and their horses were as much a natural part as the very soil they walked on. They disliked with a vengeance the little grey Ferguson tractor John Taylor had put at their disposal, his hope being that its occasional use for simple tasks would gradually bring about their acceptance of the inevitable. It was a forlorn hope, and this suited me just fine too.

Whether it was straw sheaves to be transported for stacking at harvest time or potatoes to be carted from field to 'pit' in the autumn, Johnny and Joe always found an excuse to delegate the tractor-driving to me. Meanwhile, they got on with the same jobs in their customary way. It was a dodge to which John Taylor obligingly turned a blind eye.

Those months at Acredales would prove to be some of the most satisfying of my life. Despite increasing mechanisation, the pace of life on that particular farm was still influenced, if no longer dictated, by the few remaining Clydesdales. No matter how pressing the task, horses, willing as they were, could only be driven so hard. The horsemen instinctively knew what their animals were capable of and would never contemplate trying to exceed those limits. Rest periods, then, were necessities for a horseman which did not apply to a tractor driver. Many were the 'meenit times', or refreshment breaks, I spent being regaled by Johnny and Joe's yarns about the old days, while engulfed in pungent reek from the stumpy little pipes jutting Popeye-style from the corners of their mouths. There was something deeply comforting about sitting behind a hedge with nothing to compete with the twittering of sparrows but the old boys' chortles and the sound of their horses munching on tufts of grass, while a tractor, like a portent of so-called progress, groaned at its labours in a distant field.

Another welcome aspect of the second half of 1958 was that, with no further studies to concern me, I had more time to spend with Ellie. Since its unpromising start some eighteen months earlier, our relationship had blossomed into something quite special, although we were still too young to fully appreciate it. Without really noticing, we had progressed from being high school sweethearts, somehow surviving the transient ups and downs that can scupper such youthful liaisons, to becoming, not just an 'item', but best friends as well.

Ellie's mother, now in her forties, still displayed ample evidence of the stunning good looks she must also have been blessed with in her youth. It followed that she exercised great caution before allowing her daughter to go out with me. I had passed many weekend evenings sitting in her front room watching *Gunsmoke* or *Take Your Pick* (Ellie's mother was a big fan of TV westerns and game shows) while she discreetly weighed me up. Then, when sufficiently satisfied that I was a decent lad who would treat her daughter with due care and respect, she gave her permission for us to step out on our own – but only on condition that we walked directly to visit my own parents on the other side of town. They, Ellie's mother decreed, were also entitled to get to know Ellie before allowing their son to take *her* out. Indicative of a strict German upbringing, she showed a sense of good, old-fashioned rectitude that some considered was rapidly disappearing from post-war Britain.

She also possessed a ready sense of humour, which leaned towards the slapstick and had been inherited by Ellie. For example, when watching TV, mother and daughter would shriek in delight when one of James Arness's adversaries fell off his horse or Michael Miles finally succeeded in making a contestant blow it on the 'Yes-No Interlude'. In contrast, my own mother's humour was of a less effusive kind. Yet she was just as given to a sudden fit of the giggles as Ellie, so they got on famously from the start. And despite my father sensing Ellie's lack of enthusiasm for his piano playing – which he subjected her to on her very first visit – he welcomed her warmly into our little family circle as well.

As Kimber had recently returned home on completion of his national service, he and my sister Minnie soon formed a foursome with Ellie and me. One of East Lothian's many natural charms is its quietly spectacular coastline, so, after I passed my driving test, we'd borrow Dad's old Austin Ten of a Sunday and go on a picnic jaunt to one of the sandy beaches at Gullane or North Berwick. Naturally, Kimber and I would talk endlessly about jazz, leaving Ellie and Minnie to prepare the sandwiches and brew tea on a little meths burner. Simple, innocent, yet unforgettably happy times.

Competing with Ellie's affections as a source of good cheer for me was the knowledge that Kimber's return would finally allow us to get on with forming the band we had first talked about in my grandfather's cattle shed a couple of years earlier.

*

'Wee Bob' Sandie had been one of the leading 'tippers' with Haddington Boys' Pipe Band during the years Kimber and I marched in its ranks. Consquently, Bob's drumstick dexterity was already well known to us, but only so far as his ability to rattle a snare drum was concerned. I had lost touch with Bob while he was away studying chemistry at university in Edinburgh, where, by happy chance, he had also been bitten by the jazz bug. Hearing that we were forming a band, he now got in touch to offer his services behind the full drum kit he'd bought from a fellow student, who, according to Bob, just happened to be even more skint than he was himself. The appearance of the kit reflected the meagre sum Bob had presumably paid, but the sounds he produced from it echoed those of the great Gene Krupa himself – to our eager ears, at any rate.

'Yeah, outta sight!' was Jim Douglas's reaction to Bob's introductory drum break after setting up his kit in a store room above Fred Faunt's little fruit-and-veg shop in Haddington.

Bob had joined Jim, Kimber, Jack and me for the first practice session of the Hidden Town Dixielanders – or as much of the band as we had managed to assemble so far. Sadly, we'd already abandoned hope of being able to recruit a pianist, since the only one we knew was a girl who accompanied the hymn-singing at a local Sunday school, and she was about as jazz-minded as one of Fred Faunt's cabbages. Jim, however, promised us that he had solved the remaining problem: his chum who played bass in the skiffle group (of which Jim was still a member) would be coming along just as soon as he'd finished work for the evening.

Sure enough, while we were huddled round a portable record player, each trying to absorb his individual instrument's contribution to the Muggsy Spanier Band's version of *I Wish I Could Shimmy Like My Sister Kate*, in came our promised bass player.

John Logan's reputation as a jazz aficionado preceded him. We had been told by Jim that he'd had the enviable good fortune to attend a concert by Louis Armstrong and his All-Stars in London a few years earlier. John had been doing his national service in south-west England and, Jim maintained, had a mate who'd gone temporarily blind a couple of times drinking the rough 'scrumpy' cider the West Country is famous for.

Seeing the legendary Louis Armstrong live and being a buddy of someone who got blind drunk on cheap booze! What better credentials could an aspiring jazzman have? We were ready to welcome John as a messiah, yet our faith was seriously challenged the moment he entered the room. Instead of the big bull fiddle we had been expecting, John was lugging a plywood tea chest with a broom handle and length of string attached. We glared at Jim.

'Well,' he shrugged, 'it sounds fine in the skiffle group, so...'

'Aw relax, lads,' John chuckled. 'Nobody'll notice the difference.'

Not if they're blind, I thought. Maybe deafness would be a help as well.

John was still chuckling. 'Come on,' he said, placing one foot on the tea chest while tensioning the broom handle and string for action, 'play anything you like. I'll latch on. No problem.'

In the event, the sounds John managed to pound from his tea chest bass were more musical than the wails, fluffs and grunts produced by Kimber, Jack and me in our first attempt to fuse as a Dixieland front line. The tune we'd chosen was, inevitably, *The Saints*. It was a melody everybody knew, and with the added attraction of having a simple chord sequence to improvise round. All the same, our front line's efforts could most generously be described as undisciplined, and would have bordered on the shambolic but for the steadying influence of the rhythm section. Wee Bob laid down a rock-solid beat, while Jim and John displayed ample evidence of the cohesion they had developed through playing together in the skiffle group.

And I had to admit that John was right; once the band was blasting away, his tea chest did adequately fulfil the function of a real bass fiddle. But, I reckoned, even if its sound was passable, its appearance would be regarded as a joke by jazz buffs.

John was a printer with the local *Courier*, and at twenty-five the oldest member in our group. He was also a married man with the start of a brood of little Logans to support. It was unlikely, then, that his family finances would stretch to something so frivolous as purchasing a double bass just to satisfy the pretensions of a few wannabe jazzers who might never appear beyond the confines a local greengrocer's store room. So, we'd have to accept that it would be a tea chest bass or nothing. Or would it?

There is a saying that patience, time and money accommodate all things. We had no alternative but to be patient, and trust time to turn John's thoughts towards finding the money to buy a proper bass – more essential demands upon his domestic budget notwithstanding.

*

By the end of just a few practice sessions we found ourselves relying progressively less on trying to imitate what our idols were playing on record. Instead, each of us did his own thing and let his ability to improvise dictate the outcome. After all, that's what jazz is all about, and even though our attempts were rough-and-ready, at least we were giving free rein to creative impulses that were original. Of course, we were also aware that many jazz standards featured set arranged passages which all bands were expected to adhere to, and we took time to work those out as well. Although there was no denying our solo work still owed more to unbridled enthusiasm than to mastery of our instruments, we were beginning to show signs of a mutual awareness in our ensemble efforts. We were actually starting to sound like a jazz band – or at least a reasonable impersonation of one. And boy, were we having fun!

Jazzmen have always claimed there's no bigger buzz – leastways not a legal one – than playing as a combo when everyone hits the elusive 'sweet spot' together. Not yet eighteen, I wasn't particularly up on buzzes, legal or otherwise. Nevertheless, even our faltering attempts at creating a marriage of spontaneous ideas generated feelings in me that were positively electric. I can only describe the experience as something akin to being both a piece in and a solver of a jigsaw puzzle, which isn't manifested as a still picture, but as an ever changing kaleidoscope of sound. I had never felt so alive, and I guessed this went for the other lads as well.

'This calls for a celebration!' John declared one evening after we'd completed our most rewarding rehearsal yet. 'Let's all head across the street!'

Opposite Fred Faunt's shop stood the Victoria Inn. Nowadays, the quaint old building houses an award-winning eatery called The Avenue, but back then 'The Vic' was best known for its spit-and-sawdust bar – one of the most popular watering holes in town.

In response to John's suggestion, I owned up to two concerns I believed were shared with Jack and Jim. The first was that the three of us were under the legal age for entering licensed premises, the second that we had no money. Glumly, Wee Bob admitted in suitably scholarly parlance that he was a temporary victim of the latter impediment too.

John, however, assured us there was no need to worry. 'The drinks are on me!' he grinned. 'Yeah, and in The Vic, if you're big enough, you're old enough!'

True enough, the appearance of a trio of callow youths wandering in with three other chaps who might have been their older brothers drew hardly a second glance from the mob of imbibers corralled along the length of The Vic's bar. John asked Kimber and Wee Bob to help him fetch the drinks, then gestured towards the far corner of the room.

'Better grab that table,' he told me. 'And save three seats for us.'

When it's your first time in a pub, trying to give the impression that it isn't can be difficult. As we sat down, I glanced at Jack and Jim to see how they were coping.

Jim, being the youngest, should by rights have appeared the most self-conscious. The opposite was the case. Maybe it was a sign of his village upbringing. Gifford is a sleepy little place nestled in the lower slopes of the Lammermuir Hills. In the Fifties, it was still populated for the most part by the same ilk of down-to-earth country folk that had been its lifeblood for centuries – shepherds, farm workers, woodsmen and an assortment of rural artisans. Those inclined to an occasional alcoholic refreshment (which was likely to be the vast majority) would habitually spread their custom between the village's two homely hostelries, The Goblin Ha' and The Tweeddale Arms. As both of these establishments occupied prominent positions at the hub of the community, it was my guess that Jim and his pals, like generations of Gifford youths before them, would be well accustomed to swapping quips and leg-pulls with their elders as the latter made their way in or out of either boozer.

My hunch proved correct.

Jim gave what I initially took to be the V-sign to a flat-capped old character propping up the nearest corner of the bar. 'Peace, daddy!' he called out. 'How're they hangin'?'

The old boy acknowledged Jim's greeting with a wink and a sideways nod. 'Fairly plumb, son. Fairly plumb.'

The personal nature of Jim's salutation, which enquired after the gravitational attitude of the elderly gentleman's genitalia, and the elderly gentleman's genial response, suggested a state of mutual familiarity.

'Friend of yours, Jim?' I asked.

He raised a nonchalant shoulder. 'Never fuckin' clapped eyes on him before. Nah, just checkin' he's hip to the scene.'

Point made.

I turned to Jack, who was pulling a half-smoked cigarette from the top pocket of his jacket. He tapped the back of a burly fellow sitting at the next table.

'Got a light, pal?'

Without interrupting the conversation he was engaged in, the fellow produced a cigarette lighter and held it over his shoulder. Jack kindled his dowt and handed the lighter back.

'Thanks, pal.'

'Never knew you smoked,' I remarked.

Jack popped a piece of chewing gum into his mouth. 'Gotta blend in,' he said. 'Make yerself inconspicuous.'

Point taken.

So much for my concerns about the three of us being underage. Seemed I had spent too cocooned a life, and it obviously showed. Jack pulled another blinked fag from his pocket and lit it from the one he was smoking.

'Here … relax, man. Ac' nat'ral and nobody'll notice ye.'

Old Johnny and Joe at Acredales had occasionally cajoled me into sampling the black 'Bogie Roll' they smoked in their little pipes, but one puff of the noxious shag always made me gag. Theirs was a taste I'd already given up trying to acquire.

But, if anything, the sulphurous tang of the cigarette smoke presently filling my mouth was even more nauseating. Still, needs must. The trick now would be to act natural without actually throwing up.

'Got pale ale for you three,' John informed us as our pints were placed on the table. 'It's what we call boys' stuff – a bit weaker than the heavy.'

Jack was patently miffed. 'Heavy's never done me any harm before!'

'You can have mine,' said Wee Bob, swapping glasses. 'Pale, light, heavy, brown, black, green, red or tartan – bevvy's all the same to me when it's for nothin'!'

'Spoken like a true student,' John said. 'But better make the most of this freebie. It'll likely be the last you get from me for a while.'

John's final remark bothered me. Could it be that he was about to secede from the band? And just when things were shaping up so promisingly too. Anyway, I had distinctly more urgent matters to focus on for now...

Being confronted with your first pint of beer in a public bar is a daunting experience. It looks like a hell of a lot of liquid to be downed, particularly if you're not partial to the taste. I had tried a glug from a screwtop bottle someone smuggled into our hut at cadet camp a while back, and the effect on my senses remained with me. It reminded me of the smell on Dad's breath when he came home from the pub: a pong reminiscent of the one that rose from the ground when Clydesdales were relieving themselves. And that exploratory slurp at cadet camp had tasted the same. Straight horse piss.

'Cheers!' said the lads. We clinked glasses. 'All the best!'

So, here I was, the epitome of a true jazz musician, sitting with a lit fag in one hand and a glass of booze in the other. The eyes of my peers, if not the entire bar, were on me – or so I thought. Nothing else for it now but to follow Jack's advice and hope I wouldn't make a complete arse of myself.

The air was blue, with tobacco smoke and the language of the clientele in fairly equal measure. Likewise, toilet odours mingling with the acrid smack of beer slops helped reinforce a pervading aura of squalor. But it was a cosy kind of squalor. The Vic was a no-frills pub, and judging by the profusion of cigarette butts on the floor, that's how the regulars liked it. Good news for me. I took a furtive drag of my ciggy, stifled a minor convulsion, flicked the dog-end onto the deck and stubbed it out with my foot. First hurdle cleared. Now for the horse piss...

There were two important points my inexperience had made me overlook. The first was that, unlike horse piss, beer contains alcohol. The second was that human taste buds can become accustomed to – and even grow to like – stuff that tastes remarkably similar to horse piss, especially if it has the power to intoxicate. It's just a question of perseverance, as well as employing a goodly measure of mind over matter. This dawned on me after I'd downed a couple of mouthfuls of pale ale without puking. The onset of a pleasant dizziness then eased things along – once, that is, my mind had overcome the matter of nature urging me to spew my guts up. And once the pleasant dizziness had worn off, an irresistible urge to converse with my fellow man took over. And the more irresistible this urge became, the less it mattered which fellow man got an ear-bending.

Just one visit to the toilets found me making several new friends en route, and several more on my way back. Stalwarts of The Vic every one, their salutations were invariably along the lines of, 'You're one o' them young buggers kickin' up a rammy across at Freddie Faunt's there, aren't ye?' All the same, a hearty slap on the shoulder usually followed, and so did a pint of ale on two occasions. Or was it three?

By the time I made it back, only John remained at our table. Jim, I noticed, was holding court over what had grown into a huddle of flat-capped old characters at the corner of the bar. Laughter was in abundant supply, as were half-full glasses. Or were they half-empty? Nearby, Wee Bob, his drumsticks a blur above a bar stool, was giving a master class in paradiddling to anyone who would listen – or at least buy him a drink.

I sat down, and after I'd got an eye focused on John, I took a swig of Dutch courage and asked him straight out if he was leaving the band.

'*Leaving*? I've only just joined, son!'

'Yeah, but what you said to Wee Bob – you know, about this maybe being the last time you'd buy the boys a drink...'

John burst out laughing. 'I'd buy the boys a drink every night, *if* I had the spare loot. But I don't have the spare loot every night, every week, or even every month.' He went on to explain that, apart from music, his other great hobby was shooting, and it just so happened that he'd bagged two wild geese and a roe deer the night before. That didn't happen very often, and on this occasion he'd flogged the game to a local dealer for a good price – enough to give the wife a peace offering, with a few bob left over to treat the lads in the band to a pint. 'Mind you,' he said, 'if it had been a skiffle group practice tonight, *they*'d have got the pints instead.'

My brain now joined my eye in the focusing stakes. 'Shooting, eh? Got a gun, have you?'

'A bit bloody difficult shootin' geese without one!'

'Hmm,' I hummed, pensively. 'Expensive things, guns, I suppose?'

'Good ones cost a fortune – shotguns that is.' John stuck his chest out. 'Yes, and I've got one o' the best. Twelve-bore Italian – pump-action – engraved walnut stock wi' silver inlay – the works! Aye, the wife did her nut when I brought it home. Said she could've bought a fleet o' prams wi' the money.'

My brain was now giving my open eye seeing lessons. 'Hmm,' I hummed again, calculatingly this time.

'What ye thinkin'?' said John.

I stroked my chin. 'Only that it's surprising how good horse piss can taste after a while.'

Just then, Kimber appeared from the midst of the multitude. 'Fag?' he said, pushing an open packet of Capstan towards me.

I wrinkled my nose. 'No thanks. Nah, to be absolutely honest, I don't really like smoking.'

He and John exchanged the knowing looks of two ex-national servicemen. 'Only a matter of time,' they smiled. 'Only a matter of time.'

It also proved to be only a matter of time before John succumbed to gentle, though relentless, persuasion and part-exchanged his fancy shotgun for a more modest model. He used the surplus from the transaction to purchase a proper string bass – the surplus remaining, that is, after he'd bought his wife 'a wee treat of her choice'. Which, he was at pains to point out, was *not* a new pram!

* * * * *

CHAPTER TEN

'METRONOMES DON'T SWING'

Things developed surprisingly swiftly after John bought his double bass. At the next rehearsal, Jim turned up with a banjo. This, despite his long declared aversion to an instrument he described as 'a musical (but only just!) frying pan.' All he said in mitigation was that he'd been given this one for nix by some mouldy old cat who was about to bin it anyway.

To describe a banjo to the uninitiated would be to suggest a small, shallow-bodied drum with a fingerboard protruding and a set of strings stretched fiddle-style over the whole. Jim pointed out that the 'skin' had been missing from the drum element of this particular example, as had the strings. But, hey, no sweat; it had been merely a case of re-skinning it (a skill he learned from his ex-army drummer Dad) and attaching four new strings. But we shouldn't forget, Jim cautioned, that there remained the pain-in-the-arse chore of learning to play the bloody thing, since the tuning, and consequently fingering, of a banjo is different from a guitar's.

Grunts and shrugs of resignation ensued, but with a hint of disappointment too. As pleased as we were with Jim's guitar accompaniment, particularly on slower and more mellow numbers, it had always been agreed, albeit tacitly, that the strident sound of a banjo was needed to provide an extra bit of bite for the up-tempo stuff. Especially so since our rhythm section lacked a piano.

'How long d'you reckon it'll take to learn?' I asked Jim.

Instead of replying, he sighed, slung the banjo strap over his shoulder, peered numbly at the strings, then plucked out a few discordant plinks and plonks.

In an attempt to cast light on the gathering gloom, John suggested, somewhat suggestively, that a lad of Jim's age must already have mastered the wrist action required for high-speed banjo-strumming. It followed, he deduced, that we probably wouldn't have to wait all that long for him to adapt the technique to the latest task in hand – if we saw what he meant.

While we sniggered, Jim glowered, smirked, gave one of his short, staccato laughs, then sang out:

'O-o-o-oh, de Camptown Races, heah Ah come,
Doo-dah! Doo-dah!
Caught ma goolies on de barbed wire fence,
Oh! de doo-da day!'

Without even glancing at the fingerboard, he unleashed a flurry of chords that would have done credit to the great George Formby at his window-cleaning best.

'Ah'm playin' in F!' Jim hollered. 'Come on in!'

Wee Bob led the charge with a four-bar drum break, followed by Kimber blaring out a trumpet fanfare which we recognised as the intro to one of jazz's favourite flag-wavers. Maryland, My Maryland has emerged under various names since starting out as a German Christmas carol called O Tannenbaum. It has also been adopted as an anthem by bodies as diverse as combatants in the American Civil War, supporters of Manchester United Football Club, members of the international socialist movement and, of course, the eponymous US State. But it's unlikely it could ever have been performed with greater gusto and unbridled glee than it was by us that evening. And all thanks to Jim and his banjo.

Naturally, we were keen to know how he'd mastered the fingering so quickly.

'It was a piece o' cake,' he shrugged. 'A tenor banjo's tuned the same as a fiddle.'

'Hell's bells, if I'd known you played the fiddle,' John bristled, 'I'd've collared you for a few lessons on this big fella here. Save myself a lotta bother.'

'Play the fiddle? Me? Yeah, tried it once, but packed it in. Naw, I've about as much idea of playin' a fiddle as playin' a banjo.' Jim waited for a few mystery-deepening moments to pass before revealing that all he'd done was re-tune his banjo strings to match the first four of his guitar's six. Purist banjoists might not approve, but who the hell gave a shit about purist banjoists? Certainly not guitar players who'd been railroaded, as he put it, into cookin' up music in a fuckin' fryin' pan!

Despite his protestations, it was obvious that Jim had thoroughly enjoyed the boost his banjo had given the band for that particular tune – as it would for others of similar stripe. Although never likely to be a purist, Jim had just shown he had an aptitude for playing an instrument that not all guitarists could master. And vice versa.

Saddled with an image tied to 'Oh! Susanna' minstrel shows and cheeky-chappie music hall acts, the banjo is much maligned by many in the serious jazz camp, though arguably more by non-participating 'experts' than by musicians. In any case, it would be the most frigid of souls who could listen to a banjo without a smile creasing his chops and a tap tickling his toes. This was the quality we now welcomed into the band.

We were in high spirits exiting the alley beside Fred Faunt's shop that evening. Until we were approached by a middle-aged man who looked as if he had something less uplifting on his mind.

'I was standin' havin' a pint by the window over there in the Vic,' he said. 'Heard you lads playin' *The Red Flag* –'

'That'd be *Maryland, My Maryland*', Kimber quickly corrected.

'Whatever ye say, laddie, but in the Labour Party it's *The Red Flag*. OK?'

Just as we were preparing to be dressed down for jazzing up the hallowed canticle of British lefties, the man smiled and introduced himself as entertainments convenor of the local Cage Bird Society. He didn't know a crotchet from a canary, he confessed, but any band that could bring a spark to that doomy old Marxist dirge had to have *some*thing going for it. Anyway, to the point – his organisation was planning to run a fund-raising dance soon, and would we consider accepting an invitation to provide the music?

Consider accepting? We didn't even bother to ask if there was a fee!

*

Haddington's British Legion Club was situated in premises behind Halliday's ramshackle old garage in Market Street. It wasn't exactly in the same prestige league as the grand ballrooms of the Mecca Dancing chain. And it wasn't exactly in the same capacity league as even the local Corn Exchange, since its function room could accommodate only fifty dancing couples, at a pinch. But as far as we were concerned, the 'Legion' hall had become the Taj Mahal with a dance floor.

With just three weeks to go before our first engagement, we crammed in as many practice sessions as we could. Even so, our repertoire still consisted of only a dozen tunes. Hardly enough to see us through two one-hour sets.

'There's a liquor licence,' said Jack, who, despite being a chap of few words, always seemed to have the appropriate few to contribute when it came to bar-related matters.

'No, I reckon we should adopt a strict no-drinkin' policy,' Kimber countered. 'Can't afford to get bombed out of our first gig for bein' pissed.'

'Yeah, OK, fair enough,' Jack conceded, chewing. Jack was always chewing – even when playing his trombone. I wouldn't have been surprised to see a big bubble coming out of the bell during one of his solos, though it never did. 'But actually,' he went on, 'I was thinkin' more about the punters.' He then exposed the studious side of his nature by reasoning that, by the time we started our second set, most of the customers would be sufficiently tiddly not to notice *what* we were playing, far less that we'd already played it – probably more than once.

We all agreed he had a point there. Hmm. It was still a bit risky, though.

Silence heralded an interlude of concerted thought.

Wee Bob was first to come up with a result. 'Twelve-bar blues,' he said about two seconds into the think-in.

'Eh?' we chorused

Our science-graduate drummer slipped straight into scholarly mode. 'Basic mathematics, intit? You guys can play in three keys now – four with a struggle – and a twelve-bar blues is a twelve-bar blues, whatever the key.'

Jim, like the rest of us, was none the wiser. 'So, where do the maths come in?'

'Easy. When you're stuck for a real tune, you make up a simple riff – you know, a wee repeated phrase – play it ensemble-like a couple of times on the chord sequence of a twelve-bar blues, stretch it out wi' solos, then all together again for some ride-out choruses. A few real tunes later, you're maybe stuck again, so you make up another riff in another key – give it another name over the mic – same routine.'

'So, where do the maths come in?' Jim reiterated, speaking for us all.

Wee Bob was becoming exasperated. 'Jesus wept! Three or four keys multiplied by an infinite number of different twelve-bar riffs equals the end of a limited repertoire. Get it now?'

We did indeed, and it made perfect sense.

'Goes to show it pays to have a boffin in the band,' said John with a shrug. 'Aye, and they say all drummers are bonkers.'

Bob responded with a coy smile. 'Ah well, just because a person's a genius doesn't mean he's not nuts.'

We bowed to Bob's superior intellect and left it at that.

*

Before we got the ball rolling on the big night, the Cage Bird Society's entertainments convenor took time to inform us that 'the crowd' would be comprised mainly of his fellow members, their friends and their respective wives: a more mature and dignified congregation than the herds of young animals that frequented the Cornie on a Saturday night. There would be no jiving or doing 'The Creep' here. Strict-tempo dancing was the done thing in The Legion. It followed that we'd have to remember to introduce each number accordingly – quickstep, foxtrot, slow foxtrot or whatever. Wattie Frater and his Hawaiian Serenaders had played for the last function, and they had set a standard that everyone would expect to be matched tonight.

'Ha-Hawaiian Serenaders?' I checked, first-night butterflies morphing into fruit bats.

'That's right. Ye *can* play tangos, can't ye?'

'Tangos?' Kimber queried. 'But they're Argentinian, no?'

The convenor cast him a confused look. Kimber cast me a despairing one.

'Well, we – um – we know *The Isle of Capri*,' I submitted, speculatively.

The convenor greeted this geographical compromise with a sigh of relief. 'That's near enough, son. Better kick off wi' a quickstep, though. Save the hula-hula stuff till later.'

'I might've been wrong about the no-drinkin' policy,' Kimber told me out of the corner of his mouth. 'We're gonna need all the help we can get here!'

Oh, and there was just one other thing the entertainments convenor wanted to mention before we started. Did we see that big, tall bloke down the other end of the hall? 'The spivvy-lookin' gadgie wi' the kipper tie, flared trooser and shiny shoes? Him wi' the lassie dressed up like a Christmas tree fairy?'

We indicated the affirmative.

'Well,' the convenor continued, 'he's a special guest – member o' one o' our sister societies in Edinburgh. Breeds prize-winnin' budgerigars, him. He's a Pole – stranded here after the war. Very famous in cage bird circles, like. Aye, ye've maybe heard o' him. Name's Wojciech Tworzewski-Kalinowski – somethin' like that. But life's too short. We just call him 'Budgie'.'

'Very interesting,' Jack muttered, still chewing, 'but we don't play mazurkas.'

If the convenor had heard that barbed quip, he pretended not to. 'Just so long as ye watch yer tempos, boys. Budgie's a prize-winnin' ballroom dancer as well, ye see. Hence his lassie all dolled up there in the sparkly frock wi' frilly petticoats and everything. Aye, a stickler for the strict tempos, him.'

With that, the entertainments convenor told us to 'take it away', then took himself away 'to give the missus a wee whirl round the floor, like.'

'You announce the first one,' Kimber said in my ear, 'and we'll take turn about after that.'

'Announce? *Me*?' I hadn't seen this one coming. I was seized by memories of the beak mocking my scripture-readings during school assembly. 'But I mumble! I don't –'

'Better make it a quickstep like the man said,' Kimber cut in. He handed me the mic. '*At The Jazz Band Ball* should do it.'

No escape now. I blurted out the essential info to the waiting dancers as rapidly as I could, then stomped the first tune in without pausing to draw breath: 'A-one, two, a-one, two, three, four!' And we were off!

Even if I'd been clued up on the regulation tempo for a quickstep, getting it right in the heat of this particular moment would have been little short of a miracle. That said, counting it in too slowly would have been the lesser of two evils. At least the hall wouldn't have taken on the appearance of a demolition derby track.

'Too fast, boys!' the entertainments convenor yelled as he and his missus swept past like a whirlwind. 'Too bloody fast!'

It was also too bloody late. Getting a bunch of young jazz musicians to play faster is never a problem, but attempting to do the opposite would be as futile as emulating the efforts of King Canute himself. So, we closed our eyes to the pile-ups on the dance floor and gave it welly. Indeed, as befitted the title of the tune, this jazz band was having a ball. And let the devil take the hindmost!

Budgie, the prize-winning Polish ballroom dancer, didn't waste any time in voicing his displeasure. He strode (or rather limped) up to us and snapped, 'How you 'spec peoples dance so fast? Partner been standink my feet.' He pointed to his once-immaculate patent leather shoes. 'Pumps complete fockt!'

Kimber attempted to stem the incoming tide with an apology, but Budgie was having none of it.

'Kvickstep needink *exac*' two hundred beat for minute!' He indicated his wristwatch. 'You basters doink two hundred tventy!'

He tossed his head, about turned and strutted (or rather hobbled) off in the direction of the bar.

Although the incident caused a few behind-the-hand sniggers in the band, it had also taught us a valuable lesson. Two, in fact. Firstly, unless your audience is composed exclusively of jazz-orientated types, playing for dancing means just that, and it can have certain conditions attached that weren't around in the brothels of old New Orleans. Secondly, if you're being paid for a gig, even as modestly as we were, the customers' wishes have to be respected. Well, within reason anyway.

On this occasion, reason extended to playing a couple of waltzes. Kimber's past experience in the RAF dance band got us out of that corner. But we drew the line at Eightsome Reels. *And* any hula-hula stuff. On the other hand, we thought it prudent to address the tango question with a compromise.

The basis for my having suggested *The Isle of Capri* to the entertainments convenor was that it was the first tune with even a vague Dixie-cum-Latin link that came to mind. The problem was that, even if the Latin American rhythm normally employed could be tangoed to, the feature only lasted for the first chorus or two. Thereafter, it was a case of swinging it all the way through, with the Latin beat reprised to wind proceedings up. This created something of a dilemma for a bunch of greenhorn jazzers trying to play for strict-tempo dancing.

Still, when necessity knocks, the mother of invention invariably enters. In this instance she took the form of Jack, who, while Kimber and I deliberated the dilemma, stepped resolutely up to the mic:

'Ladies and gentlemen, grab yer partners for a jazz tango ... wi' foxtrotty bits.'

'Candid and concise' was always Jack's motto, and it had never been more effectively applied than just then, as we were about to learn.

'*Jazz* tango?' I twittered, flapping. 'But there's no such thing.'

'That's right,' said Jack. 'As Sergeant Jimmy used to tell us at cadets, bullshit baffles brains. Stomp it in!'

Again, there was no escape, so stomp it in I did. And if the stomped-in tempo turned out to be acceptable to the dancers, all credit would be due to the nerves tugging at my stomping foot. Not that it ultimately mattered, as it seemed none of the customers wanted to admit being unfamiliar with this avant-garde fusion of dance routines. The floor was filled with enthusiastic tango-foxtrotters, and none more appreciative than the middle-aged couple who approached us at the end.

'I've danced many a jazz tango,' the lady gushed, 'but that was the best *ever*.'

'Absolutely,' her husband confirmed, 'and you got the foxtrot segue just right as well.' He spoke with the authority of a true connoisseur.

I glanced over at Jack, who gave me a 'see, bullshit *does* baffle brains' wink. I couldn't help thinking he would make a fine drill sergeant – or at least a politician. But I knew he had his heart set on going into the brewing business, for which it was becoming ever more apparent he also possessed the right credentials.

This isn't to say the presence of a bar had made the punters, as Jack had predicted, tiddly enough to be more tolerant of our limitations as the evening wore on. In truth, we noticed no-one in even a mildly inebriated state – with the possible exception of a certain Polish breeder of prize-winning budgies. Following his quickstepping experiences earlier, he'd limited his movements to elbow-bending on a bar stool. The small, water-like shots he was throwing back were, according to Jack, almost certainly vodka, an Eastern Bloc firewater not too well known here yet, but endowed with pain-killing properties at least on a par with Scotland's own national drink.

In any event, once our second set was properly under way, an atmosphere of relaxed jollity had descended upon the British Legion hall. A fairly straight-laced dance had developed (or degenerated, depending on your point of view) into a knees-up-cum-singalong, and we could be reasonably satisfied with the contribution made by our music, rough-and-ready as it was.

Audience participation of the vocal variety was generated by a young local girl called Nita Cowley, who sat in with us for a few numbers. Nita was already quite an accomplished jazz singer, on the brink of establishing a successful professional career. But, more importantly for us at the time, she also knew how to 'work the punters' when it came to stirring up a bit of a ding-dong. And the fact that we only knew a few of her songs didn't prove to be too much of a problem. On the contrary, busking along behind her helped familiarise us with the rudiments of 'winging it' – one of the most essential tools in any jazz musician's kit. Also, it cut down on the number of twelve-bar blues we had to cobble up.

By the time we had played the final chord of the National Anthem (it was expected of audiences to stand in homage to the monarch at the conclusion of 'public events' in those days), we knew we had successfully negotiated some lower slopes of the long learning curve that lay ahead. Every hesitant step had been an adventure in itself, but the Hidden Town Dixielanders were on their way up.

We were so pleased with ourselves that we even took encouragement from the backhanded compliment paid by Budgie, the prize-winning Polish ballroom dancer.

'I been enjoyink your music,' he slurred as he swayed up to us on his way out. 'For me, much happiness, OK?' Then, with a pained expression and a glance at his feet, he said, 'But you need makink proper tempo.' He took a threepenny bit from his pocket and lobbed it onto the skin of Wee Bob's snare drum. 'Here – save up buy fockink metropole!'

* * * * *

CHAPTER ELEVEN

'THERE'S JAZZ IN THEM THAR HILLS'

Although the fee was modest, we'd taken much from that first gig, not least the confidence to accept further engagements. The only snag was that no offers were forthcoming. The solution? We'd run our own dances. In a city, we'd probably have sniffed out a disused cellar or a room above a pub to start a jazz club in. But we lived in the country, and even if we could have found equivalent premises, the population in any of the county's towns wouldn't have been big enough to support such a venture on a regular basis. The solution? We'd take our 'jazz club' on the road.

We were sufficiently realistic to recognise that we weren't yet well enough known to fill large venues such as the local Corn Exchange. Those were the domains of big names like the Clyde Valley Stompers, and even strictly non-jazzy outfits like the aforementioned Watty Frater and his Hawaiian Serenaders. So, the search was on for premises more in keeping with our limited drawing power.

'I know the very place,' Jim Douglas enthused. 'Just up country a wee bit from Gifford. It's no very big, right enough, but gets good turn-outs for the Saturday night hops. Yeah, and it'll be cheap to rent too!'

It sounded like the perfect location for having a go at being our own promoters. Well worth checking out. At the first opportunity, I duly cycled up to Gifford, where Jim jumped on his bike and led the way. Onwards and upwards toward the foothills (or 'hillfits' as they're known locally) of the Lammermuirs we pedalled. The air was crisp and the autumn shadows welcome as we puffed and panted our way through lush woodlands blanketing the glens of Yester, the ancient estate whose rolling acres garland the village. It's widely acknowledged that there are few places more idyllic in the whole of Lowland Scotland. But Jim and I didn't hang about to take in the scenery. We were on a mission.

Longyester Farm straddles what could fairly be described as the tree line which runs along a contour of the hills some distance south of Gifford. The farmstead itself is as mellow and fetching as the age-old stone from which it is built, but the landscape behind takes on a much more rugged and, by definition, treeless appearance. This is sheep country, climbing ever more steeply towards the bald, domed summit of Bleak Law. It's aptly named; hardly what you'd expect to see as a backdrop to a popular dance hall. Yet there it was, a barn-like, wood and corrugated iron structure standing four-square and solitary a mile or so beyond the farm. And 'solitary' was the operative word.

'Who the hell would come to dances in a ramshackle old shed like that?' I gasped. I looked around, wide-eyed, 'And way out in the sticks like this!'

Jim clearly didn't share my puzzlement. '*Every*body comes to the dancin' here. Shepherds and the like – tractormen and hinds – hill folk – and plenty from Gifford as well. Oh aye, *every*body comes to the Longyester dancin' on a Saturday night!'

'But how do they get here?'

'Pushbikes, motorbikes, cars, tractors – maybe even a horse or two.' Jim gave a chuckle. 'Aye, and Ah've even heard o' a bloke comin' on a motorised lawnmower once. Brought his bird in the grass box!'

I was lost for words, but Jim could tell I wasn't convinced that this was a venue likely to advance the popularity of an ambitious but unheard-of jazz band. 'Tellin' ye,' he insisted, 'we'll go down a bomb here!'

'They'll expect Eightsome Reels,' I muttered. 'Gay Gordons, Strip the Willow and all that teuchter stuff we were forced to learn during Scottish Country Dance classes at school.'

With neither warning nor apparent reason, Jim then made a seamless shift into hipspeak: 'No pressure, daddy. Ah'm wise to a coupla cats in the village – box players. They're still *well* into that Brigadoon groove. *Really* missed the blast-off, they did. Yeah, and they'll be cool for an interval spot or two.' He remounted his bike and pushed off in the direction from which we'd come. 'Leave it to me, Pops!' he yelled over his shoulder. 'No pressure! Dig?'

It was only then that a shuffling sound drew my attention to the motive for Jim's sudden slide into jive talk. An old man with a flat cap, open smile, tombstone teeth and a dead rabbit dangling from his hand was standing behind a drystone wall, just out of my immediate line of vision.

'The Douglas laddie's right,' he grinned. 'Ye'll go doon a bomb here.'

I smiled, thanked him for his encouraging words and, pedalling off, waved him goodbye.

Still grinning, he waved the rabbit.

*

And Jim did indeed turn out to be right. Just as he'd correctly predicted that John's tea chest bass would suit our purpose (admittedly temporarily), so would he prove to be correct in his assertion that Longyester Hall would be the scene of our next step up the ladder of success. It hadn't seemed that way when we arrived for the gig, though.

'What's *that* all about?' Jack mumbled, chewing – and smoking.

'What's *what* all about?' Wee Bob asked.

Jack nodded towards a hand-printed notice outside the door of the hall. It read:

'NO TACKETIE BOOTS ALLOWED ON THE DANCE FLOOR!'

('Tacketie', by the way, is the Scots word for 'hobnailed').

We stared at Jim for some sign of reassurance.

When none was offered, John heaved a resigned sigh and said, 'Well, at least if they don't like us, gettin' kicked out'll be a mite less painful.'

The scene inside the hall presented no surprises. It was what it was: an empty shed with a raised platform at the far end. Still, the wooden floor, in keeping with the stipulated footwear code, appeared to be in fair enough nick.

Jack, however, did notice something worthy of comment. 'What the hell's *this*?' he grunted, while peering down at a clump of tiny black pellets at his feet.

'Crap,' Jim replied, in a matter-of-fact way. 'Sheep, ye know. Up here, they'll just wander in sometimes – if somebody leaves the door open, like. Yeah, an inquisitive beast, yer average sheep.'

'So,' John said, 'why all the fuss about tacketie boots, if sheep shite's legit?'

Jim pulled a that's-just-the-way-it-is shrug.

Jack, meanwhile, had allowed his eyes to wander over the floor. 'And there's lumps o' the stuff *every*where!'

Wee Bob was nodding his head in amazement. 'Aye, and the punters are expected to just dance around it, I suppose.'

'Nah, they'll never notice,' Kimber pooh-poohed. 'Saw it in Germany, except it was pigs there. Once the dancers spread it around a bit – the first number should be enough – it'll have the same effect as Slipperine. And it's free!'

'And sheep shite smells better than pig shite as well,' John submitted, dryly.

'If, in fact, *better* is an appropriate word to use in this context,' Wee Bob appended in learned tones. 'Shit, chemically, is shit, and differences in smell vis-à-vis species are essentially academic.'

As was becoming our wont, we bowed to Bob's superior intellect and left it at that.

An hour after the scheduled start of the dance, not even one customer had turned up. Jim, however, had forewarned us. A few punters might drift in before closing time at the Gifford pubs, he'd said, but only a few. Like the residues of inquisitive sheep, that's just the way it was here. Consequently, we'd decided to make use of the slack time to practice some new numbers. It was at the end of one of those that I noticed the old man who had spoken to me from behind the drystone wall on my earlier visit. He had now swapped his dead rabbit for a shovel and was scooping up sheep droppings from the floor.

'He's the hallkeeper,' Jim informed us. 'Old Wullie.'

I gave him a wave and a smile of recognition.

In return, the old boy pointed to the contents of his shovel. 'Sheep shite,' he grinned.

'Yeah, a bit dangerous,' I called back. 'Slippy – could make the dancers fall about, eh?'

He shook his head. 'Naw, naw, Ah want it for ma leeks, son. Makes them grow like fuck!'

And so it was due more to horticultural prudence than to health and safety considerations that the customers, when they did eventually start to arrive, were presented with the prospect of strutting their stuff on a largely crap-free dance floor. They'd have noticed if it had been otherwise, since the entire central area was left empty, the lads lining up on one side of the hall, the lasses flaunting their assets on the other.

This was the custom at public dances in the country back then. I'd noticed the same ritual in Haddington's Corn Exchange the night I went to hear the Clyde Valley Stompers. On that occasion, the demarcation lines became blurred after a while – after a measure of 'coupling up' came about because of familiarity breeding more … well, more familiarity. The same was to happen in Longyester Hall, the shedding of inhibitions gaining momentum as the effects of pre-dance warm-ups in the Gifford pubs kicked fully in.

Half an hour after closing time at the Tweeddale Arms and Goblin Ha', the hall was packed solid with inhibition-free customers. What's more, none of them were bothered about strict tempos, or even being told the type of dance coming up. Quicksteps and foxtrots were all the same to them – sources of a beat to which they could apply their individual interpretations of dancing. And if it didn't look all that elegant, so what?

'Ye see now why they ban tacketie boots,' Jim yelled in my ear mid-way through a particularly spirited stomp. He motioned towards the far corner of the hall, where three young guys were acting as if they were in a snake pit and trying to annihilate the residents with their feet. But they were thrashing about rhythmically and in the cheeriest of humour, while the absence of flying floor boards indicated that they had complied with the conditions of entry. Having fun was what it was all about, and everyone was in the same mood.

What these customers lacked in dancing finesse was more than made up for by an insatiable appetite for having a hot time, and they didn't hold back in their vocal demands for us to keep the boiler stoked. This was an energetic bunch par excellence; a credit to the invigorating air of the Lammermuir Hills – and to the beer taps and gantry bottles of the Gifford pubs. Boy, were we were glad to see the eventual arrival of the two squeeze-box-players Jim had organised to give us a break!

Clearly as keen to be part of the jollifications as the dancers, no sooner had they strapped on their accordions than they were up on the stand belting out a foot-tapping medley of Scottish favourites for what they'd announced as a Dashing White Sergeant. En masse, the punters took to the floor and went straight to it, but with a complete absence of the courtliness we'd been taught to observe during those dreaded Country Dance lessons at school. This isn't to say that these *real* country dancers didn't know what they were doing. They were obviously well acquainted with the accepted steps and routines, but treated them with an attitude untrammelled by any convention of prim society.

Of a sudden, the hills were alive with the sound of a hall full of whirling, birling, wheeling, reeling, *hoochin'* and *wheechin'* ravers. And, as if to confirm that news travels fast in the 'hillfits', the two box-players were soon joined by three more accordionists, a drummer, piano player and a couple of fiddlers. A tartan jam session was in full swing, and although the tunes were the same as those I'd heard since childhood on the BBC's *Scottish Dance Music* programme, the difference was like comparing the schooled tiptoeing of a dressage horse to the thundering hooves of a free-running mustang. In the parlance of seasoned American jazz musicians, those weekday sod-busters and cow-punchers knew where the Saturday night bodies were buried. And if any of them were confronted by a melody they didn't know, they improvised. They made their input blend and they made it swing. Jazz by any other name? Call it what you may, they had the joint jumping – literally.

It was the first, but wouldn't be the last, time I'd feel the sting of being upstaged by the support group. 'Follow that!' would have been the challenge laid down by less generous musicians at the end of their spot. But instead of marching off triumphantly through the crowd, these lads took up station in front of the stage and shouted their appreciation of our efforts to maintain the temperature they'd set. Despite the lack of red lights, a hotter time could hardly have been had in the teeming Storyville quarter of old New Orleans. And here, in the Nowheresville remoteness of Longyester Hall, there wasn't a single hooker to be seen. Not even a wanton sheep.

Old Wullie the hallkeeper drew me aside as we were leaving at the end of the gig. 'They say half the population o' Gifford was conceived against the back o' the hall here efter the dancin', son.' He moved in closer and whispered with a lascivious leer, 'Aye, Ah just seen another pair at it the noo!'

*

We ran a few more dances during the final months of 1958, progressing from the rural isolation of Longyester to Gifford village itself, then boldly onwards and upwards to West Barns Hall on the outskirts of the fishing haven of Dunbar, and eventually to one of the county's more select venues, the Harbour Pavilion in the prestigious seaside resort of North Berwick – the Biarritz of the North. Still unsure of how many people, if any, would be attracted through the doors, we took the precaution of hiring a bus to transport our core fans (mainly our families) to the gigs. The band travelled with the fans, who paid for the hire, which conveniently covered the inconvenience of our not having a bandwagon – a problem that would have to be resolved soon enough, nonetheless.

Although we didn't make much money for our efforts, we always managed to cover the cost of renting the halls, with a bit of pocket money left over for the lads, and a few quid into a kitty earmarked for investment in a decent mic and amplifier of our own. None of those venues had house PA systems, so it was a case of salvaging what bits and pieces we could from one of the local junk shops. Make do and mend, as ever. And even if the sound quality from our clapped out old 'speakers was rubbish, we took some consolation in telling ourselves that, if we had been aiming for a genuine 1920s sound (which we weren't), this would have been the way to do it.

While we couldn't have foreseen it at the time, those few do-it-ourselves dance promotions would never be surpassed for the pure, simple satisfaction of playing the music we loved, and doing so for no other reason than to enjoy ourselves and see others sharing our fun. There were no egos to feed, no greed to cater for, no selfish ambitions to compete with. It was a truly family effort in every respect. Jim's mother and my own would be on money-taking duty at the door, giving freely of their time and never complaining about the abuse they were occasionally subjected to. Fortunately, though, their matronly demeanour served to cool down those potential trouble-makers who turned up slightly overheated after the pubs came out. No need to hire bouncers with two redoubtable mums on the door!

Even the journeys home in an ancient Bedford Duple bus, with owner Ian Glass himself at the wheel, provided moments to savour. Ian, tall, dark and with matinee idol good looks, was a stalwart of the Haddington Amateur Operatic Society and needed no encouragement to show off his rich baritone voice to a captive audience. As a rule, we supercilious young jazzers, still high from belting out the last few choruses of *South Rampart Street Parade*, would not have cared much for being assailed by medleys of unhip refrains from *Oklahoma*, *Carousel* or, worse still, *The Pirates of Penzance*. In those happy circumstances, however, we lapped it up. Or at least gave that impression. Ian Glass, you see, was a big fellow and also a stalwart of Haddington Rugby Club.

* * * * *

CHAPTER TWELVE

'CROSSING BRIDGES'

New Year's Eve, or Hogmanay, was still the most widely and enthusiastically celebrated date on the Scottish calendar. While a Christmas Day break was not yet regarded as a universal entitlement, it was a long-held tradition that no-one, except hospital staff and those in the emergency services, would be required to work on New Year's Day. And for good reason, as I would shortly discover.

Up to now, I hadn't taken much interest in 'first-footing', an age-old Scottish ritual that begins as soon as midnight has struck on the last day of the year. Being regarded as too young to partake of strong drink, for which I had no taste in any case, my father had never expected me to join him in trying to be the 'first foot' to cross the thresholds of our neighbours' homes. On those expeditions, the first-footer would carry, according to custom, a bottle of whisky in one hand, a lump of coal in the other, and a chunk of dense, currant-crammed 'black bun' in his pocket. The coal was to bring luck to the visited house, the black bun to give sustenance and, though never admitted, to help soak up an extravagant intake of whisky. A fine theory, which, tucked up cosily in bed as I had always been, meant little to me. Until the Hogmanay of 1958.

My mother, a strict teetotaller, was not keen on having strong drink in the house. While liking a good laugh, she preferred it to be generated by alcohol-free humour. She wasn't in favour, therefore, of having the boozy Hogmanay merriments that went on in other people's houses replicated in hers. For that reason, she made no objection when Dad went first-footing at the witching hour. This allowed her to go to bed, undisturbed by passing revellers who regarded a light shining through any window as an open invitation to the next party on their rounds. On this occasion, however, things didn't quite run according to routine.

It had all started out normally enough for me, albeit with an unexpected serving of honey-tainted food for thought in late afternoon. My mother had suggested that I should ask Ellie to join us bringing in the New Year. My sister had already invited Kimber, so it would be 'nice', Mum thought, to have everyone together, with a late-night snack of traditional fare prepared in anticipation of 'the bells' ringing out at midnight.

As expected, Ellie's mother made it clear that I would have to deliver her daughter back home safe and sound by 1.00 a.m. at the very latest. She would not normally allow Ellie to be out at such a late hour, and particularly at New Year, when, as she pointed out, the place would be swarming with drunken louts. I duly promised to do her bidding. She could depend on me. She had my solemn word.

The sun was dipping low in the sky when Ellie and I arrived about half way across town. The streets were busier than they would normally have been on such a chilly winter's evening, as folk scurried about buying last-minute supplies of food and drink for the festive night ahead. True to the old Scots trait of being reluctant to act publicly in any way that might be construed as romantic, I was disinclined, when out walking with Ellie, to hold her hand – in daylight anyway. Of course, her sense of mischief always prompted her to take some sort of amorous initiative herself, whenever she thought enough people were around. This is precisely what she did by grabbing my hand when we reached the end of the High Street. But instead of drawing attention to my awkwardness by starting to giggle, she looked me in the eye and said bluntly, 'Poohsticks!' She then hauled me off in the opposite direction to the one in which we had been heading.

'*Pooh*sticks?' I queried. 'What the blazes are Poohsticks? And where the hell are we going now?'

Ellie said nothing until she had dragged me along Hardgate for about a hundred yards, then turned right onto the Victoria Bridge, which spans the river towards the eastern edge of town. She stopped half way across and leaned over the parapet, inviting me to do likewise.

'Did you never read *The House At Pooh Corner* when you were wee?' she said. 'You know, the Winnie-the-Pooh story?'

'Winnie-the-*who*?'

'Pooh – the teddy bear who liked honey – and all his friends, like Tigger, Piglet and Eeyore.' Ellie frowned. 'You *must* have read about Pooh Bear and his chums.'

'I have a mental warehouse of very limited capacity,' I confessed with a shrug.

'Could we have that in plain English, please?'

'Well, for the past six years I had so much heavy-duty stuff crammed into my nut, from the likes of Chaucer and Shakespeare to Virgil and Homer – and I had to translate that pair's stories from Latin, incidentally – that anything unlikely to be of future use was ejected to make room for it.'

Ellie shook her head sceptically. 'But Pooh Bear and his friends wouldn't have taken up much space.'

'Let's just call Chaucer and Shakespeare cuckoos in the nest, then. Anyway, it's about time they got the elbow. Yeah, and

Virgil and Homer can get the heave-ho as well. So,' I smiled, 'now's Pooh Bear's chance. What's the sticks thing all about?'

Pooh and his pals, Ellie explained, would play a game of dropping twigs into the water on the upstream side of their bridge, then hurry over to the other side to see whose twig emerged downstream first.

'Wow, can't wait to give it a go!' I breezed, before gawping down at the ground, feigning disappointment. 'Aw dammit, can't see any sticks, though.' I waited a moment, then nudged her with my elbow. 'Maybe we could use your shoes instead, eh?'

But Ellie was not in the mood for such shallow banter. I had thought her unusually withdrawn since collecting her that evening. Something was bothering her, but she seemed reluctant to say, so I decided to let her gather her thoughts without any more attempts at levity. Who knows, she may have been plucking up courage to give me the elbow, just as I'd resolved to do with Chaucer, Shakespeare et al a couple of minutes earlier. The prospect hit me like a punch on the nose. For all that our relationship was still an uncomplicated one, born of innocent adolescent attraction, it had become very important to me, and I didn't relish the thought that it could be about to end. The feeling intensified as I recalled that all the early advances had been made by me. All that silly hundred-lines-for-running-in-the-corridor stuff. Maybe Ellie had only been humouring me ever since. Maybe she still thought I was a creep.

Hunched over the parapet, I gazed down at the slow-flowing water, my mood matching the gathering gloom of evening.

By my side, Ellie was staring at the river as well. 'Australia,' she muttered after a while.

'Come again?'

'Australia,' she repeated.

Puzzled, I turned to look at her. 'Australia? What about Australia?'

118

Ellie breathed in deeply and released a slow, heavy sigh. 'Just that we're going there, if things work out right ... or wrong. Depends how you look at it, I suppose.'

'*We*'re going to Australia? But ... but who's we?'

Ellie's eyes were still fixed on the river below. 'Me,' she replied, then swallowed hard and said, 'I mean, along with the whole family – Mum, Dad and the boys.'

I could hardly believe what I was hearing. This was a bolt right out of the blue, and it hurt. 'But why?' I gasped. 'And ... and when?'

Ellie remained silent, absorbed in her own thoughts again.

The person she referred to as 'Dad' was, in fact, her stepfather, the Haddington man her widowed mother had married in her native Germany after the war. He had been serving there in the RAF at the time. 'The boys' she had mentioned were her three step-brothers, all correspondingly younger than her, their ages ranging from about six to ten. Ellie's bond with her mother was as strong as would be assumed between a young woman and her child who had survived the hardships of a war-devastated homeland, then endured with dignity an often hostile reception in their adopted country. Her relationship with her stepfather was, understandably, less close, although she had always shown him the respect he deserved. As for her stepbrothers – well, they were boys, she was a girl and a big sister to boot, so the prevailing rapport was as might be expected.

Ellie emerged from her reverie after a minute or two and told me her stepfather had talked about emigrating to Australia for years. However, the talking had never lasted long, so she had always taken it as no more than that – idle daydreaming, destined to come to nothing. That was how her mother seemed to have taken it as well. Then, a few weeks ago, a newspaper ad for '£10 Assisted Passages' to Australia had prompted her stepfather to send for an application form and, wonder of wonders, to actually fill it in.

I felt a weight lifting from my shoulders, even if only slightly. 'So, it's not definite yet, then? I mean, the application has still to be accepted, right?'

Ellie gave me a sympathetic smile. 'Well, Dad's pretty confident it will be.'

My spirits sank again. Ellie had just turned sixteen, so I guessed there might not be any legal obligation for her to emigrate with her family, if she chose not to. But how would a girl of her age survive on her own here in Scotland? In any event, I knew she wouldn't contemplate putting half the world between herself and her mother, no matter how much she disliked the idea of going to Australia. Her fate, and mine, appeared to be sealed.

'That's that, then,' I shrugged. 'You're going to be a Sheila.' I pointed down to the river, then said with as much good humour as I could fake, 'Unless you've decided to jump, of course.'

Ellie responded with a half-hearted little laugh. 'If that's the only alternative, I think I'd rather go to Australia.' Hesitantly, she pulled an envelope from her coat pocket. 'Dad asked me to post this. I've been carrying it about for over a week, wondering what to do.'

I looked at the envelope, then enquiringly at Ellie's face. 'Is that the… ?'

'Application form? Yes. Otherwise known as a Poohstick.' Ellie calmly ripped the envelope in two. 'Now Pooh*sticks* – plural!' She then crumpled up both halves as tightly as she could and lobbed them into the river.

While my head was being bombarded by thoughts of the possible implications of what Ellie had just done, I hurried over with her to the downstream side of the bridge. Both lumps of paper emerged at exactly the same time.

'Seems there are no winners,' I blurted out, realising too late that I sounded like a prophet of doom.

'No winners,' Ellie murmured. She paused, then added, '...or maybe two?' She said nothing more. She didn't need

120

to. She looked up at me for a second, before lowering her eyes.

In those few moments, I had been gently wrenched from the self-absorbed naivety of youth and placed firmly into confrontation with one very important aspect of growing up: there was a lot more to this boyfriend-girlfriend thing than just holding hands – or even being bashful about holding them in daylight. The realisation gave me a jolt. A big one.

'But – but what'll happen now?' I flustered.

The look on Ellie's face was innocence personified. 'Happen? How d'you mean?'

'Well, your Dad … he's bound to wonder when he doesn't get any feedback, isn't he?'

Ellie shrugged. 'Knowing him, he'll probably just think his application's been rejected.'

I was far from convinced. 'Yeah, but he's just as likely to phone the Australian Embassy and ask what's going on.'

Ellie smiled the smile of the unconcerned.

But misgivings were peppering my conscience like shotgun pellets. 'Let's face it,' I persisted, 'he's *bound* to phone the Oz Embassy … isn't he?'

Ellie started to snigger. 'I just thought – one of Winnie-the-Pooh's chums was called Kanga, the mother of Roo.'

'So?'

'Kanga and Roo.' Ellie was laughing now. 'Kangaroo – Australia – get it?' She nodded towards the two balls of paper floating down river in a pool of lamplight. 'Kind of ironic, eh?'

I scratched the back of my head, thoroughly bewildered. 'You've a weird sense of humour, Ellie – you really have.'

'And a big sense of determination as well,' she said, as if to herself.

I pressed her about what she would do if her stepfather did eventually smell a rat regarding his Ten Pound Pom application form.

121

She gave the top of the parapet a resolute pat. 'As the saying goes, we'll cross *that* bridge when we come to it.' Then, looking up at the sky, she said, 'Anyway, it's nice and dark now, so you're safe to take my hand and walk me back across *this* one.'

* * * * *

CHAPTER THIRTEEN

'THE HOGMANAY TWO-STEP'

Although I was sure Ellie hadn't meant me to think I was the primary cause of her decision to torpedo her stepfather's plans for a new life Down Under, I couldn't help suspecting that her feelings for me had made *some* contribution. A more serious element had entered our relationship, and I found it a bit confusing. On the one hand I was weighed down by a feeling that I wasn't up to handling such a commitment, and on the other I was walking on air because Ellie hadn't elbowed me after all. I could now stop beating myself up with that old, nagging fear that she thought I was a creep – and a creep with questionable motives into the bargain. I resolved to concentrate on the more wholesome option: I would repay with interest Ellie's confidence in me. This would also involve redoubling my determination to justify her mother's trust. I was a lucky lad, and I would act accordingly.

Just a few hours later, Ellie was leading me by the hand like a chimp with rag doll tendencies. This is how it came about...

The evening had passed uneventfully, the only difference from any other evening we had spent at my folks' place being that this one lasted longer. Dad treated us to his usual piano recital when he came home from the pub, before the telly was switched on for Andy Stewart, Robert Wilson, Jimmy Shand and the other *White Heather Club* regulars to churn out traditional tartan entertainment for the last hour of the Old Year. Meanwhile, Mother served up a selection of her home-made fare: black bun, clootie dumpling, shortbread and scones, with plenty of hot tea. No alcohol!

As soon as Big Ben had struck twelve, the TV was switched off and all hatches battened down in preparation for Mum's self-imposed incarceration. She said goodnight to everyone and reminded me that Ellie's mother was expecting her home no later than one o'clock, so we'd better be on our way. That's when matters took an unexpected turn.

'Hold on a minute!' Dad said as I was helping Ellie on with her coat. 'What's the big hurry?'

It had been apparent all evening that Dad had had quite a few practice nips in the pub earlier, then probably a few more on furtive trips to the kitchen cupboard where his Hogmanay whisky bottle was stashed. We always heard the tap being turned on after he'd been out of the room for a minute, suggesting that the level of liquid in the bottle was being topped up. I'd caught a glimpse of him doing this on previous Hogmanays, and I'm sure Mother had as well. Her view would have been that he was going to drink the same amount of whisky anyway, so it made little difference whether it was diluted or not.

'The night's young, boy!' he told me through a grin radiating the glee of creeping inebriation. 'Where d'ye think ye're goin'?'

Mother answered for me: 'He's taking Ellie home – now!'

'Nah, nah, nah,' Dad objected, Dutch courage on the rise. He took me by the elbow and shepherded me towards the door. 'He was eighteen last month,' he called over his shoulder.

'He's a man now – pub-legal – so it's high time he got into training!' With Mother still trumpeting her disapproval, Dad gave a wheezy chortle and spirited me into the night.

My awareness of what happened after that diminished with every house we visited – and there were probably only three in total before I threw in the towel. First impressions were of our immediate next-door neighbours making us welcome with firm handshakes and hearty greetings of 'Happy New Year!' A glass of whisky was thrust into my hand. Then, while following the sound of a record player blaring out Scottish Country Dance Music, we progressed through to the living room to join a crowd of people, most of whom I had never clapped eyes on before. For all that, they greeted me like a long-lost friend. More handshakes. More whisky into my glass. Lots of laughter. 'Here, son,' a happy, elderly face said, 'have a dram oot o' ma bottle.' A woman appeared in front of me with a jug of water. 'Better thin that doon a bit, dear,' she smiled. 'Easier on yer guts.' A hand slapped me firmly on the back. I turned to see another happy face, this one belonging to the secretary of the local Cage Bird Society. 'Fancy seein' you here. Aye, an' Ah see yer glass is aboot empty an' all. Let me top it up for ye!' Another woman appeared, this one with a bottle of lemonade. 'Ah noticed ye squirmin' there, pet. Terrible taste the whisky, eh?' She poured a dash of lemonade into my glass. 'That'll make it go doon better.' Still the Scottish Dance Music blared. Still the handshakes, back-slaps and raucous laughter. Except everything was becoming a bit fuzzy. Surreal, almost.

Dad appeared out of the haze. 'Must be gettin' along to old Davie's now. Always expects me.' The farewells were even more hearty than the welcomes had been, although the welcomes at old Davie's were heartier still. Same routine. More whisky, handshakes, laughs, Scottish Dance Music. A mass of people bound together by the glue of New Year bonhomie. Even sworn neighbourhood enemies had become bosom buddies. What's more, husbands were publicly kissing wives, though never their own. Scottish reserve didn't slacken off *that* much, even at Hogmanay.

The fuzziness I had experienced in the first house had now developed into double vision – occasionally undulating into the triple variety. How could so many people squeeze into one small room, especially a spinning one like this? Noticing a vacant chair in the corner, I wove my way towards it. A restraining hand gripped my shoulder. 'Never sit doon, lad,' the hand's voice said. 'Ye'll never get up again!' I swallowed the precursor of a puke. Pure whisky, with lemonade undertones. Dad arrived at my side, accompanied by two doppelgängers. 'Enjoyin' yerself?' they asked, beaming. 'Come on. Must visit old Tommy now. Always expects me.'

If I got as far as old Tommy's, I remember nothing of it. All I remember is recalling the words of wisdom Dad had given me on the night I went to see the Clyde Valley Stompers in the local Corn Exchange: 'It's when the fresh air hits them that the piss artists go doolally!' But I didn't go doolally, just into some sort of limbo.

I came to lying on our own bathroom floor. I was hugging the pedestal of the lavatory pan, my cheek pressed against the merciful coolness of its porcelain. I was moaning. The words I was moaning were: 'Blow ma nose … soft.'

The next words I heard were Kimber's. 'Aye, it's better oot than in. Boak it up. Ye'll feel the better for it.'

Wise advice, no doubt, though a tad belated. The burning sensation in my nostrils suggested that I had already boaked up a bucketful, and straight whisky at that. Even the lemonade undertones were absent.

'Blow ma nose,' I moaned afresh, '…soft.'

The next words I heard were my mothers. 'An absolute disgrace! Drunk as a newt! And all *your* fault!'

'Sh'nuzzing t'do wiv me,' my father's voice slurred. 'Like I tol' you, he – *hick*! – heeza man now.'

'He's an *idiot* now,' Mother snapped, 'just like you! Leading him astray like that. I mean, what will the neighbours think?'

'Wuzza neighbours that fuckin' did it!' Dad retorted, resorting to an expletive he would only contemplate using in front of my mother when wallowing in the good will of Hogmanay.

'And your language is just like your breath,' mother came back. 'Foul! And did you ever think about Ellie sitting here waiting while you were out teaching your son to be a common drunk?'

Mention of Ellie's name and the sudden recollection of the promise I'd made her mother must have had the effect of a pail of cold water being chucked in my face. The next thing I knew I was standing outside the house, attempting to convince my mother that I was quite capable of seeing Ellie home, while Mum tried her best to do the opposite. She reminded me that Kimber lived on the same side of town as Ellie, so it would be much more sensible if he acted as her escort. 'At least,' she declared, 'he can walk in a straight line!'

'Sho can I,' I protested. 'L-look...'

'*Walk*? You can hardly even *stand*!'

'Juzz wee bit dizzy. Juzz, ye know – be OK once ... *brrrrp*! ... once...'

As the New Year night began to swim before my eyes, Ellie materialised by my side. It would be all right, she assured my mother. She would see to it that I got her safely home – or words to that effect. What Mother's response was I can now only surmise, because my next memory is of arriving at Ellie's front gate in rag-doll-chimpanzee mode.

'Well, we made it,' Ellie panted. 'First time I've walked two miles to cover one, though.' She released my hand and patted me on the head. 'Thanks for a *lovely* evening.'

'Shmy plezzer. Gotcha home nize'n – *ick*-em! – nize'n safe too.' I attempted a self-congratulatory wink. 'Promiz izza promiz, eh?'

Ellie checked her watch. 'Hmm, even if it *is* three hours late.' She glanced at an upstairs window. 'Let's hope my folks are sound asleep.'

Another short blackout later, I came round hanging over a fence behind Ellie's house. I was vomiting, no hands, into her neighbours' back garden. More nippy nostrils, but this time without accompanying moans. I mean to say, the last thing I wanted to do was disturb Ellie's folks! A grunting, gasping sound behind made me look round, just in time to see Ellie's rear end disappearing through the top opening of a kitchen window.

'Sh'musht've forgotten her bloody key,' I muttered, before setting off on the long stagger home.

I soon became aware that a solitary street light about a couple of hundred yards ahead seemed to be getting no closer. Now I knew what Ellie had meant when she said it was the first time she'd walked two miles to cover one. But I persevered with monocular determination, even clearing the mist from my brain for long enough to dub my ambulatory challenge the Hogmanay Two-step – two steps forward, one step sideways, two steps back.

One way or another, though, I made it home and into the arms of Morpheus, eventually to be awakened by shafts of watery sunshine burning into my eyelids. I was lying spreadeagled on my bed, still fully clothed, a muffled bass drum pounding inside my head, my mouth tasting like the proverbial sumo wrestler's jockstrap.

'Never again,' I groaned. 'Never, *ever* again.'

As I pulled a pillow over my face to shut out the daylight, my mind was mugged by the sudden realisation that, tomorrow, I would begin my career as a civil servant: an Executive Officer in the Ministry of bloody Labour! I was tempted to allow the pillow to do its worst.

'Where did it go wrong?' I whimpered. 'Where did all go wrong?'

* * * * *

CHAPTER FOURTEEN

'OF DANDELIONS AND OYSTERS'

As much as I'd enjoyed working at the farm, I must admit there had been occasions when the five-minute plod along the road on a dark, rainy winter's morning hadn't seemed all that attractive. But it was a walk in the park compared to the half-mile trudge into town in identical conditions to catch the seven-fifteen bus to Edinburgh. How blissful the sweet smell of silage, the wholesome hum of dung and the warm, contented ambience of a shed full of cud-chewing cattle seemed when compared to the inside of a bus packed solid with wet-coated, soggy-shoed, fag-reeking, bleary-eyed commuters, trying gamely to convince themselves that life could be worse.

'Smoke?' Jack Blair asked, proffering an open ten-pack of Players Navy Cut.

'May as well,' I shrugged. 'Can't do any more harm than all the second-hand fug in here anyway.'

Our trombone player was also about to commence his new career. As I had always expected, he'd chosen to devote his life to the beer industry, and had secured a position in the lab of McEwan's Brewery, not far from where I'd been told to report myself that morning.

Stuart House was a multi-storey, neo-Stalinesque office block in Semple Street, a typically nondescript little backwater in Edinburgh's Fountainbridge area. This part of the city was best known back then for its North British Rubber Works, the municipal meat market, Alexander's sprawling garage and coach works, streets lined with the drab tenement flats where Sean Connery spent his childhood and, of course, McEwan's Brewery. It was a brisk twenty-five minute walk from the bus station.

'See you on the bus tonight,' said Jack as we went our separate ways. 'If we catch the same one.'

'Yeah. If not, see you at the bus stop in the morning.'

*

It would be an exaggeration to say that I was seen as a freak by the teams of civil servants working away behind the grey sheet-metal partitions that formed the corridors and divided one office from another inside Stuart House. I couldn't help but suspect, though, that I was being looked at differently from the way a *normal* recruit would be. It was the anomaly of being a direct entrant Executive Officer, of being fast-tracked into that elite class, and the first ever to be afforded the privilege. If I wasn't exactly a freak, I was a novelty, and worthy, therefore, of being given a thorough once-over. I was most acutely aware of this when entering the typing pool, where I suddenly became a greenhorn gladiator, thrust half-naked into a tiger pit.

My tour of the building had started in the basement mail room. This, according to the personnel officer to whom I had reported on arrival, was the hub of the network through which all incoming pieces of government paper (and there were sackfuls!) would pass every day. We duly followed the mail-delivery route up through the floors, along the corridors and into the various departments and offices that together comprised the Scottish HQ of Her Majesty's Ministry of Labour.

The more my tour progressed, the more I asked myself why the hell I was I there. A fish trying to swim up a sand dune couldn't have felt more out place, or conspicuous. But then I would remind myself that this was my first day. First impressions could be misleading. I had to give things a chance. Make the most of the situation. Give it my best shots, and hope for the best as well. That had been my motto at school, and it had always seen me right. Besides, I couldn't allow myself to forget that I was in a privileged position: an Executive Officer at just eighteen years of age, whereas many of those I was being introduced to had had to spend much of their lives clawing their way up to the same rung on the ladder.

'Grades – that's what it's all about,' said the grey-suited, fifty-ish EO (let's call him Mr Smith) into whose hands I'd been passed by the personnel officer at the end of my tour of the building. Mr Smith would be my overseer and mentor throughout my training. 'Yes, grades. The very skeleton of the entire civil service. Take away the grades system and the whole show collapses.'

'Just like the army, then,' I ventured. 'But without the uniforms.'

Mr Smith appeared not to have heard that. He looked at me over the top of his glasses, reminding me of old A.B. Anderson, the headmaster whose career advice had been responsible, albeit indirectly, for my ending up here in the first place. 'You're a Grade Five, the lowest grade of EO, and I'm a Grade Four. You're answerable to me, and I'm answerable to the Grade Three who occupies a more senior position in this particular branch of Scottish HQ.' Mr Smith cleared his throat. 'Do I have aspirations to occupy his desk one day? Of course I do. That's the game of musical chairs we all play.' He gave me a smile. '*If* we want to progress in our careers, that is.'

'Right,' I nodded, returning his smile, which I hoped wouldn't look quite so contrived as his own.

Mr Smith swivelled round and opened a drawer in the metal cabinet behind him. He extracted a file, laid it neatly on his desk and pulled out a document, which he then handed to me. This, he stated, was a copy of the Official Secrets Act. 'You can read it if you want, but I'd suggest you skip all that rigmarole. Save us both a lot of time.' He hunched his shoulders and shot me another smile, but more a supercilious one this time. 'After all, the powers that be aren't about to change anything *you* don't happen to like, so you may as well just sign it.' His smile widened, tentatively. 'Can't become a member of Her Majesty's government otherwise, hmm?'

'Right.' I said again, though heaving a sigh instead of returning his smile. In for a penny, I thought, then appended my moniker.

Mr Smith stood up, reached over his desk, grabbed my hand and gave it a hearty shake. He was grinning genially now. 'Welcome to the club! Ah, and on that very subject...' An afterthought guided him back to the filing cabinet. Another piece of paper was passed over to me. This, he said, was my union membership form. 'May as well just sign that as well. It's compulsory, to all intents and purposes.'

'So, is this what they call a closed shop, then?'

Mr Smith ignored that. 'Your subs are deducted automatically from your salary. Nothing for you to bother about.'

'Except that someone I don't know is getting a slice of what I earn every month. I hope this doesn't seem impertinent, but why?'

A stern look heralded a snappy retort. 'Who do you think negotiates our pensions – Santa Claus?' Mr Smith sat down, rested his elbows on the desk, leaned forward and buttressed his fingers. 'You're a member of the establishment now, Mr Kerr. Certain conditions apply, and one of them is playing by the rules ... without question. But,' he continued, a thin smile returning to his face, 'there are also certain *inducement*s.' He presented me with yet another sheet of paper. 'This is your membership form for what we call our *perks* club. It's exclusive to civil servants, naturally.' He drew a finger fleetingly down the page. 'All sorts of concessions – shopping discounts at most of the leading stores, reductions on travel, all kinds of insurance, overseas holidays, London theatre tickets, restaurants, top hotels, even the price of new cars.' He cleared his throat again. 'I'll, ehm – I'll give you a copy of the complete list when you've, uhm...'

'Signed?' I pointed to the dotted line and looked him in the eye. 'Here?'

'Quite.'

It was now reaching the point where every time I put my name to paper I saw the words 'Freedom Forfeited' flashing before my eyes.

Mr Smith looked at his watch. 'Well, my goodness, lunchtime already.' He stood up again and ushered me towards the door. 'I take it you know your way around the trendy Fountainbridge eateries?'

'Intimately,' I lied.

'Fine, see you back here in an hour ... precisely, hmm?' Apparently siezed by another afterthought, he paused with his fingers clasping the door handle. 'You, uh – you mentioned our similarity to the armed forces, didn't you?'

'That's right. The grades – like the army ranks – privates, NCOs, officers all the way up from Second Lieutenants to –'

'Generals and beyond?' Mr Smith nodded with the speed of a pecking sparrow. 'Yes, yes, yes, precisely the same system. We're all part of the same officialdom, the same *establishment* I alluded to a moment ago.'

'Except for the uniforms?' I offered waggishly.

Once again, Mr Smith appeared not to have heard. He moved in close and said in tones that were a curious mix of confidentiality and swagger, 'Generals come and go, as indeed do prime ministers. But we, Mr Kerr, we civil servants are here forever.' A wink of almost masonic caginess closed one of his eyes. 'Never forget who *really* runs the show, OK?'

At this, he opened the door and motioned me through.

'Thanks,' I said, trying to give the impression of being impressed. 'I'll remember that.'

'Oh, and talking of uniforms,' he called after me, 'the sports jacket and flannels you're wearing are fine – for a counter clerk in one of our public offices, perhaps – but get yourself a grey suit. You're an Executive Officer, so try and *look* like one!'

*

The bus home that evening was just as packed as the morning one had been, but Jack and I managed to grab a seat next to each other all the same. Jack was not the greatest of conversationalists. Never likely to bore you with idle chit-chat, I found him to be a good travelling companion – even if he spent much of the journey poring over the day's crossword in *The Scotsman*.

'Anything exciting happen in your new job?' he mumbled after a while.

I had to think for a bit. 'Well, I signed the Official Secrets Act.'

He didn't look up from his newspaper. 'Yeah? What's that?'

'Can't tell you,' I chuckled. 'It's a secret.'

'Mmm-hmm,' Jack droned, chewing on his pencil, 'it would be, right enough.'

'You're not listening, are you?' I said.

Jack was too engrossed in his crossword to reply.

I let a couple of minutes pass. 'How about you?' I asked. 'Anything exciting happen in *your* new job?'

At last, Jack raised his eyes, glanced at me, smirked and said, 'Can't tell you. It's a secret.'

I smiled at the notion that matters of greater social significance might well bubble away daily in McEwan's test tubes than many of those destined to lurk hush-hush in the heads of civil servants for a lifetime. In any event, it was clear that Jack preferred to let his brewery job lie where he left it at clocking-off time, and I was only too happy to follow suit. Tomorrow morning would come around soon enough.

*

After a few days, it was as if we had been following the same routine for years, and I could see how people might become so numbed by the daily commute that they didn't even notice it after a while. Hamsters in a wheel, scurrying hypnotically towards a dandelion-leaf pension. It would be a treadmill worth pounding, I supposed, if you actually enjoyed your job, as I suspected Jack did, for all that he never admitted it. So, despite my initial misgivings about being a civil servant, I resolved to apply myself even more positively to the task of making my nascent career an enjoyable and fulfilling one. But I had to draw on previously untapped reserves of optimism to keep myself focused. Being unable to foresee anything even remotely creative in the job was the problem, and the ability to ignore this in favour of keeping that dandelion leaf firmly in my sights was one I feared I might never acquire.

My first few weeks at Stuart House found me sitting in with members of staff in the various departments, observing and absorbing how the system worked, getting a feel for what the Ministry of Labour was all about – which included trying to become a fitting cog in the 'grade' mechanism Mr Smith had laid so much importance upon. Although nobody said as much, I could tell there was an underlying feeling that I was a young usurper, a wet-behind-the-ears upstart who had no right to be leapfrogging the very people who were obliged to show him the ropes they had spent years learning. They all came across as genuinely nice folk, nonetheless, and did their best to make an inherently awkward situation seem otherwise. I took much from that. If they could cope with my presence, I would have to make an equal effort to fit in.

Jack and I managed to meet up for lunch most days, which made a welcome break from the routine, given that this soon became a routine in itself. The 'trendy Fountainbridge eateries' Mr Smith had so flippantly referred to turned out to be, for us at any rate, a little milk bar in Lothian Road, where the staple fare was a bowl of minestrone soup and a buttered roll. Or, for a special treat of mince and tatties, we'd occasionally visit the canteen above the SMT Bus Workshop round the corner in Reigo Street. This was executive living all right! But, then, how many other EOs in Stuart House were saving up to buy a bandwagon?

A month or so into my 'training', I was sent to London on a one-week induction course. Along with a dozen more new Grade Fives from various regions in Britain, I sat through day after day of lectures in a spartan room overlooking Euston Road. The main aim of the speakers (each one a Grade Four or better) seemed to be to press the importance of the civil service as a national institution, the invaluable role of the Ministry of Labour within a 'caring society' and, perhaps most crucial of all, how grateful we should be to be part of a government machine that was the envy of every other country on the planet. Brain washing, or just preaching to the converted? Neither, as far as I was concerned. I recall taking little from that course but a sense of having felt the pulse of a state-run behemoth which kept on growing because that was how the system thrived. This was the civil service.

At the end of my week in London, the Ministry of Labour was beginning to seem more and more an unnecessarily vast bureaucracy with a nationwide network of employment agencies attached. In essence, a human-resources version of Parkinson's Law. But perhaps I was just miffed because my fellow initiates had voted against my suggestion of spending our final night digging some jazz at the Humphrey Lyttelton Club in favour of trooping along to see Agatha Christie's 'Mousetrap' at the Ambassadors Theatre. Just miffed? Maybe, but I couldn't help but suspect that there really was something essentially lacking in my suitability for employment as an Executive Officer in one of Her Majesty's government departments.

But I would persevere with renewed vigour, believing that, if nothing else, I owed it to my parents.

*

'Ah yes, I recall your mother and father well,' said the manager. 'Yes indeed, they both worked under me in this very office before the war.' The manager, pushing sixty, of medium build and slightly portly, was the epitome of a senior civil servant, though affable, in an officious sort of way. His staff referred to him by his initials – C.J., or something like that, as far as I can remember. He smiled a reflective smile. 'Yes, your parents actually met here, if I'm not mistaken.'

I had just turned up to begin a spell of work experience in Edinburgh's 'engine room' of the Ministry. Tollcross Labour Exchange was an austere Victorian pile, every inch as unwelcoming on the outside as it was depressing within. Popularly known, like every other labour exchange in Scotland, as 'the broo' (idiomatic interpretation of *bureau*), the Tollcross office was the biggest in the country and therefore merited Grade Two status, as did the manager.

C.J. moved swiftly on from the subject of my parents to point out that his was the only Grade Two labour exchange in Scotland. It followed, he added with a modest little cough, that he was the only manager in Scotland to hold the second highest grade attainable. He was leaving me in no doubt that I was in the presence of someone who, when likening the grade system to a skeleton, was the living manifestation of a neck vertebra – or at least a collar bone.

I dipped my head in mute acknowledgement. From what he said next, I took it that C.J. had worked his way up from the foot – or at least the ankle. He informed me that I was an extremely lucky young man, and he hoped I appreciated the fact. Why, in his day, a chap couldn't just become an EO after a brief interview, no matter how well he had done at school. Hadn't my parents already mentioned this? he asked in a rhetorical kind of way.

I confirmed that they had, opting not to tell him that just about every person I'd met since joining up had said the same, either directly or by insinuation. 'I do feel very lucky indeed,' I told C.J., fingers crossed behind my back.

He fell silent and stared gravely at his desk. I sensed he was thinking back over the long years of endeavour and dedication it had taken him to get where he was today. I sensed right.

'Just think,' he said, looking up to offer me an encouraging smile, 'you're still only eighteen. Eighteen and already a Grade Five.' He raised a hand and indicated the four walls of his office in an 'all-this-could-be-yours' sort of way. 'Only three more promotions to go, eh?'

I glanced at the walls, painted government green like all the other walls in this dismal old building. But at least there were no white tiles extending to dado level as in the public areas I'd passed through. I glanced at the window, curtainless and with uninterrupted views of a stark, smoke-stained tenement across the street. But at least the window had no bars. Yet I couldn't resist the thought that, if I seriously believed this to be the best I could expect from a career in the civil service, I'd walk over to that window and jump out right now.

'Ah yes, a very lucky young man indeed,' C.J. nodded. He stood up, gestured towards the door and said, 'The world's your oyster. It's been opened up for you, my boy, so go and grab it with both hands.'

I didn't know much about oysters, except that they had a reputation for being pretty slippery little buggers. It struck me, then, that old C.J. had come up with an apt metaphor; an unwitting one, almost certainly, but no less appropriate for all that.

* * * * *

satchels chained to their wrists, and only their sports jackets for protection. They blithely regarded the outing as a bit of a skive, a welcome excuse to escape the dreary confines of the office for a few minutes every week. I was 'volunteered' to join them, not because it was thought I'd be any use helping fend off a heist, but rather because my presence in the office wasn't considered particularly essential in any case.

So, the intrepid trio would weave their way through the traffic to the bank in Brougham Street at the opposite side of Tollcross junction, with me following behind at a strategic distance. My orders were to stand outside the bank (again at a strategic distance) and keep an eye open for potential robbers, while the 'boys' were inside stuffing their bags with loot. And there's no denying it would have made any hood's day to get his mitts on such a bundle, even if it meant blowing away a handful of government punks in the process.

Such were the gangster-movie scenarios I entertained myself with while keeping a lonely vigil at the corner of the street. The closest to dodgy-looking characters I noticed, though, were a group of students making their merry way, portfolios in hand, to Edinburgh College of Art a bit farther up Lauriston Place. It struck me as ironic that I could easily have been one of them. I looked at my grey suit, then at their baggy jumpers, paint-daubed jeans, long hair and post-adolescent attempts at beards. A uniform by any other name? Probably. But did I envy them their carefree demeanour? No, not really. Well, I didn't *think* so anyway.

Swiftly clearing such unsettling considerations from my head, I focused again on images of old James Cagney movies, with jazz blaring out of speakeasies on the south side of Chicago. Soon, as happened so many times every day, I was preoccupied with thoughts of the Hidden Town Dixielanders and how we were shaping up as a band...

*

Keenness to improve was a passion we all shared. Practicing our individual instruments could be done in the privacy of our own homes, but developing as a band was a case of rehearsing as often as possible. And herein lay a problem; we were running out of places to rehearse. Complaints from neighbours resulted in our being asked to end our tenure of the premises above Fred Faunt's fruit-and-veg shop. The same happened after we'd made use of an upstairs room in the local RAF Club for a month or so.

It appeared, however, that our troubles were over when we managed to wangle access to a little-used pavilion in the grounds of Tynepark House, a seen-better-days Georgian edifice occupying a sprawling plot of land by the banks of the river. Its location, on the outskirts of town, was well out of earshot of potential complainers. Another plus was that we weren't being asked to pay rent. All we'd have to do was devote twenty minutes or so at the end of each rehearsal to play for the residents of 'the big house'. The fact that those residents just happened to be a bunch of young tearaways didn't seem to worry the staff, so we saw no reason to be bothered either. Tynepark, you see, was what society euphemistically termed an 'approved school' for the setting-right of teenage girls who had strayed from the straight and narrow. This was St Trinian's with a Scots accent.

The school's principal, or 'head screw' as her charges preferred to call her, was an enlightened woman. She believed that relaxing the strict rules of the establishment for a brief boogie once a week would help prepare the girls for eventual release from a life of corrective supervision, or 'their stretch' as her charges preferred to call it. For obvious reasons, boys were barred from the environs of Tynepark, so it followed that the young female detainees – some of whom made the tigresses in the Stuart House typing pool seem like pussycats in comparison – had to make do with each other as partners on the dance floor.

For the most part, the nearest any of them came to succumbing to the temptation of asking the lads in the band for a 'favour' of any kind would be an occasional attempt to bum a fag. This, despite the Tynepark staff being careful to ensure that the girls kept at a prudent distance from us. But what the girls lacked in freedom, they made up for in resourcefulness. Indeed, according to Wee Bob the drummer, one enterprising lass even got close enough to make a request from behind the back cloth of the little stage we played on. Hers wasn't a request for a particular tune, though.

'Ah suppose an elopement's oot o' the question,' she'd whispered to Bob, promptly qualifying her proposal with: 'Just a quick knee-trembler at the side o' the pottin' shed, like!' We never did establish whether or not this anecdote was merely a figment of Bob's scholarly imagination – or perhaps even just wishful thinking. Whatever, the Tynepark arrangement went without any serious hitch, until another offer of rehearsal facilities came along. This one really was too good to refuse.

*

The Lotus Club was situated in the centre of Musselburgh, a bustling town immediately to the east of Edinburgh, with traditional ties to the fishing and coal mining industries. George Dixon, the club's owner and also the proprietor of a local furniture shop, had heard about the Hidden Town Dixielanders on the grapevine. Being a shrewd businessman, he recognised the potential benefits of combining our youthful ambitions with his own desire to successfully diversify his commercial interests.

He told us that the club, previously the Arcadia Cinema, but now, as the local newspaper proclaimed, 'The Newest Dance Hall in Town', was doing fair enough business at weekends, but was dead during the week. His conclusion was that the canny folk of Musselburgh were not yet sufficiently sophisticated to feel comfortable about letting their hair down at the end of a working day, with the start of another just a short sleep away. The enlightened citizens of Edinburgh, on the other hand, weren't lumbered with such outmoded hang-ups. What's more, they had long been enthusiastic patrons of live jazz. Just think of the massive support enjoyed by bands featuring Sandy Brown and Alex Welsh before their departure for London earlier in the decade. *And* Edinburgh was only five miles from Musselburgh, centre to centre. All the Lotus Club needed, George Dixon deduced, was a jazz band to act as a magnet. And since the Hidden Town Dixielanders hailed from nearby Haddington, the way ahead could not have been clearer.

The theory met with our approval, so Mr Dixon duly offered a deal: we could use the club for rehearsal purposes on Sunday afternoons, absolutely free of charge, if we agreed to play for the public one night per week. It was an experiment, as we would appreciate, so no fee could be guaranteed. Instead, we would be paid a percentage of the door money – sixty-forty in our favour. The offer met with our approval, so the deal was duly sealed.

While the rehearsal arrangement worked out well, the midweek gigs were a disaster. There were usually more band members than customers, and of the few punters who did turn up, most showed little interest in what we were playing. On top of that, almost all of them came courtesy of complimentary tickets, so our cut of the take amounted to sixty per cent of peanuts.

By way of compensation, we did have one celebrity customer – and he actually paid to get in as well! Edinburgh's Bobby Neill was, in that autumn of 1959, the current British featherweight boxing champ. Although his boy-next-door appearance and retiring manner belied the tough nature of his profession, he did display all the slick footwork of a boxer at the peak of his game while cutting a rug with his ladyfriend. However, on the evenings Bobby did grace us with his presence, he and his partner were invariably the only clients. If his main objective was to enjoy a bit of relaxation away from the attentions of his legions of fans in the capital, he had certainly come to the right place. Any illusions we may have had about turning the east side of Edinburgh into an ersatz version of the south side of Chicago were soon dashed. We couldn't even attract enough jazz fans to turn the Lotus Club into an ersatz version of the pavilion at Tynepark House.

'What you boys need is exposure.' Thus spoke George Dixon on the night he finally pulled the plug on our midweek gigs. 'Tellin' ye, lads – take it from a shopkeeper – ye need a shop window to bring yer stuff to the notice o' the public at large. Yes, get yerselves on the wireless!'

Anyone gifted with telepathy would have read our thoughts in response to Mr Dixon's well-meaning advice: 'Yeah, thanks, George – we'll train up a few pigs for aerobatic displays at the same time.'

But such negative a reaction, though understandable, was to prove unjustified...

*

The Record Exchange in Edinburgh's South Clerk Street was a little shop specialising in second-hand jazz albums; a mecca for enthusiasts like ourselves, whenever we had a few quid to spare. One Saturday afternoon, shortly after the termination of our Lotus Club 'residence', Kimber and I were ambling back towards the city centre, chatting away about the content of a couple of LPs we'd just bought. We were passing by the Empire Theatre in Nicolson Street when something grabbed our attention. It was a billboard featuring a curvy young starlet called Jackie Collins.

'What d'ye think?' I said.

'Aye, no bad. But forget it – ye couldnae afford her.'

'No, no, not the bird. I'm talking about what she's gonna be hosting.'

Kimber looked again at the billboard, did a double take, then squinted at me. 'Carroll Levis Discovery Show? You surely don't mean the –'

'Band? Absolutely! Why not? It could turn out be the showcase old George Dixon said we needed.' I pointed to the wording at the foot of the poster. 'See – the winner gets a spot on BBC radio!'

Kimber gave a quiet chortle. 'Nah, I've heard that show on the wireless often enough. Comedians, guys whistling *If I Were a Blackbird* like Ronnie Ronalde, close-harmony vocal groups, animal impressionists and Elvis mimics. Yeah, plenty of that. But jazz bands?' He shook his head. 'Don't think so.'

'Well, there's a first time for everything.' Fired by a sudden flare-up of reckless optimism, I made for the door. 'I'm gonna nip inside and put our name down.'

Nobody was more surprised than we were when, on the hallowed stage of the Empire Theatre a few weeks later, our version of *Down By The Riverside* prevailed over the performances of ostensibly more likely candidates: Scottish tenors and tartan-sashed sopranos, kilted accordionists, classical pianists, a Hebridean harpist and the inevitable clutch of Elvis wannabes. We were even rated above a uniquely gifted sword swallower, whose novelty act climaxed with *Nearer, My God, To Thee*, played on a saw. As Jackie Collins so succinctly put it in her summing-up, 'The saw shtick is one thing, honey, but sword swallowing won't cut it on national radio!'

We just hoped the efforts of six young jazzers from a little farming town in East Lothian would.

* * * * *

CHAPTER SIXTEEN

'A LONG DAY IN THE SMOKE'

We had left Edinburgh on the early-morning London train, the tickets provided for the six-and-a-half-hour journey stipulating that we would be returning by the last train on the same day. Clearly, 'Auntie' BBC didn't waste licence-payers' money on anything but the bare essentials in exies for talent-show hopefuls.

The Playhouse Theatre, located in Northumberland Avenue, near Trafalgar Square, was where the all-winners programme would be recorded for the Light Programme, the forerunner of today's Radio One. Backstage goings-on during rehearsals were just as chaotic as those we had experienced during our regional 'heat' in Edinburgh. The prevailing atmosphere was one of adrenalin-charged excitement, though ranging in manifestation from trouser-wetting panic among the ranks of undisguised rookies to exaggerated indifference in the case of a lamé-suited quartet of pop-singing narcissists who were at pains to give the impression that they'd seen it all before. We placed ourselves nearer the trouser-wetting end of the spectrum. This wasn't because we were unduly nervous, but rather since we felt more akin to that camp than to any of the no-business-like-showbusiness types present. Some of the latter, including the four we had dubbed The Up-themselves Brothers, had actually applied stage makeup ... for a radio programme!

By six o' clock, a full house was being entertained to a preview performance (really a final rehearsal) before the actual recording took place between 6.45 and 7.30. The legendary Carroll Levis, a rotund Canadian of jovial mien, introduced the acts with effortless charm and faultless timing, despite having been conspicuously absent from proceedings up to then. The mark of a true professional? He certainly left no-one in any doubt that he was the star of the show, and in so doing was setting a precedent that would be emulated by opportunity providers like Hughie Green and Simon Cowell in decades to come. Where there's talent, there's gold – for the discovered, occasionally; for the discoverers, nearly always.

We had regarded our participation in the show as an adventure, a chance to go on an expenses-paid trip to London and to experience the buzz of taking part in a nationwide broadcast. Our deliberately uncomplicated arrangement (we knew our limitations) of *Down By The Riverside* had gone down well with the live audience, although, to be fair, they had given an equally encouraging response to all the performers, even to those who had dropped more jitters-induced clangers than we had. The defining factor for us, though, was that we didn't expect a spot on the Carroll Levis Discoveries programme to turn us into stars overnight. Jazz was too erudite a scene for that to happen. All we hoped for was that appearing in this famous shop window would help attract more customers to whatever engagements we might now be booked for back home in our little corner of rural Scotland.

So, satisfied that we had done our best in that regard, we hightailed it out of the Playhouse Theatre and set off to take in some live jazz.

*

A short taxi ride beyond the august precincts of Trafalgar Square took us into the heart – or, some would say, intestines – of Soho, London's infamous 'square mile' of neon-flickering sleaze. Great Windmill Street at night becomes about as seedy as any thoroughfare in this merry maze of depravity. What better place, then, to find a jazz club? The one bearing the name of New Orleans-style clarinettist Cy Laurie was located in a basement which shared an entrance with a strip club and a boxing gym. Over the street stood the Windmill Theatre, universally known for its barely-legal nude *tableaux vivants*, or 'living (female) statues'. Habitués of those jazz-nurturing clip joints and cat houses in turn-of-the-century Storyville would have felt right at home here.

Cy Laurie's Club was essentially a big, grubby cellar, a few moth-eaten couches set against the walls its only concession to creature comforts. Not that the current crush of creatures seemed to care. These weren't the debauchees who trawled the streets and alleyways above, but a cross section of the city's bedsit community: young people who were here to jive the night away, and with luck (at least in the case of the males), to obtain for free what the debauchees above were prepared to pay for.

The featured band was fronted by a baby-faced young Yorkshireman called, appropriately, 'Kid' Shillito, a disciple of fellow trumpeter Ken Colyer, who was long acknowledged as Britain's champion of all things 'purist' in traditional jazz. Like Great Windmill Street itself, the band oozed echoes of New Orleans, although it's unlikely that many in the audience had more than a passing interested in such trivia. Their mission was to let the music motivate their feet, and even the highest-steppin' Basin Street mamas of old would have been pushed to match their antics on the dance floor. In the steamy gloom of the cellar, they appeared as a blur of gyrating bodies, and the more frantic the tempo, the more energy they seemed to draw from it. Indeed, this was like a gathering of dervishes set on whirling themselves into oblivion.

Still, we enjoyed the spectacle *and* the music. But we were country lads with an unkickable fresh-air habit to feed, so we couldn't dally too long down there before coming up for a fix. Just as significantly, though, time was short and there was one particular place we were determined to visit before catching the train back to Scotland...

The Humphrey Lyttelton Club's home was also a basement, but with a respectable address at 100 Oxford Street, the bustling avenue which marks the northern boundary of Soho and boasts some of London's most fashionable shops. Although still affectionately known as Humph's, the venue had recently changed its name to Jazzshows Jazz Club, with a policy of presenting an ever-changing programme of top bands, seven nights a week. Its patrons ranged in type from the less bohemian of London's bedsit brigade through middle-aged jazz diehards to ostensibly 'hip' American tourists.

On this occasion, the Alex Welsh Band was billed as the main attraction, and if any Americans present happened to be Chicagoans, they'd have thought they were back home in the windy city the moment they took their first step down the Jazzshows stairs. Trumpeter Alex Welsh, a native of Edinburgh, had managed in the few years he had been in London to assemble a group of British musicians who could produce a particularly free-swinging, hard-driving brand of Dixieland like no other band outside America. Close your eyes and you might have been listening to a recording made by one of the star-studded line-ups led by the man whose name had long been as synonymous with Chicago-style jazz as the city itself, the fabled Eddie Condon.

Although by no means palatial, and while also possessing that distinctive mustiness common to most cellars, Jazzshows did seem a more listener-friendly place than Cy Laurie's. Whether by design or chance, the jive monkeys, though having claimed most of the floor area as their own, had left a patch immediately in front of the band free for those keener to treat their ears than pound their feet. Since the stand was only about a foot high, those customers positioning themselves close enough could actually imagine they were part of the band. Which is what we did, and what an experience it was!

As fate would have it, the two albums Kimber and I had bought on the day the Carroll Levis Show first beckoned back in Edinburgh had been recorded by the Alex Welsh Band only a year or so earlier. *The Melrose Folio* and *Dixieland to Duke* had been played so often during breaks in our rehearsals since then that we knew by heart the subtleties and nuances of every one of the tracks. Now we were standing within inches of the featured musicians as they reproduced their distinctive versions of jazz evergreens like *Dippermouth Blues*, *King Porter Stomp*, *Cornet Chop Suey*, *Ostrich Walk* and *I'm Coming Virgina*.

We savoured every note from Alex Welsh's punchy lead (his Wild Bill Davison roots showing!), the silky-smooth trombone work of Jack Teagarden-inspired Roy Crimmins, and Edinburgh-born clarinettist Archie Semple's uncanny ability to emulate, not only the individual styles of his heroes Edmond Hall and Pee Wee Russel, but sometimes both at once! This was all pure magic to our ears, and we would gladly have lingered there all night, but for the realisation that the last train home would already be fired up and waiting. Never dreaming that any of us might one day perform in this hallowed temple of jazz, or, even more fancifully, play alongside such world-class musicians, we took our leave of the erstwhile Humphrey Lyttelton Club and grabbed a taxi for King's Cross Station.

*

The only sustenance we'd had time to snatch during that long day in London had been a few packets of crisps and an occasional handful of peanuts. Now, comfortably seated in the compartment we'd grabbed for ourselves (no open-plan, walk-through carriages in those days), we wolfed into a heap of soggy bread slices spread with whatever mush was flavour of the day at the King's Cross snack bar. Awful as they were, no food fit a king could have gone down better than those British Railways sandwiches. Even if we hadn't yet reached the required standard musically, we were at least learning to *eat* like professional jazzmen. And another prerequisite was about to be added.

'I fixed up something to help celebrate our first broadcast,' wee Bob the drummer announced as soon as we'd scoffed the last of the King's Cross doorsteps. He stood on the seat and produced a large bottle from his bag on the rack above. 'It's a certain *potion* I prepared at the uni – something we chemistry students brew up in the lab for special occasions.' He cleared his throat. 'Ah-hem, when the coast is clear, so to speak.'

'Looks like water, man,' said Jim, scowling.

'Looks can be deceptive,' said Bob, winking. He poured an equal measure of his potion into a half-empty bottle of lemonade. 'Here,' he said, and handed me the bottle, 'have a couple of slugs and pass it around.'

I shot him a leery look.

'Don't worry,' he smiled, 'there's plenty more where that came from.'

When I regained consciousness, the train wasn't moving, but the inside of the compartment was.

'Don't worry,' I heard wee Bob say again, 'we've only stopped at York station. Routine stuff. We'll be away again in a minute.'

'*York?*' I blinked. 'But that's half way home!' I shook my head, trying to focus. 'How long was I out?'

'Oh, two hours or thereabouts. Aye, it happens with the old ethanol, ye know.'

'*Eth*anol? But – but that's the rocket fuel speedway bikes run on!'

'No, no, you're thinking about *meth*anol. Nah, never drink that – it's poison.'

I looked to my right. There was Jack, sitting beside me, just as he'd been during the sandwich-scoffing interlude, except he was now out cold, head back, mouth agape, breathing in intermittent bursts. I looked to my left. There was Jim. Ditto. I looked over at Bob. He was smiling, just as he'd been when he passed me the spiked lemonade.

'What the hell's ethanol?' I croaked. I glanced round the compartment again, my head clearer now. 'And where's Kimber and John?'

'Pure alcohol is the answer to question one, and away to the lavvy is the answer to question two.'

'The lavvy? At the same time?'

'Yeah, I think they had a puke comin' on.' Bob allowed himself an impish little chortle. 'Kimber and John. Ex-national servicemen, ye know. Drank you three senseless easy enough. Thought they could out-bevvy me as well. Aye, right,' he laughed, 'but beware a chemistry student bearing gifts.' Bob held up two almost-empty bottles. 'Guess which one contains the straight lemonade...'

'But, for God's sake, you might've *killed* us!'

Bob was nonchalance personified. 'Naw, no chance. It's an old students' game. I wouldn't have let you drink too much.'

At that very moment, my eyes were drawn to the window, which framed a picture of a wheyfaced John pushing a porter's barrow rubber-legged along the platform. Spreadeagled on the barrow was Kimber, comatose.

I glared at Bob. 'Wouldn't have let us drink too much, eh!'

Bob's head was bobbing with silent laughter. 'Seems to have done John's brains no harm,' he wheezed. 'I mean, he must've worked out it would be impossible to drag somebody in that state along the corridor from the shit house.' He stood up and helped me to my feet. 'Come on – better go and find an empty compartment to haul them into.'

* * * * *

CHAPTER SEVENTEEN

'HITTING THE ROAD'

By the time our Carroll Levis Show spot was broadcast, I was doing a stint of work experience in the offices of the Ministry of Labour Professional and Executive Register in Edinburgh's George Street; a more upmarket address than the Tollcross 'broo', but a 'broo' nonetheless. Rightly or wrongly, the Ministry had a policy of segregating the elite of the unemployed from the proles, yet the dejected looks on the faces of men genuinely in search of a job were exactly the same. Those on the Professional and Executive Register were, however, spared the indignity of having their misfortune exposed to their peers. No shuffling forward in line to collect their dole money, no interviews except in private. Everything, in fact, was conducted as discreetly as possible, which, ironically, seemed to exacerbate the aura of despondency that pervaded the place. While I considered myself fortunate to be a member of staff as opposed to one of the 'customers' (many of whom had academic credentials far superior to my own), it was good to know I would only be there for a few weeks.

I was also glad of my involvement with the band: a creative hobby which provided a welcome contrast to what was becoming a predictable daily grind. As anticipated, the radio exposure of the Carroll Levis programme didn't turn us into overnight stars, but it did trigger bookings from farther afield. Good news though this was, it also focused attention on a long-standing problem: transportation.

We had been invited to Newcastle-upon-Tyne by the city's New Orleans Jazz Club, which held Friday night sessions in a local pub. The club was run by the Vieux Carré Jazzmen, whose name was borrowed from the 'French Quarter' of New Orleans and also signified the 'purist' type of traditional jazz they were dedicated to preserving. We had our doubts about the reception our less 'uncorrupted' style would be given by the club's regular clientele, but an opportunity to appear in a real jazz club for the first time was one we weren't about to refuse.

It was also the first time we'd feel unable to impose upon family and friends to help get us to the venue and back. A two-hundred-mile round trip was involved, so asking to borrow their cars or expecting them to subsidise the hire of a coach was out. We'd have to rent a van. Despite the outlay, which would consume much of the fee we were being paid, there was a feeling that travelling in something akin to a bandwagon of our own would add a touch of 'on the road' authenticity to the occasion. We'd be experiencing what it was like to be a *proper* touring band – even if only for one night.

The gig itself went surprisingly well, the audience giving us a typically warm Geordie reception, and the Vieux Carré boys showing no outward sign of contempt towards our less traditional approach to playing traditional jazz. The club encouraged young musicians to sit in with the band, and one who had a blow that evening would become, within a few years, one of Newcastle's best-known sons. It would not be as an earthy-sounding trombonist, however, that Eric Burdon would make his mark, but as lead singer of the Animals on their massive international hit, *House of the Rising Sun*, the lyrics of which immortalised a knocking shop in, aptly enough, the Vieux Carré district of New Orleans.

High spirits had been much in evidence during our three-hour journey to Newcastle, and after what had proved to be a more than satisfactory jazz club debut, spirits were higher still on the way home – for the first hour or so, that is. To save money, the van's insurance had been limited to cover only one driver: me. I was about to learn the hard way that, once a post-gig downer sets in, the exuberance of on-the-road musicians tends to fade pretty rapidly, and in unison. For the remainder of the trip north, the laughter and joke-telling that had filled the van up to then would be replaced by snoring and, in a low-pitched harmony of sorts, farting. I bade myself welcome to what it was really like to be a member of a proper touring band – particularly the member who's saddled with the driving.

*

Based in the tiny gatehouse of Drygrange Mansion near Melrose in the Scottish Borders, the eponymous Border Dances was one of the biggest dance-promoting organisations in the whole of Britain. The brains and driving force behind the enterprise was Duncan McKinnon, whose partiality to a drink or ten had earned him the nickname of Drunken Duncan. Ace tippler though he may have been, the fact remained that Duncan had built his operation from nothing to a point where he now controlled an empire that was running dances in as many as thirty different venues throughout Scotland and the north of England every weekend. He was a very important man, high on the list of promoters that even the most eminent of London booking agents would contact when arranging a northern tour for a band. We could hardly believe our luck when Border Dances offered us an engagement which, if successful, stood a chance of being repeated on a regular basis.

The Hidden Town Dixielanders had been presented with an opportunity to say goodbye to being essentially amateurs and indulge their hobby on a semi-professional basis. Being paid a guaranteed fee for playing jazz would now be the norm instead of the exception. Still, it was a foregone conclusion that those fees would be appropriately modest until we'd proved we had the drawing power to merit a rise. A businessman like Duncan McKinnon hadn't become successful by throwing money at turkeys. Equally, our accepting engagements on the Border Dances circuit would involve travelling considerable distances, so it would be only fair for the boys in the band to be rewarded with an appropriate share of the spoils. Continuously handing over a large slice to a van-hire company would soon take the gilt off the gingerbread.

But how could we buy a wagon of our own? The band had nothing in the bank, and we weren't sufficiently flush individually to chip in for even a down payment on an old banger. Then Lady Luck appeared, but in the most unlikely of guises…

'I hear tell thoo'll be needin' a peedie bus,' said my maternal grandfather in his lilting Orkney brogue. 'For gettin' the boys aboot tae play at the dances?'

We were paying one of our regular family visits to his farm at Bonnyrigg, a few miles south of Edinburgh, and I presumed it had been my mother who had told him about the bandwagon situation, probably just as a casual remark.

Grandfather and I were alone in the scullery of the farmhouse, where, rather than go to the barbers and part with a couple of bob, he periodically risked his ear lobes by asking me to trim what little hair he had left. I confirmed that we were indeed in need of a peedie (or small) bus of some kind, but it looked as if we'd have to make do with hiring a van until we'd set aside enough from the band's earnings to buy one.

'Weel then, come thee wi' me,' he said, as he got up from his chair and swiped a dusting of clippings from his shoulders. 'I've likely seen the very item.'

Ten minutes later we drove onto the forecourt of the local filling station, and there, in the middle of a line of second-hand vehicles, was his 'very item'. Described on the windscreen as a Ford 'Utilicon' Estate Car, it was in reality a little E83 half-ton delivery van, factory-converted into a six-seater people carrier, complete with side windows. Although ten years old, it appeared to be in good condition.

'A fine-like peedie bus, boy, eh?' said Grandfather, his tombstone teeth bared in a self-congratulatory grin. 'Yass, the very dab, if thoo asks me!'

I agreed that it would suit our purpose fine, even if it might be a bit of a squeeze to get the boys *and* all the gear in. But anyway, I shrugged, that was all fairly academic right now.

Grandfather squinted at me. 'Academic? It's no tae be a *school* bus as weel, is it!'

'No, no,' I laughed, then gestured towards the little Ford's windscreen, on which the sum of £200 was painted large and white. 'What I mean is, they'd have to knock a hundred-and-ninety quid off, because a tenner's about all I could stump up right now.'

'Yass, yass, fine that,' Grandfather said absently, appearing more interested in weighing up the slick-looking young man now heading our way across the forecourt. Old-time farmer that he was, he had done enough real horse-trading in his time to make what followed an object lesson in how to wring the best possible deal out of a used-car salesman. Not only did he manage to browbeat the fellow into accepting twenty pounds less than the asking price – 'Ten per cent discoont for cash, boy!' – but also twisted his arm into parting with a 'luckpenny' in the form of a complimentary roof rack – 'For the bandsmens' musical implements, thoo kens.'

The deal finally done, he handed me the vehicle's registration documents, then promptly took them back again. Like Duncan McKinnon of Border Dances, old Tom Muir hadn't got where he was today by throwing money at turkeys – not even a closely-related one. He told me that, before he'd part with the papers, I'd have to pay him back every penny of the purchase price, in six equal monthly instalments.

Six? A quick flurry of mental arithmetic came up with the conclusion that I'd need to hand over thirty quid every month. My civil service salary couldn't cope with that, and there was no way of forecasting how much the band would be able to contribute. Panic stations!

A large, banana-fingered hand rested on my shoulder. There was no need to fret, Grandfather said. The peedie bus would be mine to use as I saw fit in the meantime. And the conditions he'd set weren't intended to be a millstone round my neck, but a first lesson in how to be a businessman. He could weel imagine, he said, how big a pain in the arse travelling from Haddington to Edinburgh and back every day in a crowded service bus must be, not only for me, but for everyone else too. So, all I'd have to do was find five of those everyone-elses and charge them the service-bus fare, but for transportation in chauffeur-driven comfort. He nodded towards the newly-purchased Ford Utilicon. 'See what I mean, boy?'

As gross an exaggeration as 'chauffeur-driven comfort' may have been, once word got round that seats were available in the 'peedie' bus, I could have had the pick of many more passengers than there were seats available. Anything, it seemed, would be an improvement on the existing sardine-can drudgery of the daily commute. And the fares of the chosen five did indeed add up to an invaluable contribution to my monthly repayments to Grandfather. His business acumen had served me well, while simultaneously solving the band's mobility problem.

*

The venues used by Border Dances were, typically, town halls, corn exchanges, drill halls and the like; no-frills municipal facilities centrally placed within each locality, reasonably cheap to hire and capable of accommodating several hundred dancers. Our first booking for the organisation was a Saturday night hop in the Borders wool-mill town of Galashiels, its Volunteer Hall known affectionately on dance nights as the 'Gally' Palais. We appeared as support band for American rock 'n' roll idol Gene Vincent, whose star was twinkling slightly less brightly some four years after the release of *Be-Bop-A-Lula*, the hit that had first won him transatlantic fame. He was still drawing big crowds in early 1960 for Border Dances, though. Crafty Duncan McKinnon had a knack of catching the right fish at the right time – whether on its way up river or down.

It's fair to say that the 'Gally' Palais crowd that night (certainly the female element) was more taken by Gene's gyrations in black leather jeans than by anything an up-and-coming jazz band could offer in the way of visual titillation. But at least passive indifference was better than being booed off the stage. This gig gave us our first lesson in measuring success by not being on the receiving end of verbal, if not physical, abuse; playing at Saturday night hops in rural Scotland did have its hazards – particularly after closing time at the pubs. We left Galashiels that night in notably lower spirits than when returning home from the Newcastle jazz club, yet hopeful that the neutral reception we had received might still warrant further bookings from Border Dances, and grateful that only our egos had been bruised.

As it transpired, Duncan McKinnon didn't immediately flood our diary with repeat engagements, but we had at least made our way onto his list of bookable bands and were assured our services would be called upon again – though at Duncan's sole discretion. This, undeniably, was the prerogative of powerful men. Any worries I may have had about consequent shortfalls in my monthly repayments on the bandwagon were, however, soon allayed. News travelled fast within what was still a relatively small live-music scene in Scotland. We were soon contacted by two other dance promoters, both keen to exploit the growing popularity of jazz bands in parts of the country where local combos were still thin on the ground.

Bert Ewing was an ex-ballroom dancing champion, who, since hanging up his pumps, ran dances in public halls in his native north-east of Scotland; an operation akin to Duncan McKinnon's, though on a more modest scale. His main venues were in bustling Aberdeenshire farming hubs like Huntly and Inverurie, where, as might be expected, Saturday night audiences were by nature enthusiastic and invariably large. Bert, as shrewd as he was amiable, was always likely to be on a winner in those towns. Yet he also had the distinction of having made one of the region's least bustling locations into perhaps the most popular rural dance venue anywhere in Scotland.

Mintlaw Station appeared, at least when arriving there in the dark, little more than a scattering of houses at a crossroads deep in the bucolic Buchan countryside. As its name suggests, the place denoted a stop on the soon-to-be-defunct Aberdeen-to-Peterhead railway line. But, more significantly, it was located at the centre of a thriving agricultural area made up of many small communities – but only Mintlaw with a dance venue suitable for hosting touring bands. Bert Ewing was a canny man!

Some sixty miles to the west, the elegant country town of Elgin was the business base of cafe proprietor turned band impresario Albert Bonici, whose importance would eventually eclipse that of the mighty Duncan McKinnon himself. In July 1960, Mr Bonici would open a dance hall called The Two Red Shoes, adjoining his Park Cafe in Elgin. A couple of years later, the Beatles were fated to play their first Scottish date there, to a very sparse audience and for the princely fee of £42. However, the occasion became enshrined in popular music history when the Fab Four's first single *Love Me Do* stormed the charts soon after. The Two Red Shoes became essential to every name band's Scottish itinerary, and Albert Bonici, who'd had the foresight to be appointed the Liverpool group's sole Scottish booking agent, soon had his £42 'gamble' amply rewarded.

In the spring of 1960, however, Albert was still promoting dances in Elgin's Drill Hall, and at similarly unpretentious venues in neighbouring towns, such as Nairn, Forres and Keith. What's more, as a jazz enthusiast himself, he was happy to give promising young bands a break.

*

There's a saying that when a pleasure becomes a habit, it ceases to be a pleasure. We were to discover that the same can apply to a hobby when it becomes a profession – even a *semi*-profession. As a songwriter of yore advised rainbow-chasers: 'You'll find your happiness lies, right under your eyes, back in your own back yard.' And it's true that the simple enjoyment we had derived from those first, tentative gigs in our home patch was unlikely to be improved upon or, in some respects, even repeated 'on the road'. Still, the buzz of playing together had not diminished, particularly now that the band was really starting to knit as a musical unit. All our dedicated practice may not have made perfect, but it had certainly buffed off a lot of rough edges. Nevertheless, while sitting for hour after hour in a cramped bandwagon on the way to a gig can be bearable, and occasionally enjoyable (if the scenery outside and the humour inside are conducive), the return journey is almost certain to become a drag. And the longer the journey, the bigger the drag.

The typical Ewing or Bonici venue was almost two hundred miles distant from our home base; a good six-hour haul for our fully-laden little Ford, considering its puny ten horsepower engine struggled to top forty miles per hour – downhill. When I say six hours, that's excluding the two-and-a-half-mile crossing over the River Forth. This was four years before the opening of the Forth Road Bridge, so the crossing could add hours to a journey, depending on how long the hapless traveller had to wait for the ferry. On a Sunday, the first one sailed at 7.30 a.m., and we found that anything up to two hours could be spent huddled in the pre-dawn chill of the bandwagon, parked in a row of long-distance trucks on the slipway at North Queensferry.

Ah, those long-distance trucks, all heading south from the big north-east seaports. Invariably, we'd find ourselves stuck behind one for mile upon mile after passing Aberdeen, the melted ice dripping from the lorry polluting its slipstream with the stench of putrefying fish. Given that our peedie bus hadn't the poke to overtake, the only alternative was to take the foot off the gas until a cushion of relatively fresh air had been established between ourselves and the offending vehicle. But this would only result in our being overtaken a couple of minutes later by another member of the same convoy.

'Piscatorial purgatory,' as drummer Bob so lyrically put it.

'Would make ye honk!' guitarist Jim more idiomatically opined. He added that he was about to prove the point.

It should have been a relief, then, to pull into the North Inch transport cafe on the fringe of the fair city of Perth, the only all-night truck stop on the route. If there had been a league table of 'greasy spoon' cafes, this one would surely have qualified for the top – or bottom, depending on how the ratings were formulated. Although rough and ready, at least the eating area (sausage, bacon, fried egg and baked beans the house speciality) had a more wholesome ambience than the toilets, which bore evidence that Jim hadn't been the first in several nights to succumb to the side-effects those dreaded fish wagons – or, dare we say, the house sausages?

* * * * *

CHAPTER EIGHTEEN

'THERE'LL BE SOME CHANGES MADE'

Jack and Bob were the first to leave the band, not because they couldn't take the rigours of travelling to and from those far-off weekend engagements, for they were as hardy and keen as the rest of us in that respect, but simply because of priorities. The band was taking up more and more of our spare time, and it was time that neither Jack nor Bob could commit to without adversely affecting day job and university studies respectively.

A young Edinburgh trombonist called George 'Ozzie' Oswald took over from Jack. Though his preferred style was perhaps a tad on the 'modernist' side for an outfit like ours, Ozzie adapted well and quickly became one of the boys. The drummer's stool vacated by Bob was immediately claimed by our old Haddington Boys' Pipe Band chum Derek Dewar, who had first introduced me to the 'real' jazz of Louis Armstrong in *The Glenn Miller Story* movie. Before upgrading to a full drum kit, Derek had been rattling a washboard for the same skiffle group from which Jim Douglas and our bassist John Logan had graduated. For an ex-piper, Derek proved to be a surprisingly capable drummer, booting the band along in fine style.

But no sooner had the new line-up started to gel than Ozzie received a call to join the arranging staff of the world-famous Ted Heath Orchestra in London. Then Derek was forced to pull out, his training as an engineer at a local mill involving weekend shift work which clashed with the band's travels. Suddenly, it seemed our growing popularity, modest though it still was, might actually spell the end of the Hidden Town Dixielanders. Where were we going to find yet another replacement trombone player and drummer now? Certainly not locally.

*

On Sunday evenings, when back home from our latest trip and refreshed after a few hours sleep, Kimber, Jim and I had often made a point of popping into the Royal Mile Cafe in Edinburgh's High Street. The attraction wasn't the coffee, good though it was, but an extremely competent seven-piece band fronted by Eric Rinaldi, the proprietor's trumpet-playing son. They played in the Chicago style favoured by that other Edinburgh-born trumpeter Alex Welsh, whose band we had lapped up live in London after our Carroll Levis Show broadcast a few months earlier. And I must say the Royal Mile Cafe boys, most of them still in their twenties, were doing an excellent job of maintaining Edinburgh's reputation for nurturing this gutsy brand of Dixieland jazz.

We soon became friendly with Eric and his sidemen – Jack Duff (clarinet), Kenny Ramage (trombone), Tom Finlay (piano), Alex Marshall (guitar), Ronnie Dunn (bass), Sandy Malcolm (drums) – and with other Edinburgh jazz musicians who dropped in from time to time to 'dig the scene'. One of the regular visitors was a forty-something-year-old drummer called George Crockett. Affable, avuncular, well-mannered, quietly-spoken, neatly-dressed and a gentleman in the truest sense of the word, he was the very antithesis of the popular image of a jazz drummer. To add to George's enigmatic stamp, he worked on one of the popular national dailies as a journalist, another profession not automatically associated with the more decorous of human qualities. George had never married, but was devoted to jazz, and particularly to the flavour served up in the Royal Mile Cafe on Sunday nights. While he hadn't the reputation of being the most technically-gifted drummer in town, he did have a jazz pedigree that made him worthy of being set on a pedestal by young aspirants like ourselves.

George Crockett had actually played and recorded with the most revered of Edinburgh's previous generation of jazz musicians before their departure for London. He had worked with the aforementioned Alex Welsh and his clarinettist partner Archie Semple in the early Fifties, and with clarinettist Sandy Brown and his trumpet-playing accomplice Al Fairweather as far back as 1946. He had even been on back-slapping terms with Tam (later Sean) Connery when the muscular young coffin polisher was employed as a bouncer at Oddfellows Hall, the home of one of Edinburgh's trailblazing post-war jazz clubs. Although George was a living legend in our eyes, he came over as the epitome of modesty, never mentioning his involvement in Scotland's jazz history unless specifically asked, and then only with unaffected reserve. He was, however, most generous when it came to sharing his considerable knowledge of Chicago-style jazz.

I still have a rare ten-inch copy of the Eddie Condon Band's *We Called It Music* album lent to me by George around that time. Whenever I offered to return it, he'd say something like, 'No hurry. I've been listening to these guys since the 1930s. I've soaked up everything I can – now it's your turn.' Coming from anyone but George Crockett, this last statement could have been taken as something of a derogatory dig, but he meant no offence, and none was taken.

Someone else who was unstinting in his enthusiasm for sharing the benefit of his collection of jazz records was Kenny Ramage, the trombone man in the Royal Mile Cafe band. Tall, ebullient, well-built and with a pair of lungs to match his physique, Kenny played in a hot, driving style reminiscent of Trummy Young, but minus the growls and rasps Young employed when playing with the Louis Armstrong All-Stars. Kenny, though having the reputation of being a bit of a wild man, was happily married and lived in a ground-floor flat overshadowed by a railway embankment in the Seafield area of Leith, the old Port of Edinburgh. There's no doubt his long-suffering little wife deserved a medal for putting up with the all-night record-playing sessions her husband habitually presided over for the delectation of his musician pals. As the communal intake of cheap wine progressed, the louder the record player blared. It was said there were two infants in the Ramage household as well, but since they never stirred during these 'music-appreciation gatherings', it was generally presumed they were either deaf or heavily sedated.

Two of Kenny's favourite albums were *Coast Concert* and *Jam Session – Coast-to-Coast*, featuring such American giants of the Dixieland idiom as trombonists Jack Teagarden, Abe Lincoln and Lou McGarity, clarinettists Edmond Hall, Peanuts Hucko and Matty Matlock, trumpeters Bobby Hacket and Wild Bill Davison, drummers George Wettling and Nick Fatool, plus the essential catalyst himself, Eddie Condon on guitar. The longer the session lasted, the more those two albums would be played, ultimately as if on an endless loop. Even today, over half a century later, I regularly listen to them, every track a timeless masterpiece in its own right. The magical mystery of brilliant jazzmen making it all sound so easy – happy-go-lucky yet soulful – well-knit yet free-and-easy – each musician's on-the-spot improvisations bouncing off and melding simultaneously with the others'. Perfect Dixieland, or jazz of any hue for that matter.

George Crockett and Kenny Ramage, while having personalities as different as chalk and cheese, shared the same good taste in music, and it was always an enlightening experience to be in their company. Imagine, then, our delight when they offered to join the Hidden Town Dixielanders.

'I need the bread, man,' was the frank reason given by Kenny. 'Yeah, with a litter of fuckin' bread-snappers to feed, you always need more bread, man.'

George was more gracious, though no less honest, when revealing his motive. 'The phone isn't ringing all that often at the moment, so yes, it'll be nice to have a few gigs to look forward to. Thanks, boys.'

Bingo! We were back in business. OK, we would have to repeat the breaking-in rehearsals we'd so recently run through with Ozzie and Derek, but George and Kenny were experienced musicians and wouldn't take long to get to grips with what we were doing. But then Kimber, one of our founder-members, dropped the bombshell that he was about to quit the band as well. We had known for some time that he hoped to start his own business with a fellow joiner, if ever the opportunity arose. The news that it was actually going to happen came as a real jolt, nonetheless. The two workmates had been offered suitable premises at a reasonable rent *and* a lucrative manufacturing contract which, given due dedication, would provide a foundation on which to build a secure future for their fledgeling firm. Opportunity had knocked twice on the same day, and Kimber knew it would be a long time, if ever, before it knocked so loudly again.

At a stroke, an end came to a succession of adventures that began as fumbling 'jam sessions' round my Dad's piano, progressed to entertaining bullocks in my grandfather's cattle shed, survived the two years Jim and I kept the dream alive while Kimber completed his national service, and eventually saw a bunch of keener-than-accomplished country laddies evolve into a unit that was now being accepted, however provisionally, into the ranks of a discerning musical brotherhood. We were hugely indebted to Kimber for his input (our early jazz education would have been sketchy indeed but for those albums he brought back from Germany), and we had always valued his companionship and unflagging enthusiasm. Things would not be the same without him.

But the band had assumed a momentum of its own now, and it would have been a waste of so much effort and commitment not to keep that impetus going. A new trumpet player would have to be found – somewhere, and soon. And who better to tell us who, where and when than George Crockett? Nothing happened on the Edinburgh journalism and jazz scenes that he didn't know about, and he fortuitously happened to know right then of a young horn man who was available and would fit the bill nicely.

Enter Alastair 'Al' Clark, a twenty-three-year-old sub-editor with *The Scotsman* newspaper, who had cut his jazz teeth playing with local bands involving trombonist Bob Craig and other ex-Sandy Brown alumnae. George had struck gold for us. But, he cautioned, there was a snag – or a bonus, depending on our point of view: Al had a chum who played pretty slick 'stride' piano, and our trumpet player elect would prefer it if he joined our ranks as well.

A snag? If this was a snag, then we would form a snag-appreciation society. So, enter Bob McDonald, a medical student who had just turned twenty-one and could tickle from the ivories some Fats Waller licks my father would have given his right hand to emulate; probably his left hand, too, if my mother had anything to do with it.

Yet one snag *was* created by this most welcome addition to our personnel. We were now a seven-piece band, but with only a six-seater bandwagon. As ever, though, the will was there, so we'd surely find a way of solving this latest problem too.

* * * * *

CHAPTER NINETEEN

'THE LAST POST FOR MY FIRST POSTING'

It was now the summer of 1960 and, training complete, I had been assigned to my first post as a bona fide Executive Officer in the Ministry of Labour. My biggest dread had always been that, when this time came, I'd be bundled off to some remote outpost, such as Stornoway labour exchange in the Outer Hebrides. Not that I'd have minded living on the island of Lewis; given my Orkney heritage, I'd probably have felt perfectly at home there. But being domiciled in the Western Isles may not have been all that conducive to continuing my jazz-playing activities – certainly not with the Hidden Town Dixielanders, based almost 300 miles away in mainland south-east Scotland. It was with no small measure of comfort, then, that I found myself posted to Edinburgh, back to Scottish Headquarters in Stuart House, where, I presumed, expert eyes would focus on my progress.

Had Stuart House been part of the H.J. Heinz empire, the department I had been drafted into would have been responsible for canning the beans others had harvested and cooked, if 'cooked' isn't an unfortunate term to use in relation to government statistics. A team of half-a-dozen Clerical Officers (COs) – mostly young females, but including a couple of out-to-grass WWI cavalry veterans – would gather and pigeon-hole monthly reports and unemployment figures submitted by every labour exchange in Scotland. All relevant categories were sorted: shipbuilding, farming, mining, fishing, steel production, whisky, textiles, tourism, etc. Eventually, two elderly EOs (Grade Fives, like myself) would check what had been categorised, append notes where approriate, then pass the files over to me.

Meanwhile, I would have spent a few hours each day reading. First of all, I'd scan the morning's newspapers for anything related to Scottish employment/unemployment trends and the state of the country's industrial health in general. I would outline such items in red, before finally handing the pile of papers over to the clerk responsible for cutting out the marked articles and pasting them onto sheets of foolscap for filing. The civil service union had long since ensured that strict demarcation rules applied in this regard: an EO could read and mark newsprint, but punitive action would be risked if he encroached upon a CO's right to clip and paste.

No sooner had I finished with the newspapers than the latest edition of *Hansard* would be delivered to my desk. This official publication is a transcript of all Government debates that have taken place in Westminster during the previous day. A fairly daunting volume, given that the pages present an unabridged version of every blast of hot air that has crossed the floors of both Houses of Parliament – Commons *and* Lords. My job, as with the daily papers, was to scour the contents for anything which might refer to the interests and activities of the Ministry of Labour in Scotland.

Talk about looking for needles in haystacks! This was more like rummaging for feathers in a barrel of treacle. Oh yes indeed, many were the moments I told myself that less harsh sentences had been passed on convicted criminals.

And the purpose of all this stats-crunching, paper-shuffling and departmental navel-gazing? In a nutshell, so that the Controller of the Ministry in Scotland could be armed with all the gathered information for his monthly meeting in London with Ted Heath. No, not the bandleader who had recruited our trombonist Ozzie Oswald, but the Member of Parliament who was the current Minister of Labour and Britain's future Prime Minister. But how could our Controller make himself sufficiently familiar with all those reams of info? Well, he couldn't. No-one could, unless of course it was presented to him in a nutshell. Which is why the mountain of paperwork so painstakingly produced by the department I worked in was ultimately handed over to me. It was up to me to collate the gathered details and condense them into a two-page résumé, which in turn would be used by our Controller to brief the Minister.

Although it didn't occur to me at the time, this was quite a responsibility to be entrusted to a nineteen-year-old. Yet, how important was the content of that monthly résumé in the wider scheme of things anyway? Probably the only time Ted Heath would cite it would be when answering a question during a rarely-pertinent House of Commons debate. Then the process would start all over again – *Hansard* recording what he'd said, the national press reporting it. Thus, round and round ad nauseam my hobby-horse on the civil service roundabout would go.

In hindsight, though, I suppose the process did provide me with some valuable experience in creative writing. This isn't to suggest that I fictionalised any of the contents of those monthly reports. It was for politicians who availed themselves of the facts to indulge in such jiggery-pokery, if so inclined. I must stress, however, that I never noticed anything untoward in this respect, and even if I had, I wouldn't admit it. I'd signed the Official Secrets Act, don't forget!

What I *can* say absolutely freely is that I knew within myself that repeating the routine of compounding these billets-doux month after month would eventually drive me to distraction.

*

Jeffrey's Audio House was a hi-fi and record shop in Earl Grey Street, just round the corner from Stuart House, and I'd occasionally pop in of a lunch hour to have a look for any interesting new jazz albums. On one such day, I was browsing away when a slim, business-suited chap in his forties came from behind the counter and asked what types of jazz I was interested in. He introduced himself as Bryce Laing, the owner of the shop and a jazz buff to boot. During the ensuing chat he told me he had recently started his own record label, Waverley, on which he planned to showcase Scottish artists of various musical stripes. When I mentioned my involvement with the Hidden Town Dixielanders, Bryce's ears pricked up. His so-called studio, he confessed, was actually only the back room of his shop, but he had just installed some up-to-date recording equipment, which he hoped would improve the quality of sound he was able to produce. Would we be willing to come in and put the new gear through its paces for him?

Would we? Would he like to try and stop us!

A few evenings later, our new line-up was in the Audio House 'studio' and rarin' to go. The personnel comprised a front line of Al Clark (trumpet), Kenny Ramage (trombone) and myself on clarinet, with the rhythm section made up of Bob McDonald on piano, Jim Douglas (banjo), John Logan (bass) and George Crockett (drums).

The pride of Bryce Laing's new sound equipment was an AKG C24 stereo microphone – the very latest and the best, he assured us. It also turned out to be the *only* mic in his armoury. So, with the C24's pick-up pattern set to 'circular', Bryce placed us in something resembling a ring around its floor stand. After a few dry runs and some repositioning of bodies, he finally had a sound balance he was happy with. But before he'd commit anything to tape, he had a favour to ask: would we mind taking off our shoes? This, he explained, was to prevent the sound of our foot-tapping being transmitted through the floor boards to the mic's super-sensitive 'ears'.

Primitive though all this may have seemed to us, Bryce knew exactly what he was doing. When he finally played back our contribution to his tests, we certainly couldn't criticise the sound quality he had coaxed from his equipment. And the band's efforts hadn't come over too badly in Bryce's opinion either. To our surprise – and no less delight – he said he was sufficiently pleased with what we'd played that he'd decided to release some of the results on record. Two singles would be issued, one coupling *Stars and Stripes Forever* with *Ice Cream*, the other pairing *Waltzing Matilda* with *Coney Island Washboard* (the latter track featuring a vocal by seventeen-year-old Jim Douglas). There was, however, one proviso Bryce wanted to add: The Hidden Town Dixielanders was, he felt, a tad too 'parochial-sounding' for commercial purposes, so, if there were no objections, he'd like to change the name of the band to Pete Kerr's Dixielanders. There were no objections.

*

When the discs were released a couple of months later, they didn't exactly set the record-buying world on fire, but, like the Hidden Town Dixielanders' spot on the Carroll Levis radio show the previous year, they did help raise the profile of the new band with dance promoters. In addition to the usual town hall and corn exchange type of venue, we found ourselves being booked into proper ballrooms, such as the Fountainbridge Palais in Edinburgh and Aberdeen's Beach Ballroom. It's true that such engagements weren't all that frequent, but they *were* steps in the right direction. Whether humble hall or glitzy ballroom, however, one common necessity prevailed: we had to get there, and seven bodies into a six-seater bandwagon won't go, except on uncomfortably intimate terms.

To upsize to even the smallest of what was now being popularly termed a minibus would have meant buying a Bedford Dormobile. But the cost of a second-hand one was more than I could afford, even given a reasonable sum in part-exchange for the old Ford Utilicon. Cue make-do-and-mend again, on this occasion in the form of a basic Bedford CA panel van, of Dormobile configuration but without rear seats or side windows. A straight swap for the Ford did it, and as part of the bargain the dealer agreed to fit the necessary windows – though economic realities dictated they'd have to be of the non-opening variety. Since the ability of the boys to see out was my prime consideration, I readily agreed to this small condition. In any case, I reckoned the notoriously leaky seals on this model of van's sliding front doors would provide more than enough fresh air in the back!

All that needed to be done outwardly was to change the muddy brown colour of the bodywork to something a bit more jazzy. An afternoon with a spray gun and a tin of bright metallic-blue cellulose produced the desired result. This only left the all-important matter of rear seating to be dealt with. Some lengths of timber appropriately assembled along either side provided the basis, which, once cushioned in foam rubber and covered with bright-red faux leather, completed the transformation of the shabby old workhorse into a natty new bandwagon. Well, as near a natty new bandwagon as my limited spray-painting, carpentry and upholstering skills would allow. But at least it was big enough for purpose, and once the roof rack retained from the old Utilicon had been bolted to the roof, I thought our makeshift Bedford Dormobile really did look the part – from a respectful distance, at any rate.

*

No matter how much time I devoted to band matters, I made sure it never interfered with my work. The ethic of 'sticking in and doing well' had been drummed into me since childhood, and I had no intention of abandoning that perspective now. And it would have been wrong to openly demean the advice I had been given by just about everyone I'd met since becoming a civil servant: I was a lucky lad to have been parachuted directly into the executive box. Accordingly, there was never any danger of my not turning up fit to perform to the best of my ability, irrespective of how rigorous the band's gig schedule had been. The people I worked with relied on me to pull my weight within their team, and I wouldn't let them down. I also appreciated the fact that, if they thought I was a bit of a square peg (as well they might), they never let on. By that very same token, I fully respected my colleagues' regard for the security a civil service career provided, even though I had come to see it as a potential albatross around my own neck.

Try as I might, I couldn't banish from my mind the same two recurring questions: Did I honestly see myself climbing the promotion ladder as a labour exchange manager – first in charge of a Grade Five office, then a Grade Four, a Grade Three, and finally the Grade-two pinnacle that was Edinburgh's depressing Tollcross 'Broo'? Or was I aiming to climb the Stuart House administrative stairway that led to the office of Controller for Scotland – the head honcho whose status entitled him to a monthly chinwag with his political overlord in London?

The answer came to me one sunny autumn afternoon when I was enjoying a tea-break chat with Davie and Bill, our two WWI veterans. As ex-cavalrymen, they enjoyed listening to my yarns about old Johnny and Joe, the horsemen I had worked with at Lennoxlove Acredales before joining the Ministry. Davie and Bill never said much about their own experiences with horses during the Great War, though, and it wasn't hard to imagine why. Mind you, they didn't say much about their experiences in the Ministry of Labour either, and I guessed they simply regarded their daily routine, mundane as it may have appeared to others, as a suitably untaxing way of eventually topping up the modest pensions their wartime hardships had earned them. And who could fault them for that? They were grand old fellows, whose rapport I valued greatly.

Davie and Bill sat at desks by a window overlooking Semple Street, with uninterrupted views over the roof of Alexander's sprawling garage and coach works to the municipal meat market, then beyond to McEwan's Brewery and the North British Rubber Works. On a clear day like this, I could make out the smoke rising through the intervening jungle of chimney stacks from the steam trains leaving Haymatket Station farther away to the west. To urbanites, such a cityscape may well have been regarded as attractive, but all it did for me was induce that old feeling of being a fish out of water.

My thoughts drifted off to the rolling fields of Acredales and to what old Joe and Johnny would be doing at this moment. More than likely, they'd be busy with the potato harvest, sitting atop their carts heaped with newly-picked spuds as their Clydesdales plodded their unhurried way to the 'pit' at the corner of the field. Once their loads were discharged, they'd probably give the horses a breather and sit themselves down with their backs against a cartwheel. Stubby pipes newly kindled, they'd be all set for a few minutes of idle mutters and chortles about subjects of no greater worldly consequence than the price of Bogie Roll baccy or the spattering of horse shit on their boots. Maybe they'd have noticed Patchy McLatchie shuffling along the river bank, checking out the trout population en route to setting his rabbit snares for the night. If he looked up, they'd wave a hand and bid him a hearty, 'Aye, aye, son – fine day, eh!', unconcerned about the fact that he was half-a-mile away and wouldn't hear a word of it.

How I envied the three of them. I even envied the two Clydesdales.

I glanced out over the Edinburgh rooftops again, then around the open-plan office dotted with desks and filing cabinets that would be my potato field and riverbank until some faceless personnel officer decided I should be posted elsewhere. While I accepted it would be unrealistic to contemplate ever sharing the simple lifestyle enjoyed by Joe, Johnny and Patchy, I also realised that I had to get out of the civil service. And I had to do it before the advent of greater responsibilities and the associated tentacles of a secure career began to wring the life out of me.

*

The catalyst arrived quite unexpectedly one morning. It was a letter from John Marshall, owner of the Storyville Club in Cologne, Germany. I had happened upon his address and had sent him review copies of the band's two Waverley records, never really believing that anything would come of it. Hope springing eternal, I think I'd even sent copies to Frank Sinatra in Las Vegas! However, John Marshall had actually listened to the records and liked what he heard. His letter explained that a residency in his club had become available for the forthcoming month of December. If I accepted the terms he was offering in the enclosed contract, there would be the guarantee of a further one-month month engagement at an associate club in Mannheim, with the possibility of even more work in Germany to follow on from that.

Christmas had come early. I accepted his terms by return post.

The die thus cast, I was now faced with the thorny task of informing my employers, my parents and, fairly crucially of course, the boys in the band.

* * * * *

CHAPTER TWENTY

'WHAT AM I GONNA DO NOW?'

Since my folks had always harboured a sneaking suspicion that my true calling in life had never been the civil service, I got the impression, on breaking the news I had decided to quit, that their feelings were more of anxiety than surprise. But they didn't try to change my mind. Instead, they limited their response to asking, perhaps rhetorically, if I had thoroughly thought through the consequences of making what was bound to be a truly life-changing decision. There was no need for me to say I felt guilty about having disappointed them and hadn't meant to belittle the sacrifices they'd made to give me the benefit of a decent education. They already knew that. In return, although clearly concerned, they were sufficiently altruistic to accept that it was my life and I was entitled to make up my own mind about how to lead it – for better or for worse. Even so, I found out a while later that my mother had asked our family doctor at the time if he thought I was right in the head. His reply was that he wasn't a psychiatrist,

183

so couldn't give her a straight answer. But, he added, he knew me well enough to speculate that, if I wasn't already off my head, I eventually would be if I remained trapped in a job I disliked so much.

The tendering of my resignation to the Ministry of Labour wasn't greeted in such a conciliatory way, however. Mr Smith, the Grade Four who had been my original overseer and mentor, summoned me to his office. He was flanked at his desk by two grey suits I recognised as members of the interviewing panel from the fateful day in Drumsheugh Gardens when I'd performed well enough to earn myself a life sentence in the civil service. Mr Smith introduced the suits as his immediate superiors. It was plain I was being granted an audience with eminent men, whose very presence reflected the gravity of the situation I had plunged myself into.

Total incomprehension was the dominant element in everything the triumvirate said. I was bombarded with salvos of questions and statements loaded with puzzlement at why anyone could be so ungrateful and short-sighted as to even *think* about forsaking the unique opportunity I'd been given. More importantly, there was the image and reputation of, not just the Ministry of Labour, but the entire civil service to consider. Had I forgotten I was the first person to be granted direct entrance to the executive class? Did I not realise that my rash relinquishing of this privilege would put at risk the continuation of a radical scheme created to set *promising* young people such as myself on a fast track to the inner sanctum of the establishment? Then there was my copper-bottomed pension to consider, the executive perks, the chilling prospect of, once having left such an exclusive 'club', never being allowed back in. A concerted deep breath was drawn, heralding a few moments of pregnant silence.

Mr Smith leaned towards me, rested his elbows on the desk, buttressed his fingers, peered frowning over his spectacles and said, 'Are we *really* to believe you're serious about swapping a bright future within the protective arms of the Ministry for a life in the shady world of...' He paused to swallow, as if suppressing a vomit, then grimaced, '... *jazz* musicians?'

When my polite but determined opposition to all of these exhortations finally convinced my inquisitors that I was beyond salvation, I was dismissed and left the room to a chorus of despairing 'tuts'.

With that door now firmly closed, both literally and figuratively, it was time to tell the boys in the band about the offer from Germany which would enable us to turn professional.

If I had been trying to convince myself (and I had!) that the boys would greet my news with unbridled enthusiasm, I was in for a rude awakening. The only one who responded positively was, surprisingly enough, our drummer, 'old' George Crockett. Despite, or maybe because of, being a stalwart of the august Edinburgh newspaper fraternity, he reckoned he was ready to take a chance on being part of this German adventure. An opportunity to fulfil his long-cherished dream of a being a full-time jazz musician might never come his way again. Yes, I could count him in.

Of the others, only my old chum Jim Douglas declared any appetite for what was on offer. Jim, however, had recently been accepted as a trainee at Castle Wynd Potteries in his home village of Gifford. It was a profession which promised a bright future for someone of Jim's artistic abilities, and one his mother was extremely glad he'd entered. As a widow, with four of Jim's younger siblings to bring up, she couldn't have been happier than to have him setting out on adult life while still living at home. As much as Jim was tempted to make the German trip, there was no way he would turn his back on family responsibilities. I fully understood and respected his reasons, yet Jim's excluding himself from the venture still came as a real blow. Since schooldays, he had been an ever-present part of my involvement with jazz. Plus, he was my best pal.

Bassist John Logan was the only other remaining member of the original Hidden Town Dixielanders. While I would also miss his continued presence, I had accepted that, with a wife and young family to consider, the likelihood of his giving up a reliable job as a printer with the local paper was bound to be slim.

Similarly, Archie Sinclair, who had taken over trombone duties from pastures-new-seeking Kenny Ramage, had domestic commitments which had to be honoured. Archie, an up-and-coming advertising exec, had only recently settled back in Edinburgh after a spell working in Canada, so leaving home again, even for a few months, was not an option. (Archie would go on to form Old Bailey's Jazz Advocates, a semi-pro band destined to gain a loyal following in the Edinburgh area).

Three down, two to go…

It was always known that our pianist Bob McDonald would have to regard his jazz-playing activities as a hobby, a spare-time activity to be indulged in when and for so long as his medical studies permitted. He was also out.

This left only trumpet-player Al Clark. Al was already regarded as a journalistic star of the future at *The Scotsman*, and would let nothing, not even the promise of becoming a jazz star of the future (I spared no hyperbole!), hinder his climb up the rigging of the flagship of Scotland's press.

The seven-piece band I had agreed to provide for the German engagement was now a duo. There was precious little time left to find replacements, and I hadn't a clue where to start looking.

At this point, did I regret having jacked in my civil service career? No, not yet, but I won't deny that I hadn't experienced such severe sphincter spasms since my first attempts at giving the kiss of life to a set of bagpipes. Litigation for breach of contract loomed. Since my fellow duettist had spent years reporting on proceedings in courts of law, I decided to seek his advice.

'What the hell am I gonna do now, George?'

Even when only observing someone else worrying, gentleman George Crockett tended to look worried himself. I'd always thought this showed he genuinely sympathised with the worrier, even if he didn't get involved in offering solutions. On this occasion, however, he actually laughed in the face of my dilemma. That was another tendency of George's: when he was amused by something someone said, he would bow his head, his shoulders would start to shake and he would repeat the amusing statement through a fit of whispery chuckles.

'What the hell am I gonna do now?' he tittered.

I didn't get the joke, and I said so.

'What the hell am I gonna do now?' he re-tittered, and slapped his knee.

'It's damned serious, George! The laws of Germany shall prevail. That's what it says in the agreement I signed.' I shook my head in despair. 'I'll be extradited. Two years in a German slammer – maybe more. Stalag bloody Luft Three, here I come!'

When he was finally all sniggered out, George said if I'd been around jazz musicians as long as he had I'd realise I was shitting bricks unduly. I could take his word for it – once he'd passed the word around that a chance was going a-begging to play full-time on the Continent *and* get paid for it, I'd have more recruits lining up than even Uncle Sam and Lord Kitchener together could have mustered.

Overblown as it clearly was, his claim proved to be essentially correct. Within a couple of days, the band's ranks had been all but fully replenished by the enlistment of some of the highest-regarded jazzers in the Edinburgh area: Andrew Lauder, a young organ builder recently returned from doing national service in the RAF, played trumpet in a smooth, lyrical style quite rare among Dixieland horn players; John McGuff, in his late twenties and a builder by trade, was a trombonist of exceptional talent, his work in big dance bands having helped develop a gutsy, fluent technique that was second to none – anywhere; tubby Ian Brown, a teacher and contemporary of John's, possessed an enviable mastery of the double bass, though with definite 'modernist' leanings; Alex Shaw had an unassuming demeanour belying a CV that confirmed him as a pianist of outstanding versatility and ability. Although not yet forty (or so he claimed!) Alex had wide experience as a professional musician, not just gigging around his native Edinburgh, but as a cabaret accompanist in London, touring with the celebrated Tommy Sampson Orchestra in the late 1940s, and even 'on the boats', entertaining transatlantic cruise passengers. Alex had extensive musical 'form'.

Only one vacancy in the line-up had failed to attract any interest – that of guitarist/banjoist. Odd as it may seem, I was actually pleased. I knew that, deep down, Jim Douglas was desperate to try his luck with the band in Germany, even if it meant gambling on being allowed to return to his job at the pottery if things didn't work out. I also suspected his mother was just as aware of this as I was. She would be sensitive to the possibility of Jim forever regretting *not* having taken the chance, should he eventually discover that being a potter was not for him. I decided to put my conscience on hold while I tried to tilt the balance in favour of the band.

With Jim's passive collusion, I told his Mum a deliberate lie, albeit one I tried hard to convince myself was as white as the driven snow. I told her Jim's surprise non-participation in the German engagement was creating serious contractual complications, which might even result in the entire project being cancelled. Work permits and passport numbers had been recorded, I stressed, and there was no time to make changes.

The look she gave me was mirrored by Jim's granny and even, I fancied, by their old collie Sheila. None of them believed what I'd said. Then Jim and his mother exchanged glances, and though not a word was spoken, it was obvious she understood her son's inner feelings sufficiently well to put personal considerations aside. Not for the first time, Nancy Douglas was going 'above and beyond' to support Jim's musical aspirations and, by association, mine as well. In time, she would prove willing to extend those selfless qualities for the benefit of the whole band. And in circumstances that none of us could have foreseen just then.

*

The pangs of guilt I felt about trying to hoodwink Jim's mother for my own ends were duplicated a few days later when I was driving through Haddington. Out of the corner of my eye, I noticed a really attractive girl walking along the pavement. A quick glance in the rear-view mirror confirmed what I'd thought: it was Ellie. I hadn't seen her for some months, but not because of any serious falling-out. We hadn't even had cross words. The parting of our ways had happened more as a drift than a rift, and was due entirely to my being totally preoccupied with the band, my job and associated matters as they affected *me*. I had acted in a self-centred way that left increasingly less time to spend in Ellie's company. Seeing her again now, I suddenly realised what a heel I'd been. A complete idiot too. She was no longer the feisty little thing whose pretty face had first attracted me at school. She was nearly eighteen, and even in the few months since I'd last seen her, had matured into a young woman of exceptional beauty.

What had I been thinking about? Hadn't I realised there were others who would give anything to have a girlfriend like Ellie? And I needn't kid myself that Ellie wouldn't know this better than I did. Although naturally shy and not in the least vain, she was a girl and would therefore be well aware of the effect her looks had on the opposite sex. I'd heard she had recently started to train as a nurse at the local hospital. So, what about all those randy young doctors? They'd be falling over one another to win her attentions. And I needn't kid myself that Ellie wouldn't know this better than *any*one.

What a prize numpty I'd been. An insensitive one as well. Hell, if it hadn't been for her feelings towards me, she might never have gone to the length of sabotaging (successfully, as it happened) her stepfather's plan to emigrate to Australia. Poohsticks, indeed. I'd have to find a way to mend this broken bridge.

Posters, that was it! The Storyville Club in Cologne had asked for posters, to include a brief blurb about the band – in German. Who better to do the required translation than Ellie's mother?

The ploy worked, although I had a hunch that Ellie was as sceptical about my motives as she had been when I first gave her those lines for running in the school corridor. Conversely, her mother couldn't have given me a warmer welcome back into the fold. Being a mother, and a particularly protective one when it came to her only daughter, she would know instinctively what was right for Ellie. She clearly believed that I passed muster, despite my having kept Ellie out so late on that fateful Hogmanay. Her mother had never brought that up, nor had she mentioned my puking over her neighbours' fence while Ellie was climbing in through the kitchen window. The more I'd thought about it since, the more convinced I was that she *must* have overheard the entire episode. Yes, Ellie's mother was on my side all right, and this, I told myself, could make my attempted reconciliation with Ellie a lot less awkward than it might otherwise have been.

A few days later, I left for Germany, having exchanged promises with Ellie that we'd keep in touch by letter, which gave me more hope than I probably deserved. It was 27th November, 1960 – the day before my twentieth birthday.

As I drove away from home in the tarted-up old Bedford bandwagon, my feelings were a mix of excitement and apprehension-tinged optimism. Yet the words spoken a couple of weeks earlier by that prophet of doom Fergus were still rankling...

'Dead in the gutter,' he'd said to my parents. That's how I'd end my career as a professional jazz musician. 'Dead in the gutter ... prostitutes and rotgut booze ... the pox and cirrhosis of the liver.'

* * * * *

CHAPTER TWENTY-ONE

'SAUERKRAUT AND ALL THAT JAZZ'

'Wow!' was Jim's reaction when we stepped from our cab outside the entrance to the Storyville Club. 'We're a long way from Longyester Hall now, man!'

I was equally impressed. 'Yep, been a while since shepherds watched their flocks around here – no doubt about that!'

We had arrived in Cologne by train, having left the bandwagon in London with one of George's musician contacts, in whose Clapham flat we had spent the previous night. It had been an unscheduled, sleep-on-the-floor stopover, demanded by the sound of the old Bedford's engine, which had become increasingly rattly during the four-hundred-mile trek down from Scotland.

'Don't worry, mate,' said George's chum. 'Leave the old crate wiv me. Prob'ly jus' tappets. Yeah, an' I know the very geezer oo'll sort 'em out. Won't cost ya an arm an' a leg, neiver.'

How and when I'd be able to retrieve the old crate was another matter, but one I was happy to leave in abeyance.

Getting to Germany in time to kick off our first month's engagement was all that mattered right now, even though the unbargained-for cost of rail fares would blow a hole in my financial calculations for the entire venture. But this wouldn't be the last bothersome occurrence to blight what was turning out to be a pretty unpromising start to my career as a professional bandleader...

A few months earlier, a silky-tongued character, whom we'll refer to as 'The Lip', had wheedled himself into becoming the band's de facto manager. Smallish, straight-backed, moustache-sporting and pushy as a snake oil salesman, he had impressed me initially with his talk of the doors he could open for us. He reckoned we had the talent, he had the contacts and know-how, so it would be just a matter of letting him take care of things and we'd soon hit the big time. Unfortunately, The Lip's actions never did match his words, so I welcomed the opportunity to be rid of him that the German engagement presented. The trouble was, he succeeded in sweet-talking his way into coming with us – on wages! The pretext he quoted was that he would not only 'look after things' with the club managements we were already booked to play for, but would also act as our roving representative, responsible for securing further bookings in Germany.

I immediately voiced my concern that the expense of his 'roving' would prove to be an unsustainable drain on the band's earnings, to which he countered that revenues from the 'side deals and spin-offs' he would negotiate were guaranteed to exceed whatever costs might be involved. Common sense told me such claims were dangerously fanciful, but the guy was about the same age as my father, and I just didn't have the self-assurance to tell him to take a hike. Until, that is, the boys and I were preparing to doss down for the night on those Clapham floor boards.

Instead of fulfilling his supposed managerial duties by organising alternative transport for the remainder of the trip, he had spent the evening up town, 'entertaining' an old flame. He was clearly half-stewed when he barged into the flat and immediately launched into a verbal attack on me for not having provided reliable transportation for the band's journey from Edinburgh to Cologne. Up to that moment, he had always appeared to treat me with respect, and I had reciprocated. But he had just crapped in his own trough, to paraphrase a favourite expression of my farming grandfather's. The Lip had shown, sooner than might otherwise have been the case, that he had aspirations to be the boss. Mistake. There can only ever be one of those, and in this instance I was it. There was no indication that any of the boys in the band, several of whom were considerably older than me, would have a problem with this, but I knew if I showed any weakness now, the chances were I would eventually regret it.

Headmaster A.B. Anderson's words about making a choice between pragmatism and discipline come echoing back, as did Sergeant Jimmy's lessons on the value of making an example of someone who gets out of step with the rest of the squad.

'Transportation to Cologne for the band is all taken care of,' I told The Lip, 'so all you need bother about is how you're going to get back to Edinburgh tomorrow – at your own expense. And,' I added before he could start breathing again, 'you'd better go and get your old flame to *entertain* you for the rest of the night, because you are *not* sleeping here!'

Although what I'd just done hadn't been premeditated, it quickly occurred to me that the amount saved by not having to pay The Lip a wage for two months would go a long way to covering the cost of our revised travelling arrangements. The ill wind he'd blown had done me a favour, and had taught me a valuable lesson as well: always give snake oil salesmen short shrift on sight.

*

When we eventually piled into taxis outside Cologne's railway station, sighs of relief replaced the snores and yawns which had been the main sounds any of us had uttered since five minutes after boarding the train in London that morning. The bandwagon's jerry-built bench seats and the floorboards of the Clapham flat had taken their toll. Now, a shower, a change of clothes and, if the gods of strolling minstrels were in compassionate mood, a square meal was all we craved before starting work.

The Kaiser Wilhelm Ring forms part of a curved boulevard following the original line of Cologne's ancient city walls. Wide and tree-lined, this elegant avenue is fringed by office and apartment blocks flaunting the affluence of Germany's fourth-largest city. An unlikely situation for a jazz club? It was certainly a world apart from the seedy surroundings of the Cy Laurie place in London's Soho, and even Jazzshows' pitch on trendy Oxford Street wouldn't have compared too favourably. It didn't come as much of a surprise, then, that the interior of the Storyville Club also turned out to be a cut above.

As usual, the location was a cellar, but one that sniffed, not of mustiness and stale sweat, but of roasty-toasty German cigarettes, fresh coffee, smoky frankfurters, simmering sauerkraut and, ever so faintly, cement. This latter feature suggested the place had been completed fairly recently, and it had been done out in a snazzy style which also made its British counterparts seem distinctly dowdy in comparison. The primary motif was an old train of the fairground type, puffing statically round the walls from the entrance to the bandstand. Its carriages, painted in bright primary colours, formed booths, each accommodating half-a-dozen customers sitting either side of a table. Gaudy though this description may seem, the atmosphere inside the club, even when empty, was bright and cheery and ready-made for live jazz. Knackered as we were, we were keen to provide the necessary.

It soon became clear that 'knackered' and 'keen' were to be permanent symptoms of our condition. We would be playing from 8.00 p.m. until 2.00 a.m. six nights a week, until 3.00 a.m. on Saturdays, with three-hour matinees added on Saturdays and Sundays. The rhythm section would also have to accompany conga-drumming singer Frank Holder in his twice-nightly cabaret spots. OK, the money we were being paid was decent enough, but boy, were we having to work damned hard for every pfennig!

Frank Holder, Guyanese by birth, had been prominent on the London music scene as a Latin-American specialist since his demob from the RAF at the end of the war. Before going solo, he had been featured vocalist/percussionist with the world-famous Johnny Dankworth Band, which meant he was accustomed to working with some of the top modern jazz musicians around, including the likes of Ronnie Scott, Tubby Hayes and Joe Harriott. It followed that he must have had some misgivings about being backed by a bunch of unknown 'traddies', but it took only a few bars of *Baubles, Bangles and Beads* (hardly a trad jazz standard!) to convince him he had nothing to worry about. There wasn't much musically that pianist Alex Shaw hadn't experienced before, and his ability to handle everything from bop to boogie in virtuoso style placed him among the best Frank Holder would have mixed with. Likewise, the other guys in our rhythm section, including a quick-learning eighteen-year-old Jim Douglas on guitar, showed that booting along two-beat Dixieland wasn't all they were capable of – although there's no denying they did that in fine style too. Initial reaction from the Storyville Club audiences provided ample endorsement of that, and the management had no complaints about the numbers who were parting with their Deutschmarks to hear us either.

Nevertheless, we had only played a couple of dates as a band before leaving for Germany, so it was essential we took every opportunity now to work on our own arrangements of jazz evergreens, as well as putting an original stamp on whatever less hackneyed material we could come up with. There was no way of achieving this except by rehearsing, rehearsing and rehearsing again. I'd been warned back in Edinburgh, however, that some of the older hands I'd recruited would tell me to go and stuff myself if I asked them to work outside the stipulated hours of the gig. They'd think it enough to grind their nuts off for upwards of six hours every night. Beyond that, their time would be their own, to enjoy whatever Germany had to offer in the way of 'relaxation'. Why else, the naysayers cautioned, would these guys be making the trip?

Well, the doubters couldn't have been more wrong. All of the musicians, irrespective of age and reputation, rose to the occasion like true professionals. At least a couple of hours every weekday (apart from Mondays, which were reserved for catching up on sleep after the long, hard graft of the weekend) were spent back in the club rehearsing. This, together with the actual job of playing together night after night, soon had the band sounding much more like a well-drilled unit. And it's safe to say that my pal Jim and I, being the youngest and least experienced members of the outfit, benefitted most individually.

Andrew Lauder's tastefully understated trumpet lead left plenty of room for adding the embellishments which constitute the essence of a clarinettist's function in a jazz band. Tempering this freedom, though in a positive kind of way, was John McGuff's trombone work. When the music called for it, John, a technically brilliant player, could effortlessly lay down the basic 'tailgate' rasps and glissandi employed by most trad jazz 'bone players. But he was also more than capable of letting rip with some really fast and furious pyrotechnics. This taught me as never before the importance of listening carefully to the two brass men standing next to me. It's the key to knitting those ad-lib patterns that comprise the basis of improvisational cohesion within a Dixieland front line. An every-man-for-himself free-for-all is the last thing needed.

For Jim, just playing in a rhythm section alongside a pianist of Alex Shaw's calibre would have amounted to an education in itself. Yet Alex could not have been more generous in his sharing of tips and wrinkles about alternative chord changes, interesting tonal inversions, and generally making something special out of even the most humdrum of harmonic sequences. Jim and I knew we had a lot to learn, and we could hardly have found ourselves in a better situation to do just that.

This was the upside of all the hard work. The downside, for everyone in the band, was that we had neither time nor energy left to see anything of Cologne beyond the entrance to the club and our lodgings, a couple of blocks away on the other side of the Kaiser Wilhelm Ring.

The square meal we had been craving at the end of our traumatic journey from Scotland turned out to be the speciality of the house – Goulash Soup. This became our staple diet, and not merely because a nightly item from the menu constituted part of our fee. That Goulash really was something to write home about. Ian Brown, our epicurean bass player (with a figure to match his bull fiddle), wasn't the only one to scrounge left-overs from the kitchen once the last of the customers had left, although he was always the first.

And what of those customers? As might be expected, the average age was well under thirty, which was on a par with their jazz-clubbing counterparts in London. And doubtless their social backgrounds were much the same as well: that's to say suburbanite commuters and city-centre flat-dwellers. Their style of dancing, however, was notably less frantic than that of the whirling dervishes we'd seen in the Cy Laurie Club, less acrobatic than the typical British jive monkey, and lacked entirely the carnal shuffling of Saturday night 'Creepers' in

Scotland's rural dance halls. In essence, things were just a bit more restrained. This isn't to suggest the young people of Cologne didn't know how to enjoy themselves. They did. But in conditions tailor-made for a more tempered approach.

At one side of the Storyville Club's dance floor was the bar, from where a team of waiters conveyed drinks and food to the passengers in 'the train'. No need to smuggle in half bottles of whisky to gulp down in the gents' toilets, no need to stuff a greasy fish supper down your cake hole on the way to the dance after the pubs closed. And, perhaps not surprisingly, no drunken punch-ups either. A culture that treated its youth in a civilized way was having its trust rewarded accordingly – a revelation to those of us unaccustomed to such enlightened ways.

John Marshall, the impresario who owned the club, was a genial German with, as he said himself, a courageous approach to business. That quality would have been a must, gambling as he did on importing locally-unknown jazz bands like ours from the UK. But without putting ourselves down, I'd have to concede that the popularity of his club was probably due as much to the setting he had created than to many of his customers' appreciation of jazz. All the same, John didn't take their custom for granted. He was ever on the lookout for a chance to publicise what was currently on offer. So, when I told him my girlfriend back in Scotland was Cologne-born, a reporter and photographer from the *Kölner Stadtanzeiger* were soon on hand.

The first thing the scribe wanted to establish was an 'angle'. Simply writing a piece based on a Scottish jazz band playing in Cologne wouldn't warrant any column centimetres in his editor's view. So, since Christmas was only a week or so away, the subject of Christmas trees was the angle he zeroed in on.

I would be aware, he ventured, that the tradition of having a Christmas tree in one's house was a German one – *ja?* I confirmed that I did indeed know the custom was said to have been introduced to Britain by Queen Victoria's German husband Prince Albert. That being the case, the reporter concluded, he could safely say my girlfriend Ellie would have such a reminder of her Cologne heritage in her adopted Scottish home – *nicht*? I began to assure him that she would. '*Aber*,' he interjected, 'will she have a proper German Christmas tree stand?' My reply that I didn't know what he was talking about prompted him to send his photographer on an urgent errand to a nearby fancy goods store, to return a few minutes later carrying a small cast-iron disc with a circular socket in the middle. This, the scribe informed me, was *ein Christbaumständer*, a proper German Christmas tree stand, available in various circumferences and weights, according to the size of one's tree. '*Mein Gott in Himmel*, no German family would contemplate being without one!'

A photograph was duly taken of a grinning me holding the stand next to my ear like a hit record. The accompanying headline, when the feature appeared in the paper a few days later, was to the effect that poor Ellie, so far away from her native Cologne, not only had no Christmas tree stand, but had no Christmas tree either! Well, I figured, why let the truth get in the way of a good angle? After all, it was a bit of publicity for the band, albeit a tad indirectly, and, as the Storyville Club also got a mention, John Marshall was well satisfied too.

*

Christmas day in Germany is, above all other days in this family-orientated country, *the* day of the family, the day for being together 'at home'. Most businesses, including bars, restaurants and clubs, were closed. So it happened that Christmas day was our one and only day off in the month, and to say we were at a loose end would be putting it mildly. Besides not knowing what to do with the spare time we had on our hands, we suddenly felt out of place, far from everything familiar in this great city of almost a million souls.

Little Willy Braun, the ever-attentive manager of the Storyville Club, had long been urging us to take a close-up look at Cologne's iconic cathedral, the Dom, which was only a fifteen minute walk away by the banks of the Rhine. According to Willy, the Dom was the largest Gothic church in northern Europe, and was also Germany's most popular tourist attraction. No-one, anywhere, warned Willy, would believe us if we said we'd been in Cologne for a whole month without visiting its most famous landmark.

'Big, eh?' said trombonist John, in a masterpiece of understatement, especially coming from someone who was a builder by trade.

We were gazing at the Dom's twin spires rising heavenward from a facade reputed to be the widest of any church in the world. It was a structure, according to Willy Braun, which had also been the tallest in the world until little over half a century before, when those brassy Americans wrested the record.

'Yeah, massive,' agreed trumpeter Andrew, awestruck. Then, his thoughts drawn reflectively to his own particular trade, he muttered, 'Mmm, and just imagine the size o' its organ!'

Under other circumstances, this conjecture would certainly have elicited lewd comments about what may or may not have been evidence of Andrew having a one-track mind. Today, however, the mood among the boys was too downbeat. We were homesick, although none of us would admit it. But the fact remained, a house of God, even one as magnificent as this, was no substitute for the simple pleasures of home at Christmas. And no amount of feigning interest in ecclesiastical architecture would change that.

We wandered on, a straggle of waifs, through parts of 'old' Cologne which had been completely destroyed by Allied bombing during the Second World War. I paused to look inside the church of St Andreas, where Ellie told me she had been Christened. A mere stone's throw from the mighty Dom, this more modest place of worship had also been spared the utter devastation inflicted on its environs. I recalled Ellie mentioning that, as a toddler towards the end of the war, she had seen a dead hand protruding from the rubble in this very vicinity. It would not have been an uncommon sight; many thousands of people, women and children included, had perished in their homes under the relentless aerial pounding of Germany's industrial heartland.

But now, only fifteen years after the end of hostilities, the city, or at least this part of it, had risen from the ashes – literally. The place really had been reborn, and there was an almost palpable vigour about it, even in the near-deserted Christmas streets.

After a while, we found ourselves on the Deutzer Bridge, looking down on the river, the great Rhine barges that ply their trade all the way from the North Sea deep into southern Germany berthed along its banks for this one day of respite in the year. In the eponymous Deutz quarter on the other side of the bridge, aspects of the war's aftermath remained. Gap sites lay in wait of the redevelopment burgeoning all around, while some older buildings, having survived the bombs, still bore scars slashed by the artillery fire that ravaged what remained of Cologne in the final days of conflict.

Yet there was an air of optimism here too. Indeed, it seemed to reflect an attitude we had noticed in the young people who frequented the Storyville Club. Like the city's mushrooming new buildings, they epitomised a hopeful future born of the dark legacy of a previous generation. Germany was being helped back on its feet by the aid of its former adversaries, and the youth of the country were grasping the opportunity with both hands. It seemed strangely ironic, then, that it should be the successors of those involved in the destruction of Cologne who would rescue us from the blues brought on by our exclusion from the Christmas cheer emanating from every home we passed on our walk.

The old civil airport of Butzweilerhof, on the northern fringes of Cologne, had been taken over as an RAF station after the war, and a few of the young airmen presently stationed there were in the habit of coming along to the Storyville Club at weekends. Regarding us as welcome visitors from home, they had quickly made a point of getting on friendly terms. We found them to be a good bunch of lads, and many were the after-hours chats we'd enjoyed with them at the bar. But that was as far as our association with them went. They would head back to their base in the wee, small hours, while we shuffled off to the three rooms we shared in a tenement owned by an elderly war widow called Sophie Schreiner.

As befitted the young jazz musicians who, for some time, had been her regular boarders, the rooms were basic, verging on shabby. But they were kept scrupulously clean by Frau Schreiner, a dedicated and indefatigable lady, who must have curbed regular urges to set about some of her less domesticated residents with a broomstick – if not a hose!

Still, it would be unfair to imply that the rooms were not perfectly adequate for their intended use as crash-out pads for musical night owls. Using them to relax in was, however, another matter. The thought of sitting on the edge of a bed staring at four walls entirely bare except for a sepia print of Otto von Bismark wearing a spiked *Pickelhaube* would be enough to cast the most buoyant of spirits into depression. But that's exactly what we faced on that forlorn Christmas evening of 1960. Until, that is, we rounded the corner and saw a ten-ton RAF truck parked outside Sophie's place. Yes, the boys from Butzweilerhof, feeling sorry for us, had decided to lay on transport to take us out to the 'drome to share their festive fare. More specifically, they would have their cooks serve us turkey and all the trimmings in the kitchen, *if* we dished up our music in the mess hall afterwards.

And so we had a busman's holiday, which was just the ticket as far as we were concerned. Happy times were here again! But this wasn't to be the only treat our RAF chums had in store for us. On learning that we had already made the mandatory tourist pilgrimage to the cathedral, they undertook to end our Christmas day by showing us another, less-vaunted of the city's attractions.

The Kleine Brinkgasse is a narrow back alley, only thirty metres or so long, in the busy commercial/residential area of Cologne called Altstadt-Nord. If you didn't know of the Kleine Brinkgasse's existence, you'd probably pass by without noticing it – in daytime. But at night, even in the early hours of Boxing Day, my first impression on approaching the lane was that it must be the site of some sort of nocturnal market, so swarming with cars and pedestrians was the area immediately adjacent. Only when I noticed that the pedestrians and occupants of the cars were exclusively male did it finally become apparent why, all the way in from Butzweilerhof, our RAF guides had been smirking and sniggering every time mention was made of 'the Brink', as they called it. This place made Soho's Great Windmill Street seem like the Champs Élysées strewn with rose petals. I had never set eyes on such a seamy scene. It struck me as no wonder a chicane of two half-walls had been built at the entrance to the alley in an attempt to hide the ongoing activity behind. Most other business establishments in the city may have closed for Christmas, but not so those of the ladies trading in the world's oldest profession.

A market it was indeed. And a cattle market at that. Except the livestock on offer weren't enclosed in pens, but displayed in ground-floor windows – half-naked and alluringly lit. According to the RAF boys, there were up to a hundred 'working girls' flogging their wares on any given night in that tiny street of iniquity. As we gawped at the scrums of leather-coated roués jostling for bidding space at the windows, I was reminded of something my grandfather used to tell me when a particularly dodgy-looking lot of heifers entered the sale ring at Gorgie Auction Mart in Edinburgh: 'Even *lookin'* at one o' them is as good as a bill from the vet, boy!' I don't suppose he envisaged I'd ever relate those rustic words of wisdom to a situation like this, but I couldn't think of a more apt observation. We got the hell out of there before we were arrested for loitering by the plain-clothes cops our airmen pals said were mingling with the throngs of active cash-splashers.

It's said you can't appreciate the best of a city until you've seen its worst, and our chums from Butzweilerhof had certainly ensured our estimation of Cologne would rise dramatically after taking us, literally, to the Brink.

* * * * *

CHAPTER TWENTY-TWO

'MANNHEIM, MEIN HERR'

True to form, Willy Braun impressed upon us the magnificence of the landscape we would be passing through on the two-and-a-half-hour train journey southward along the banks of the Rhine from Cologne to Mannheim.

'Some of the most spectacular scenery in the world!' he crowed. 'Especially around Koblenz – the Rhine Gorge – the fairytale castles – the Lorelei rock, where the beautiful siren of legend lured boatmen to their deaths. *Wunderschön*! Not be be missed!'

We missed the lot.

Our last gig at the Storyville Club had started at eight o'clock on New Year's Eve, extending all the way through until eight o'clock the following morning. Admittedly, we had been backed up by a couple of interval groups, but it had still been an exhausting shift, not least because the usual no-drinking-on-the-stand rule had been relaxed to allow us to join in the communal champagne toast at midnight. Or, as fate would have it, at both midnights. Due to the time difference, Scotland's Hogmanay celebrations would be kicking off one hour later than Germany's, and it came as no great surprise that no-one in the packed audience complained when I announced that, 'to comply with international protocol', more bubbly would have to be quaffed at one o'clock local time. While this by no means signalled the onset of a night on the booze for the band, it did ease any lurking scruples sufficiently to allow us to engage with the merriment in a more liberated manner than had been our wont up to then.

Pianist Alex Shaw, retiring by nature and not normally prone to any form of exhibitionism, brought jollifications to a pre-dawn climax by hijacking Frank Holder's final cabaret spot and leading the gathered company in singalong versions of two Scots music hall warhorses. *Ye Cannae Shove Yer Granny Aff A Bus* was sung to the tune of *She'll Be Coming Round the Mountain*, and, with words in praise of a famous brand of budget cigarette, *Woodbine's A Rare Wee Fag* followed the melody line of *Who Were You With Last Night?* To his credit, Frank Holder accepted the caper in good humour and, together with the audience, tried valiantly to get to grips with lyrics, which probably would have made as much sense if they'd been written in Swahili.

*

We arrived in Mannheim railway station just as we had left Cologne: sound asleep.

The Schwabinger Künstlerkeller – nominally an *artists'* cellar, emulating the character of Schwabing, the bohemian quarter of Munich, capital of the neighbouring state of Bavaria – would be our place of business for the next month. Although Mannheim had also been severely battered by Allied bombing during the war, the street in which the club was located seemed either to have escaped the worst of the destruction or had been rebuilt in traditional style. As the city is laid out in a grid pattern, it was difficult to tell where we were in relation to the centre, if indeed there was one, in the usual sense. Anyway, we appeared to be in an area with a lively, inviting feel, which augured well. We knew that, if our Cologne experience was anything to go by, we'd be unlikely to see much of Mannheim beyond those immediate environs for the coming four weeks.

And the club itself did indeed have a distinctly 'Left Bank' quality to it. The cellar, or rather series of cellars linked by archways, had probably served originally as warehouses for the shops above. All that had been done by way of transformation was the setting out of cafe-style tables and chairs and the addition of suitably arty murals here and there. Dim lighting completed a setting in which the young people of Mannheim could see themselves as genuine Schwabingers – even if relatively un-bohemian versions. But the main thing was that the concept worked; the Künstlerkeller had a real jazzy vibe. Though completely knackered, we were keen as ever to get in the groove.

One of the highlights of our stint in Cologne had been a surprise visit from one of America's top modern jazz combos, Art Blakey's Jazz Messengers. The quintet had just given a concert in the city, were looking to unwind in the after-hours atmosphere of a jazz club, and the Storyville just happened to be the only one in town. It didn't seem to matter to Art and his boys that our stuff was at the other end of the jazz spectrum from their own. After introducing themselves, they grabbed a table and 'dug the scene' until closing time, then sat chewing the fat with us for a while. Nice guys, and not at all affected by their standing as world leaders in their field.

In Mannheim, we would get to know another jazz legend, but on a more intimate basis. Clarinettist and sax player Benny Waters, like many other black musicians of his generation, had opted to leave his native America to work within the less discriminatory attitude prevailing in post-war Europe. Now approaching his sixtieth year, Benny had lived in Paris since 1952, having been long established in his homeland as one of jazz music's most respected journeymen. The list of big names he had worked with over the years read like a veritable who's who of jazz. As well as occasionally fronting his own band, Benny had played under such celebrated leaders as Fletcher Henderson, Jimmie Lunceford and Clarence Williams. Even more awe-inspiring to a young 'apprentice' like me was that he had actually recorded with Louis Armstrong's original boss and mentor, the fabled Joe 'King' Oliver himself. Now, he would be playing guest spots with a band that had my name in front of it, and no-one had to tell me how unworthy I was of that! Yet Benny could not have been more more gracious or less condescending. He had managed to remain 'one of the boys' in many varied circumstances during his lifetime, and, to my great relief, he quickly made it obvious he wasn't about to change the habit here.

Of medium height and stockily built, Benny had bright, darting eyes and an impish smile, which gave a clue to his nature. He had been on the scene long enough to know how to weigh up an audience, and he was sufficiently pragmatic to accept that not all jazz club customers were particularly knowledgeable about jazz. Accordingly, he would build his featured sets around a mix of playing-to-the-gallery clarinet fireworks, smoochy alto sax ballads, bug-eyed scat vocals and, his favourite party piece, using the top of a small leather stool as a 'mute' to produce some wah-wah effects on his soprano saxophone. 'OK, kid,' he'd mutter to me, 'stick yo' foot out and steady ma pew while Ah bugle up a mess o' magic fo' the masses.'

We never saw Benny outside working hours. He'd arrive at the club five minutes before his first spot, and leave immediately after the last. And he was always by himself, prompting us to think he must lead a very lonely life. Perhaps sensing what was going through our minds, he came into the band room one night tee-heeing merrily to himself.

'Man, oh, man!' he tittered. 'Dat chick o' mine, she sho' is somethin'!'

'Yeah?' we chorused, wide-eyed and all ears.

'Yeah! See, Ah was givin' her a piece o' *Bratwurst* [winks], know what Ah mean? when she squeals and hollers, "Stop, Benny! Stop! Yo' killin' me, Benny!" To which Ah say – while never missin' a beat – "It's good fo' ya, honey! It's good fo' ya!"'

We stopped feeling sorry for Benny after that, although we never did get to see his chick.

As anticipated, we didn't get to see all that much of Mannheim either. Whatever its proximity or otherwise to the city's centre, the section of the 'grid' we were in had everything we needed. Our digs were just a couple of minutes' walk away from the club; a simple restaurant, belonging to the club and situated just above it at street level, provided us with our main meals; and a stroll of a few hundred metres in either direction took us to any shops that might be of interest. Favourite among those was *die Konditorei*, a cafe-cum-bakery, with display cabinets stuffed full of pastries and cream cakes fit to dazzle our unaccustomed Scottish eyes. Tattie scones and clootie dumplings these confections most certainly were not.

If we ever needed to locate old George Crockett of an afternoon, he could usually be found at a window table in *die Konditorei*, sitting back, watching the passing show, legs crossed, cigarette in one raised hand, coffee cup in the other, top lip gloriously moustached in cream. Jim Douglas soon became equally hooked on the contents of those glass counters. Disinclined to bother learning their individual names in German, Jim would simply indicate the cake of his choice to the assistant and say, '*Ein* o' them, *bitte*!' Yes, it seemed the cosmopolitan character of this part of Mannheim was catching ... sort of.

Now that we had established a working-sized repertoire, there was no need to rehearse quite so frequently as we had in Cologne, leaving more time during the day to do whatever we chose. In most cases, this was to make up for a month of too little sleep. However, the proximity of a couple of good clothes shops and an extremely favourable rate of exchange did tempt even the least dress-conscious of us to invest in a few shirts, which could be bought for a fraction of their UK price.

But this wasn't enough for Jim, who, paradoxically, was moved to forsake the hippy image he had started to develop in modish Cologne for a more gent-about-town appearance, now that he was immersed in the laid-back atmosphere of Mannheim. 'Our man in Zürich' was how a tickled George Crockett dubbed Jim when he made his entrance into the cafe above the club one lunchtime. Every inch the Teutonic dandy, he was wearing a raglan-sleeved overcoat of the finest woollen fabric, with a matching hat fashioned in what might be described as the William Tell style. Jim's new ensemble looked expensive, and he assured us it was. He revealed that the whole outfit had actually cost him just as much as it would have back home – if not more. But anyway, he shrugged, it had been worth every penny. The genuine Continental look didn't come cheap, daddy!

Imagine, then, his reaction when it was noticed by a chuckling John McGuff that the inner labels of his purchases read, 'Harris Tweed' and 'Made in Scotland'. While everyone laughed it up, the smoke coming from Jim's ears prompted George Crockett to confer upon him the nickname, 'Steaming' Jim Douglas; a handle destined to stick forever, baffling though it might seem to the uninitiated.

Perhaps inspired by Jim's transformation, chubby bassist Ian 'Brownie' Brown, never the most sartorially conscious of individuals, invested in a smart new sports jacket and trousers the very next day.

'Blew near enough ma whole stash on this gear,' Brownie boasted, appraising himself in the mirror after work that night. He was preparing to leave our lodgings with Alex Shaw to meet up with a couple of local modern jazz fans who had befriended them. 'Yeah, ace threads, though,' he declared, patently satisfied with his appearance. 'Ye get what ye pay for. Ye cannae beat class, and class costs bread!'

Such a cavalier attitude towards his finances struck us as somewhat curious, given the contents of a telegram Brownie had received from his wife back in Edinburgh just a few days earlier. He'd passed it round the band room for all to see. The message read: '*Send money quick. Kids starving.*' Brownie chortled dismissively. 'Great sense o' humour, the missus. Kids starvin'? Aye, right!'

George and I shared a room opening through a wide archway into Alex and Brownie's pad. George called the latter 'The Arab Quarter', due to the souk-like look generated by its permanent state of disarray – particularly in Brownie's space. It seemed the shambles was being rearranged when, at some ungodly hour, I was awakened by muted cursing and the sound of furniture being knocked about.

'Fuckin' new threads!' grunted Brownie. 'Pissin' rain!'

Apparently, our two quasi-Bedouins had been caught in a thunderstorm on the way back from their night on the tiles with their two modern jazz chums. Feigning sleep, I watched the goings-on through a half-open eye.

'Jacket … fuckin' squelchin'!' Brownie muttered, hauling the sodden garment off his shoulders. 'Troosers … fuckin' wringin' wet an' all!' he panted, while staggering into his bedside table and ricocheting off a wardrobe as he struggled to peel the clinging material from first one leg, then the other.

Alex, oblivious, was already asleep, spreadeagled fully-clothed on the floor.

I heard George suffocating a snigger under his duvet.

The pantomime came to an end with Brownie climbing onto a chair to drape his dripping clothes over a central heating duct which ran along the wall above the archway. I was surprised to note that, even in his 'mellow' state, he had taken the precaution of first laying some sheets of newspaper over the hot pipe.

'Ruin ma new threads wi' dust?' he'd mumbled. 'No bloody chance!'

It took less than thirty minutes for the fire to start. George and I were aroused anew by the frantic clattering of Brownie doing a fandango on his new clothes. Their damp condition had saved them from total cremation, but they were damaged beyond salvation, nonetheless.

The following morning, Brownie asked for an advance against his next week's wages. Another pleading telegram had arrived from his missus, but it transpired that a replacement set of new threads would take priority. Mrs Brown's 'great sense of humour' was clearly in a long-suffering class of its own – even for the wife of a jazz musician.

*

Although Alex Shaw had slept through his friend's little drama, he was soon to demonstrate that he was perfectly capable of producing one of his own. A confirmed bachelor, Alex shared a flat in the Leith area of Edinburgh with an older sister, who took a motherly interest in his well-being. She also looked after his loft of homing pigeons whenever he had occasion to fly the coop himself. Shortly before joining us for the German trip, Alex had had a spell in hospital for the treatment of 'an ailment sensitive to the consumption of alcohol'. Not surprisingly, his sister, anxious that his recovery should be given every chance to progress unhindered, had asked Brownie to 'keep an eye on him'. Brownie had assured her that he would look after her wee brother with total dedication at all times. 'Relax, darlin''. He'll be all right wi' me!'

For all that the boys in the band liked a drink (some more than others!), none had ever blotted his copybook by arriving on duty the worse for it. While there was never any evidence that Brownie actually *encouraged* Alex to partake of alcohol on their nocturnal rambles, it had become obvious on the night of the fire-damaged threads that Alex had managed to escape his guardian's watchful eye for long enough to get himself completely blitzed.

The inevitable hangover manifested itself in spectacular style the very next evening. A green-gilled and understandably subdued Alex coped admirably with his piano-playing responsibilities, up to the very last number of the night, when he was seized in mid-solo by a coughing fit. It so happened that the local *Karneval* season was nearing its climax, with this particular night earmarked for Mannheim's mayor and his team of municipal dignitaries to squire the current carnival queen and her attendant princesses on a round of the city's nightspots. The Schwabinger Künstlerkeller was their last port of call, and a right jolly time was being had by all. Until, at the height of his coughing spasm, Alex sneezed, and his dentures shot from his mouth to go skittering across the dance floor like a runaway clam.

A plague of mice darting around their feet would not have elicited more shrieks from the carnival queen and her ladies in waiting, nor louder guffaws from their civic-dignitary dancing partners. As for the band, it was all we could do to control our laughter enough to keep the music going. But Alex, a sensitive soul at the best of times, was mortified, scurrying about on hands and knees in a frantic effort to salvage his false teeth before they were trampled to destruction. He left the club, dentures found but dignity lost, alone and without saying a word to any of us.

For the second time in twenty-four hours, I was rudely awakened in the middle of the night; though not, on this occasion, by too much noise, but by too little air. By a total *lack* of air, in fact.

'All Ah want is a little sympathy!' Alex's voice was quivering with emotion. It also sounded oddly strained.

I could feel fingers closing round my throat, thumbs digging into my windpipe. In the semi-darkness, I blinked my eyes open to see Alex's face hovering inches above mine. His usual genial expression was contorted into a sinister scowl.

'A little sympathy – that's all Ah want, man!'

I couldn't have answered, even if I'd known what he was on about. My first concern was to breathe. But Alex's grip was tightening with every passing second, and I could already feel consciousness slipping away. Pinned to the bed and helpless, I hoped that either George or Brownie would come to my assistance, and fast. All that emerged through the half-light, however, was the sound of snoring. In desperation, I reached up and grabbed Alex's right hand, but the more frantically I tried to wrench it away from my throat, the more vice-like was his grip. The only thing I could do now was squeeze his hand with all the strength the instinct to survive would muster. There was an audible crack, followed quickly by the blessed ability to suck in air again.

'Wa-a-a-ah, ya bas–!' Alex yowled. 'Ye've broke ma fuckin' Acme!' (Alex was a habitual user of rhyming slang, and 'Acme Wringer' is the parallel for 'finger' in the Scots lexicon).

Clutching his Acme and wailing, Alex swiftly exited the room and disappeared into the Mannheim night. He didn't come back.

'He's buggered off back to Blighty,' Brownie said when he joined the rest of us for a lunchtime breakfast in the cafe. 'Came into the pad ten minutes ago, packed his bag and shot the crow.'

We sat dumbstruck as Brownie went on to tell us that, after Alex had left the digs in the middle of the night, he had found a clinic run by nuns, who had 'fixed up' his snapped little finger as best they could, until such time as he could receive proper medical attention.

'Says he's goin' back to London,' said Brownie. 'Says Frances Day – ye know, that old Yankee nightclub singer he used to play for – says she'll likely look after him.'

So much, I mused, for the tubby bass player who told Alex's sister *he* would look after him. Anyway, that was all water under the bridge now. Of a sudden, we were without a piano player. But before I set about trying to solve that problem, I thought I'd attempt to clear up one equally important point that had been bothering me for the past few hours. I quoted the words Alex had growled while in the process of throttling me:

'*All I want is a little sympathy...* What the hell was that all about, Brownie?'

Our bass player raised a nonchalant shoulder. 'Missin' his pigeons, maybe?'

Brownie then ordered himself a double cheese-burger with an extra helping of fries on the side, and a half-litre of Coke to wash it all down. Life goes on.

*

The club's management found us a local student to deputise for Alex. Young Fritz was no less delighted to be given the chance to play with us than we were to have him. While he didn't possess Alex's rare gifts as a pianist, at least he had ten functioning fingers and no pigeon hang-ups.

The final days of our Mannheim residency passed without further incident. They also passed without any offers of further German engagements. John Marshall, the impresario in Cologne, had been as good as his word, in that he had kept in touch with me regarding his efforts on our behalf. The confidence he'd had about securing at least one other four-week deal for us had been undermined by the club in question having unexpectedly decided to take a chance on an emerging trend that was beginning to spread over from Britain. Forsaking its previous commitment to jazz, the club had booked a 'beat group', which John had been informed was some sort of electric-guitar-led combo, pioneered in the provincial English city of Liverpool, of all places. Other German jazz clubs would be watching this experiment with interest, but John was sure he would be able to obtain other bookings for us in a few months – once this new 'beat' fad had passed, as he was certain it would.

Unfortunately, a few months was tantamount to forever as far as I was concerned. If I was going to keep the band together, I needed to find paying work for it *now*. While the rest of the boys spent the final day of our Mannheim sojourn on a sightseeing trip to the nearby town of Heidelberg, picturesque setting of the *Student Prince* film, I took advantage of the club's offer to use their office as a base from which to launch a last-gasp attempt at securing some immediate dates back in the UK. But every London agent I phoned had the same depressing tale to tell: they were already swamped by jazz bands, each hoping to find success in the ascendant 'Trad Boom'. The hard fact was that there were already more bands than work to go round.

The boys greeted this news with glum faces, but I suspected all of them were itching to get back home to families, friends and loved ones. I felt the same way, although with one significant complication: once the rest of the lads had renewed old acquaintances, most of them would have *some* chance of returning to their former jobs. Not me. As I had been well warned, there would be no way back into the civil service.

My prospects looked bleak, but that didn't prevent me from reflecting on the experiences of the past couple of months.

A brush with death-by-strangulation aside, those experiences had been unbelievably good. I had enjoyed the privilege of playing with and sharing the camaraderie of a group of fine musicians, who were also decent guys, totally dedicated to jazz, individual idiosyncrasies notwithstanding. I had tasted the sometimes sweet, occasionally bitter, but always edifying life of a full-time musician and bandleader. I had been afforded access to the people, ways and culture of another land. By listening to and learning from my bandmates and our esteemed guests, I had been given the opportunity to improve as a musician. But, perhaps most significantly of all, I believed that, in those two months, I had learned more about myself, human nature and how to interact with my peers than a lifetime spent in the cloistered corridors of the civil service would have provided.

Rightly or wrongly, for good or ill, this would be the conviction with which I'd now have to face the future.

* * * * *

CHAPTER TWENTY-THREE

'LEND ME A TOOTHBRUSH'

If, as its minder in Clapham claimed, my old Bedford bandwagon had never turned a wheel during my two-month absence, the only conclusion to be drawn was that it had driven *itself* into the ground. If, as the same guy asserted, he hadn't been using it to ferry himself and other musicians around, I could only assume that the crushed fag packets, cigarette butts, empty beer bottles and old issues of *Melody Maker* littering the floor were evidence that a few buskers had been using it as an alternative to sleeping rough under a railway arch. And one turn of the ignition key told me that tappets were now the least of the engine's problems. All the starting motor could do was raise a wheeze. Sighing in sympathy, I tried to slide the driver's door shut. It fell off.

'Mechanic geezer done his best, mate,' the minder shrugged. 'Yeah, an' at least he never charged ya nuffin'.' He then directed me to the yard of a local scrap dealer, who, he assured me, would tow the old crate away and wouldn't charge me nuffin' neiver.

Hark the lark!

*

I had left home on the eve of my twentieth birthday with a bandwagon, a seven-piece band and enough work to keep its members gainfully employed for two months – at least. Two months later, at the beginning of February 1961, I was back home with none of those things and no way of repeating the trick. I was a has-been before I'd even been anybody. I was washed up, a flop. To their credit, none of the lads who had declined the chance to make the German trip came out with any 'told-you-so' digs. Their attitude seemed to be that at least I'd tried. Still, I realised there would always be a 'loser' stigma attached to what I'd set out to do. And that bothered me.

It bothered me even more that I had let my parents down, as well as helping realise Nancy Douglas's worries about her son Jim's training as a potter being interrupted, permanently. Those feelings of guilt and failure were at least eased for a few days by the joy of being back home and by the warmth of the reception afforded me by my folks. As was their way, there was no demonstrative welcoming back of the prodigal son, just a continuation of family life as if I had never been away. And the only reproachful reaction to the influences of my time as a professional musician was my mother's demure lowering of her eyes when I instinctively came out with the 'F' word at the breakfast table on my first morning home. However, this tacit rebuke was countered by an almost imperceptible, though approving, smirk tugging at the corner of my father's moustache.

Ellie, too, greeted my return with customary restraint. Unlike a scene in some schmaltzy movie, we didn't rush from opposite ends of an empty street to meet half way and fall into each other's arms panting with pent-up emotion. Instead, she opened her parents' front door to my knock with the same warm but guarded air she had exhibited on the day we'd parted two months earlier. Cautiously welcoming though her manner may have been, just seeing her again made the same impact on me as when I'd first noticed her on the way home from school all of four years ago.

I knew well enough I didn't have the same effect on Ellie, but I did notice she seemed relieved to see that at least I hadn't changed. I hadn't become the flash, spivvy character my exposure to the worldly ways of big-city nightlife might have made me. Indeed, after a while sitting chatting to Ellie and her mother in their front room, I got the impression that Ellie was developing a less wary attitude towards me than had sometimes been apparent before. As I explained my disappointment at having to disband the band and my uncertainty about what lay ahead for me now, the more she seemed to look at me in a way I hadn't previously seen. She was beginning to regard me, not as that former prefect who gave her lines for running in the corridor, but as someone with a vulnerability to match his ambition. I could fail, not just like everyone else, but more spectacularly than most. Was this bringing out the maternal side of her nature? I didn't know. What I did know, though, was that there was no need to assure her I hadn't been fooling around with any fräuleins while away, any more than she needed to convince me she hadn't been dallying with any young doctors. It was just something we both accepted. And this said more about our feelings for each other than any movie-style reunion ever could.

If parting had made the heart grow fonder, it wasn't to be the last time the old adage would be put to the test, nor would it be long until it was again. It took only a few days for the elation of being back home to be replaced by the gut-churning worry about what I was going to do with my life now. The stark reality was that my career as a professional jazz musician hadn't merely entered choppy waters; it was in danger of foundering completely. Maybe the only way to salvage it would be to start from scratch. This would mean forming a new band, since it would be too much to expect all, or perhaps any, of the lads who had joined me in Germany to give me a second chance. And even if I could put a new line-up together, where would the work come from? My thoughts, like the mythical 'Oo-ya Bird', were starting to fly in ever-decreasing circles, and I feared it would be only a matter of time before I also disappeared up my own backside. For once, despite an abundance of will, there was no discernible way.

At a loss for a better idea, I was leaving the house one morning to go and ask if there was any casual work available at the farm along the road, when my father called me back:

'Phone call for you – from Glasgow – bloke says it's urgent!'

I had been so preoccupied with trying to figure out how I could continue leading a band of my own that the thought of someone asking me to join *his* had never occurred. But that's precisely what Ian Menzies, trombonist-leader of none other than the mighty Clyde Valley Stompers, wanted me to do. He explained that the Clydes were about to move their base from Glasgow to London, but a few key members of the personnel, including clarinettist Forrie Cairns, had elected not to go.

'I was wondering if you'd maybe be interested in taking his place?'

'When do we leave?' I blurted out, not even trying to conceal the note of desperation. 'I'm ready when you –'

'Well, there would need to be a wee try-out first,' Ian cut in. 'I mean, I've heard the two records you made for Waverley, and your playing sounds fine. But, you know, we'd need to see how you fit in with the rest of the boys.'

I was on my way to Glasgow for that 'wee try-out' within the hour.

*

The Clyde Valley Stompers had been in the news quite a bit since I saw them live at Haddington's Corn Exchange several years before. Most of the reports had been of a positive nature, like the account of their appearance on the bill of Scotland's first ever Royal Command Performance and various mentions of how 'Stompermania' continued to grow unabated. But the item of news I recalled most clearly was about a legal wrangle involving the Clyde Valley Stompers' name itself.

A year or so after I'd seen them in Haddington, a major split within the band had led to trumpeter Dean Kerr and soprano saxist Maurice Rose leading a breakaway group, whose intention was to claim the Clyde Valley Stompers name for themselves. Ian Menzies duly made a counter claim, a legal kerfuffle ensued, with the name eventually being put up for auction. Luck was on the Menzies side. The 'rebels' failed to register a bid before the court-declared deadline, so Menzies' opening offer of £60 was accepted. He was quoted as saying that, 'for a song', he had acquired legal ownership of a brand name for which he would willingly have paid much, much more. In business terms, buying the 'good will' attached to that name for about the same as the band's fee for a single gig was indeed an unbelievable snip.

From then on, lest there be doubt in anyone's mind about whose band it was, the billing would be *IAN MENZIES and his Clyde Valley Stompers*, with the emphasis unmistakably on the leader's name. What I didn't know when entering the band's Glasgow rehearsal room on that fateful February day was that Forrie Cairns, the clarinettist I was being auditioned to replace, had parted company with the Clydes (together with his pianist brother John and vocalist Fiona Duncan) not, as I'd been led to believe, because they simply didn't want to make the move to London, but due to a serious falling-out with Ian Menzies. So, it could be assumed that the good will associated with the business image of the band wasn't always being reflected within its ranks.

But even if I'd been aware of this, it would not have weakened my immediate resolve, which was to make a good impression in this 'wee try-out'. My entire future depended on it, and any skeletons lurking in the Clydes' cupboard were none of my business.

The band was all set up when I walked into the room, and although I took it for granted that they'd be as uneasy about the chances of my being right for the job as I was nervous about being put to the test, I was given the sort of welcome Glaswegians are renowned for. This despite the fact that I hailed from even farther east than Edinburgh!

Ian Menzies, who came over as less aloof than he'd appeared on stage and did indeed have a big-brotherly air about him, introduced me to his sidemen. I recognised diminutive drummer Bobby Shannon and red-haired banjoist Norrie Brown as members of the line-up I'd seen in Haddington. Like Menzies, they had been with the band since its formative years. Trumpeter Malky Higgins and bass player Bill Bain were, however, more recent recruits, enlisted in the aftermath of the split that had resulted in the auctioning of the Stompers' name. One thing they all had in common, though, was a natural cheeriness, and I had a feeling they were rooting for me to do well. There seemed no lack of good will here.

'Know *Beale Street Blues*?' asked Ian, once I had my clarinet reeded up and ready to blow.

I nodded the affirmative, and without further ado he kicked things off, but at a considerably faster tempo than most bands take that particular tune. Clearly, there was to be no chance of easing gently into this test.

And wow, did little Bobby Shannon belt those drums with a vengeance! After George Crockett's almost gentlemanly laying down of the beat, this was like being rammed in the back by a steam hammer. But it got the musical adrenaline going in a way I hadn't known before, and I liked the sensation. Playing alongside the two Clyde Valley Stompers horn players was also a complete change from what I'd become accustomed to of late. The sparse Menzies trombone style left a lot more space for clarinet 'fills' than John McGuff's busy approach had done. This, however, was offset by Malky Higgins employing his impressive trumpet technique to the full. He could produce notes with the velocity of a machine gun, and with an astonishing fluency of phrasing too. For me, this represented a whole new exercise in fitting into the jigsaw puzzle that constitutes the sound picture of a traditional jazz band's front line. Yet, despite my jitters, I was soon beginning to enjoy myself, and I sensed the rest of the guys were as well.

Jazzmen being jazzmen, what started out as an audition might well have developed into a full-blown jam session, if Ian Menzies hadn't put the brakes on.

'OK, let's get down to brass tacks. We'll see what you can do with *High Society* now, Pete!'

I'd been expecting this. Back at the beginning of the twentieth century, Alphonse Picou, one of the earliest pioneers of jazz in New Orleans, had reworked the piccolo part of a march called *High Society* to create his clarinet solo in a 'ragtime' arrangement of the tune. His idea caught on, and since then no traditional jazz clarinettist had been regarded as worth his salt if he couldn't replicate Picou's set piece. Consequently, learning it was one of the first things I'd committed myself to after gaining a modicum of proficiency on my very first instrument. I had played the solo on just about every gig since, so I reckoned that playing it again here shouldn't be a problem – provided, of course, my shaking fingers did what my brain told them. In my favour was the universally accepted belief that individual clarinettist should apply their own variations to Picou's original theme. With this in mind, I hoped any 'improvisations' my fingers produced of their own accord might give the impression of being intentional.

And I got away with it. Spurred on by some spirited back-beat hand-clapping and shouts of 'Gawn yersel', kid!' from

Malky Higgins, I made it through my *High Society* baptism of fire without any major clangers being dropped. The nods and mutterings of approval from the boys seemed genuine enough, but the final word would have to come from Ian Menzies. Although his smile was encouraging, he kept schtum until swapping glances with a woman who had been sitting in a corner watching and listening throughout.

'This is my wife Janet,' he said, as the typically-perky wee Glesca lass came over and shook my hand.

'That was smashin',' she beamed. 'Pure dead smashin'. Aye, and yer hair reminds me o' Charlie Gall, our first trumpet player, so it does.'

The relevance of the hair comment escaped me, but I knew Charlie Gall to be a good musician, so I took what she'd said as a compliment and thanked her for it.

'Welcome, I'm sure,' she replied. 'Ye'll fit in fine, so ye will.'

This was Ian's cue. 'So, Pete, can you be ready to leave for London in three days?'

'Lend me a toothbrush,' I grinned. 'I'm ready to leave right now!'

* * * * *

CHAPTER TWENTY-FOUR

'A-STOMPING I WILL GO'

Ellie accepted the news of my imminent departure for London in a refreshingly down-to-earth way, which eased my concerns that I could be expecting too much of her patience. The Stompers' date sheet was full for the coming three months, and all the engagements would be at venues 'down south'. This, after all, was the reason for the band moving its base to London in the first place.

'Look at it this way,' she said, '– if you'd stayed in the civil service, you could have been posted anywhere in Britain by now. And if you were a few months older, you'd have been liable for national service before it was scrapped. I mean, you might even have been back in Germany for the next two years! Anyway, I'm going to be on night duty at the hospital for a while, so we wouldn't have been seeing much of each other in any case. Off you go to London, and enjoy yourself! I'll still be here when you come back.' She paused and shot me a mischievous little look. '*If* you come back.'

There was no need for me to respond to that, and Ellie knew it.

*

The Clydes had made several forays into England over the years, and had already established a following. When in the London area, they had been in the habit of staying in the northern suburb of Finchley, in a guest house owned by a chirpy old West Country lady called Curwood. Moss Hall Crescent lies just off Ballards Lane, the main link from Finchley to the North Circular Road which, in turn, leads to all major arterial routes out of London. Mrs Curwood couldn't have picked a handier location to serve as a home-from-home for a group of itinerant jazz musicians.

Ian Menzies made a point of sharing a room with me on the first night of his band's permanent exile. Away from the other musicians, with whom we had driven down from Scotland in the Clyde's minibus, Ian showed less of the school-masterish manner which I'd noticed when first watching the band play live. Still, even though he had contributed to the banter bouncing about in the back of the wagon on the long journey south, he had seemed happier to stay in the driver's seat, keeping himself on the periphery of the fun. In essence, he gave the impression of not *quite* being one of the boys, but I hadn't been able to work out whether this was deliberate or not.

Now, in the one-to-one privacy of our room in Mrs Curwood's, his late-night conversation revealed a certain sensitivity I hadn't noticed before. I got the impression he was aware of how I might be feeling: a kid on my first day at a new school, surrounded by older, more experienced new acquaintances, and confronted by challenges that probably had me shaking in my shoes. There was more than a grain of truth in this, so I was thankful he seemed to care. If I needed a big-brother figure, I reckoned I could do worse than have Ian 'Big Ming' Menzies in the role. (In Scotland, incidentally, Menzies is pronounced 'Ming-is', hence the 'Big Ming' nickname).

Curiosity tempted me to ask him about the Clydes' history of frequent personnel changes, always resulting, allegedly, from rifts between himself and other members of the band, but I thought better of it. My policy would be to take him as I found him, and he had done nothing so far to suggest he was anything but a thoroughly decent guy. In keeping with his public image, he was a man of few words, reluctant, it seemed, to give too much about himself away. Still, he did freely tell me he had learned to play trombone with the Boys' Brigade in the workaday Finnieston area of Glasgow, had left school to become an apprentice draughtsman in a local foundry, had joined the Clyde Valley Stompers in the early Fifties and had been passed the reins when the band's original leader, bass player Jim McHarg, emigrated to Canada a couple of years later. He went on to say he had taken the band as far as it was possible to go in Scotland, both geographically and commercially, so the logical next step was this move to England, where more and, in many cases, better-paying work was available. Previous tours south of the border had laid the foundations of a fan base, had secured the Stompers a contract with Lyn Dutton, London's top band agent, and had seen them signed by Pye Records, currently the foremost jazz label in the UK.

This led neatly to the subject of my first Clyde Valley Stompers gig, which would be the recording of two tracks for Pye the very next day. I hadn't a clue about the tunes, except that they were new compositions by Ian, who told me all would be revealed at a rehearsal in the morning. No pressure there, then – and the likelihood of not much sleep tonight for me either!

*

The Refectory is a pub in Golders Green, a prominent Jewish enclave of north London, just down the road from Finchley.

The use of the pub's basement function room had been made available for the Clydes to rehearse in by Neville Nisse, the band's publicist and a local resident. Neville made a brief appearance at The Refectory that morning, mainly to grab some background material from me for routine publicity purposes, but also to wish the band well for the recording session later in the day. A good PR man knows how important it is to present a friendly image of himself to his clients, and on that basis Neville Nisse qualified as a worthy member of his profession.

Pleased as I was to meet him, I was glad when he went on his way and let us get on with the rehearsal. My only experience of playing with this group of musicians, remember, had been on the handful of numbers we had skipped through for my audition; not exactly an ideal way of getting to know one another's ways before *any* first gig, far less a crucial one like a recording session. But that's jazz, as they say, so all I could do was follow my old maxim of getting stuck in and doing my best.

It quickly became clear, though, that I needn't have lost any sleep. The 'new compositions' Ian had lined up for the occasion were actually only extended versions of riffs the band used behind the melodies of two standards that were staples of their repertoire. I recognised them from the Clydes' latest LP, a copy of which Ian had given me at the end of my audition, 'to mug up on for a couple of days'. Nevertheless, those two ostensibly new titles were set down as original works by Ian Menzies. There was nothing iniquitous or even unusual about this, of course; adding an alternative 'tune' to an existing chord sequence is a device as old as music itself. Quite legitimately, Ian would earn composer's royalties on all sales and air plays of the record.

The LP those two sides were gleaned from had been produced by Lonnie Donegan, the King of Skiffle, who, like the band itself, was Glasgow-born. He had now stepped aside to allow the Clyde Valley Stompers' recording work to be supervised by Alan Freeman. Alan (not to be confused with the radio disc jockey of the same name) was Pye's top pop-music A&R man, and had already produced a variety of hits, most notably for Petula Clark and Lonnie Donegan himself. Whatever his jazz credentials may have been, he presumably didn't recognise the Clydes' two latest offerings for what they were. He listened to the run-throughs in the studio, made a constructive suggestion or two, went up to the control room to set the balance, put each number safely in the can in a handful of takes, and bade us a pleasant farewell.

Though nervous, I had found my first recording session for a major company to have been a surprisingly laid-back experience. Afterwards, Ian Menzies went out of his way to allay any doubts I might have had about my performance by telling me, in front of the rest of the band, that it was funny how seemingly terminal set-backs could result in a change for the better. It was obvious this was a lightly veiled swipe at my predecessor. But I didn't see myself as being in competition with Forrie Cairns, a fine clarinet player with whom I was flattered to be compared, but who had an entirely different style from my own. I accepted Ian's compliment graciously, albeit seasoned with a liberal sprinkling of salt. Whatever open wounds he carried were the result of battles I hadn't been involved in, and I had no wish to be implicated now, no matter how indirectly.

The only slightly disconcerting aspect of the musical side of the recording session had sprung, ironically enough, from another compliment Ian paid me. On the first take of one of the tunes, I opened my solo with a phrase featuring a pronounced 'blue' note. Ian told me he liked that idea, before switching the order of solos so that his came before mine. Then, for the next take, he repeated note-for-note the phrase I'd previously opened with. It didn't bother me at the time, because I never played a solo the same way twice in any case. To my way of thinking, jazz without instant improvisation wasn't jazz, and that, going right back to my earliest Hidden Town Dixielanders attempts, was how I'd always regarded it, as had every other musician I'd played with – until now. But so what if Ian had 'borrowed' an idea from me? I told myself something lent to a big brother shouldn't be taken as a loss, and left it at that. More importantly, the floods of ad-lib creativity cascading from Malky Higgins' trumpet amply compensated for *any* front-line shortcomings, including my own.

*

Haslemere is a pretty little town on the edge of the Surrey 'Stockbroker Belt', about forty miles south-west of London, and it was there we headed immediately after the recording session. No grass grew under the wheels of Clyde Valley Stompers' bandwagon! My first live gig with the band was a concert the same evening in Haslemere's concert hall, yet I still knew nothing of the band's repertoire beyond the contents of their latest album – and the two numbers we had recorded that afternoon. Fortunately, there's a considerable list of time-honoured standbys with which all jazz musicians are familiar, and we managed to wing it through the two-hour show by borrowing extensively from that. We simply dug in and enjoyed ourselves in what amounted to a glorified jam session.

Perhaps it was because of this spontaneous approach that the audience greeted our efforts with a surprising degree of appreciation. Thanks to the past support of Jack Stokes, the concert's promoter, who also ran a popular jazz club in the Wooden Bridge pub at nearby Guildford, the band was already reasonably well known in this southern-English hotbed of trad. It followed that local jazz enthusiasts would have been aware of the recent changes to the Clydes' line-up, not least the departure of personality vocalist Fiona Duncan. And, without doubt, her absence alone would have necessitated a significant change to the bill of musical fare that Clydes' fans were accustomed to having served up. It was with much relief, then, that we set off back to London at the end of the evening, having had our makeshift programme accepted so warmly by the good folk of Haslemere. Indeed, there could be no denying that any less positive a response would have augured badly for the packed schedule of engagements now about to be tackled.

For the next couple of weeks, all the bookings arranged by the Lyn Dutton office happened to be within a radius which allowed us to return to home base every night – or, more often, before dawn the next day. This gave us a chance to cram in some much-needed rehearsal time at The Refectory in Golders Green. It also gave Ian Menzies an opportunity to complete the transfer of his family from Glasgow to their new London abode, a comfortable semi-detached villa in the suburb of Cricklewood. Its location was both close to Golders Green and an easy drive round the North Circular Road to Mrs Curwood's Finchley guest house, where the rest of us continued to share rooms.

In 'domestic' terms, life for me was not much different from what it had been in Germany. But since UK jazz gigs usually consisted of a maximum of two one-hour sets per night, compared to a *minimum* of six hours nightly in Germany, the work side of life was now a piece of cake. Until, that is, the travelling element was factored in. I'd already had a taste of this in Scotland, of course, but those 'tours' had normally consisted of only two or three weekend dates. Being permanently on the road, seven days a week, was a completely different matter, made even tougher when the journeys began to extend farther from London and involved several overnight stopovers per trip.

In 1961 the only motorway in Britain was the recently-completed first stretch of the M1, which ran from the outskirts of London to the Blue Boar transport cafe just south of Rugby, a mere fifty miles to the north. All other journeys had to be undertaken on the old single-carriageway trunk roads, which were slow, dangerously outdated and clogged with convoys of diesel-belching trucks. A typical one-week tour could involve a total distance of over two thousand miles, and often comprised an itinerary that might have been plotted on a map by a drunken spider. Birmingham today, Durham tomorrow, onwards to Norwich, Bristol, Liverpool, Cambridge and Brighton. Then there would be the occasional radio show to squeeze in between our everyday club, ballroom and concert dates. Somehow, we had to find time to eat and sleep as well.

Banjoist Norrie Brown was first to hand in his notice, promptly followed by drummer Bobby Shannon. It wasn't that the two longest-serving members of the band had less stamina than anyone else, but rather that they had already been through the rigours of life on the road way back when the Clyde Valley Stompers were first making a name for themselves. There had been a sense of adventure about it in those days: the fun and excitement of breaking new ground, of achieving things that no Scottish band had done before. For Norrie and Bobby, that old magic was unlikely to be recaptured in this new venture. But of more significance was that, in the band's early years, a tour had usually involved no more than a week's travelling within Scotland, and always with a return to home comforts to look forward to at the end. Norrie was married, so the current prospect of not seeing his wife and young family in Glasgow for several months at a time must have been hard to bear. And the chances of his ever being in a position to emulate Ian Menzies by setting up home in London would have meant relying on the likelihood of a substantial increase in his present earnings. It was a gamble Norrie wasn't prepared to take; nor, though a bachelor, was his long-time colleague Bobby Shannon.

I recall wondering at the time how those two experienced campaigners hadn't foreseen the likely outcome of such a disruptive undertaking as this. Perhaps only their sense of loyalty to the band, and to Ian Menzies in particular, had prompted them to make the move south. If so, it must have been of small comfort to see their old mate 'Big Ming', whom they'd stuck by through every squabble and line-up change over the years, having the wherewithal to transfer his family to a comfortable home in London while they were obliged to 'rough it' together in a single room.

Whatever, this marked the end of an era, with Ian Menzies the only member remaining from what the band's original Scottish fans regarded as the golden age of the Clyde Valley Stompers. But would things get even worse? Would the departure of these two stalwarts trigger a chain reaction? Like Norrie Brown, trumpeter Malky Higgins and bassist Bill Bain were married men, now facing separation from wives and young children back in Glasgow for lengthy periods of time. How long would it be before they decided to head home as well?

But their situation was different from Norrie and Bobby's, in that this attempt to boost the band's fortunes was a new experience for them. They were tasting, for the first time, that heady brew of adventure their predecessors had savoured many years before. Yes, they were here for the long haul ... or so they confidently predicted, and genuinely believed.

* * * * *

CHAPTER TWENTY-FIVE

'THINGS AIN'T WHAT THEY USED TO BE'

It was sad to see Norrie and Bobby leaving a band they had served so staunchly since its earliest days. Their presence throughout had been a cornerstone of the public's perception of the Clyde Valley Stompers, both visually and musically. They were also good lads: modest, sociable and gifted with a generous supply of droll Glaswegian humour. My own integration into the band had certainly been made all the easier by having their friendship and support. I would miss them.

Nonetheless, the cloud created by their departure in May 1961 did have a silver lining: it created an opportunity for Jim Douglas to resume his career as a professional musician by replacing Norrie Brown on banjo. And this made me feel good in more ways than one. I still bore a weight of guilt on my shoulders for having encouraged Jim to risk all by joining me on the German venture, only to leave him in limbo when it ended. But apart from easing my conscience, the reopening of that closed door would allow Jim and me to renew the comradeship we had enjoyed since school days. More crucially, we were still at the beginning of our musical careers and shared an eagerness to help maintain the Clyde Valley Stompers' reputation.

The same would apply to Robbie Winter, the young Glasgow drummer who was recruited to take over from Bobby Shannon. With a dynamic, unfussy style not unlike Bobby's, Robbie was also of an age to take in his stride the demands that would surely face this latest incarnation of Scotland's top jazz band.

As with my own initiation, Jim and Robbie were thrown in at the deep end by having to cope with the pressures of a recording session as one of their first gigs. I doubt it really surprised anyone that the band's previous single had proved to be a flop. Ian's two 'compositions' would have served well enough as fillers on an album, but they didn't constitute potential hit material, and hit singles were what record companies now wanted from jazz bands. This, I presumed, was why Pye Records had put Alan Freeman in charge of the Stompers' current recording efforts. And Ian Menzies was astute enough to have taken that on board.

It was equally likely that, while Ian craved the benefits of a hit single (he often talked about how his fellow Pye bandleader Kenny Ball was already investing his burgeoning royalty earnings in property), he was at a loss as to how he could create one. Churning out tried-and-tested old favourites on an LP to please the band's existing fans was one thing, but it was quite another to come up with something different and dress it up in a way that might catch on with a wider public, as indeed Kenny Ball seemed able to do at will. Yet, instead of taking time to find and develop the right material, Ian opted to head quickly back into the studio to record, not just one, but *two* singles. Maybe this was to comply with conditions of the Pye contract, but, as with all matters legal and financial, only Ian was privy to those details.

The day before the session, he asked Jim and me if we had noticed any tunes doing particularly well during our stint in Germany; tunes that hadn't yet enjoyed any chart success in the UK. Those that came immediately to mind as having been played most frequently on the jazz-only jukebox in the Schwabinger Künstlerkeller were *Play to Me Gypsy*, which I had since adopted as a clarinet feature, *Taboo* and, perhaps a mite ominously, *Auf Wiedersehen*. I was flattered when Ian suggested that *Gypsy* should be the A-side of one of the new singles, and I could see why he thought it had potential: clarinet features had a history of becoming hit-vehicles for jazz bands. Unfortunately, though, that particular bus had already left, with Chris Barber's star clarinettist Monty Sunshine and Acker Bilk taking turns at the wheel. The reason was obvious for Ian's choice of the march *Trombones to the Fore* as the B-side, but many more catchy, easily-recognised pieces of military music had already been adapted and recorded by jazz bands, so this one always risked being regarded as an also-ran.

The definition of 'commercial' was changing rapidly in popular music, and if the Clyde Valley Stompers were to graduate from being predominantly a live attraction to contenders in the contest for hit records, then a new approach would have to be adopted. Throwing darts at a dartboard in the dark wouldn't do. To be fair, though, this also seemed to be the policy currently followed by some major record companies. The singles market was peppered with all sorts of trad jazz efforts, the tunes apparently chosen for no better reason than that they were capable of receiving the standard trad jazz treatment. Not unpredictably, the resultant success rate was meagre.

So, what was learned from that hurried Pye session? Not a lot, it seemed. While time had been made available to run through the four chosen numbers before committing them to tape, the band was still a long way from being totally familiar with its bread-and-butter working repertoire. The week following this latest studio date, and barely a fortnight after Jim and Robbie's arrival, the band was booked to play a concert in the affluent resort of Worthing on the south coast of England. Many of the rough edges that hadn't been smoothed out may not have been all that noticeable in the jive-happy environment of clubs and dance halls, but playing for a seated concert audience was going to be a trickier prospect entirely.

It says much for the affection in which the band was already held in such jazz-savvy areas of southern England that our unpolished offerings were received with genuine enthusiasm. Raw as it was, our performance must have exuded enough nervous energy and excitement to prompt the audience to treat us kindly. As had been the case following my own inaugural concert at Haslemere, we headed back to London from Worthing that night in a mood of gratitude and relief.

And the memory of the experience was instantly consigned to the back of our minds by all of us. All, that's to say, except our leader. Although we would only become aware of it when an LP was issued on the Ember label some months later, Ian had arranged for Neville Nisse, the band's publicist, to have the entire Worthing concert recorded through the hall's PA system. I remember listening to the album for the first (and last!) time and wondering why on earth Ian would have been party to the release of such a poor impression of what his band was capable of. This applied as much to the sound quality as the performance. The banjo on Jim Douglas's feature, for example, was so far off-mic that it sounded as if it was being played out on the beach. As Jim was eventually to pronounce, the tapes should have been chucked into the sea at the end of the show. And I believe they most certainly would have been if the boys in the band had had any say in the matter.

But that was just one of several bones of contention that would surface in due course. Meanwhile, we committed ourselves to getting on with the job. Musicians of all persuasions live to play music, and those given a chance to make it their livelihood are doubly delighted if presented with a full diary of work. The Clydes had such a diary, and not one of the band members was anything but grateful to 'Big Ming' Menzies for giving him the opportunity to share this good fortune.

*

It was around this time that the band started travelling in two vehicles instead of one. Ian had bought himself a top-of-the-range Humber Hawk saloon, and decided that the three new boys – Robbie, Jim and myself – should travel in it with him. Malky and Bill would go on ahead with all the gear in the band's Morris J2 minibus, which, although having now clocked up a fair old mileage, was still perfectly capable of transporting the entire band and its baggage. The relief of boredom on the road is usually best achieved by the fun and games that automatically happen when everyone is piled into the same vehicle, so why Ian wanted to segregate the personnel in this way seemed strange. Still, we saw nothing sinister in it. Maybe he just got a buzz out of arriving at gigs in a smart car. Anyway, it was his own money he was spending, so who were we three rookies to question his motives? As for Malky and Bill – well, they were a happy-go-lucky pair who revelled in each other's company. They had no objections to having the bandwagon to themselves; Malky behind the wheel, pipe clenched firmly between his teeth while he entertained Bill with off-the-cuff nonsense stories about an imaginary Glasgow family called the McGubligans. When Bill wasn't holding his sides or dabbing his eyes, he would map-read. It wasn't unknown, therefore, for us to approach a roundabout in the Humber, only to see the bandwagon heading *back* up the same road. Yet the full complement always succeeded in arriving at the venue in time for the gig.

The schedule of work arranged by the Lyn Dutton Agency was punishing by any standard, but we knew that plenty of other bands would have given anything to be in our position, so we accepted any accompanying hardships without a thought of complaint. The joy of playing jazz night after night *and* being paid for it more than compensated for the negative aspects of touring. Even the variety of venues we played added spice to the blandness of life on the road. And nowhere boasted a wider variety than London itself: the ramshackle ballroom on 'hippy' Eel Pie Island; the majestic Royal Albert Hall; packed-to-the-gunnels riverboats on shuffles down the Thames to Margate; the vast indoor expanses of Alexandra Palace; the mecca of Jazzshows Club at 100 Oxford Street, where, fresh from our Carroll Levis Discoveries broadcast, Jim and I had stood starry-eyed listening to the Alex Welsh Band only a year before.

Now, we were not only playing on that hallowed Jazzshows stand, but also rubbing shoulders with those same musicians in the Blue Posts pub round the corner. For the Blue Posts was a favourite haunt of jazzmen seeking a pint and a chance to compare notes with kindred spirits. The paths of bands did occasionally cross at jazz festivals, on all-nighter jazz band jamborees and on those sunny riverboat shuffles, but the Blue Posts was a haven of relaxation unmarred by the need to get back on stage in a hurry – unless, of course, you happened to be the band playing Jazzshows that night. And, because of our work load, those were the only occasions on which we had an opportunity to cut the Blue Posts fat. Still, it was great to sample, even fleetingly, the camaraderie that exists between dedicated jazzers, successful and otherwise.

*

A girl singer had always been featured in the Stompers' line-up – Nita Cowley, Jeannie Lamb and, most recently, Fiona Duncan having successively followed the trail first blazed by Mary McGowan back in the early Fifties. Only Ian Menzies knew why this tradition would no longer continue, and it was a subject left unbroached by the band's new boys. We had enough to do familiarising ourselves with the purely instrumental content of the Clydes' repertoire. The Dutton office did go some way, however, towards appeasing any disgruntled fans by booking 'star' jazz vocalists to guest with the band on selected concert dates. George Melly, Beryl Bryden, Clinton Ford and Neva Raphaello proved themselves to be great fun to work with, universally popular with the public, and also past masters at putting on a well-rehearsed show without the benefit of any rehearsal at all. Just appearing on the same stage as them was an education in itself!

One discontinued Clydes' tradition I did query with Ian was that of having a piano in the rhythm section. The lack of a pianist, I respectfully suggested, gave the band a thinner-sounding foundation than had ever been associated with it before. Ian's response was swift and to-the-point: 'If a no-piano back line is good enough for Chris Barber, it's good enough for me!' No comment was invited, so none was made.

* * * * *

CHAPTER TWENTY-SIX

'SUMMERTIME, AND THE LIVING IS... UNEASY'

Fortunately, a tradition that wasn't being abandoned was the Clydes' annual 'summer season'. The Isle of Arran is often described as 'Scotland in miniature', boasting Highlands and Lowlands and many other scenic attributes of the mainland, all contained within a comparatively small package. Sitting serene and majestic in the Firth of Clyde some fifteen miles off the Ayrshire coast, Arran had a total population back then of about four thousand souls, more than half living in the villages of Brodick, Lamlash and Whiting Bay, which border their respective crescents of sand on the east side of the island.

Sparsely populated, tranquil and contentedly unhip, Arran was also a potential gold mine for a professional jazz band like the Clyde Valley Stompers. Paradoxical? Not in the days before cheap package holidays made it possible for the man in the street to fly off with his family to Spain for a couple of weeks every summer. In the early Sixties, it was still the long-observed custom of Clydesiders, and those who lived in the still-thriving industrial conurbations around Glasgow, to take their annual break 'doon the watter' at one of the Firth of Clyde's bustling resorts. But, unlike Dunoon, Rothesay and Largs, the seaside villages of Arran were the very antithesis of 'bustling'. In fact, there was no source of organised entertainment on the island at all. Hence Ian Menzies' shrewd decision to base the Clyde Valley Stompers there for the best part of two months every summer.

The plan was simple: hire the village halls of Brodick, Lamlash and Whiting Bay for the season, and play for dancing in each one, night about, week in, week out. Gold mine! The potential wasn't immediately obvious to me when we arrived on the island at the end of June, but when the Glen Sannox ferry from the Ayrshire port of Ardrossan unloaded its first human cargo onto Brodick pier a few days later, the shape of things to come could not have been clearer. An invasion of a vast, fun-hungry army had been launched. The 'Fair Fortnight' is how the folk of Glasgow and its neighbouring towns referred to their respective two weeks of summer respite. The first of those, at the beginning of July, was the Greenock Fair, followed for the second two weeks of the month by the Glasgow Fair itself, with the Paisley Fair succeeding that at the start of August. Half of Scotland's five million population reside in what is loosely referred to as Greater Glasgow, and it seemed at times as if half of that number had taken possession of sleepy wee Arran during the summer of 1961.

Accommodation was at a premium, with local householders letting out every available room. Accordingly, the band's lodgings in Lamlash had been arranged well in advance by Ian, or perhaps more likely by his wife Janet. The Menzies family had been assigned a spacious Victorian villa, Malky and Bill and their families two small terraced cottages, while Jim, Robbie and I shared an attic room in a little house belonging to an elderly spinster by the name of Hyslop. When I say an attic 'room', a truer description would be 'loft storage space', low-roofed, part-floored, lit by one small skylight and accessible by ladder. No staircase. No beds – just mattresses on bare floorboards. The only toilet facilities consisted of a ground-floor bathroom shared with the holidaymakers who occupied the house's only two proper bedrooms. Miss Hyslop herself, as was common practice among local house owners, lived for the duration of 'The Fairs' in a comfortably fitted-out garden shed.

Many were the nights, drenched in sweat after playing to a packed village hall, that we three loft-dwellers would gladly have swapped our cramped, stuffy quarters for the comparative luxury of Miss Hyslop's hut. But we didn't complain to Ian. After all, we were the band juniors, and only had ourselves to consider. Accommodation was scarce, so if compromises had to be made, it was our lot to make them. Besides, we were being paid our full wages for spending a couple of months playing jazz on a beautiful holiday island, with only three or four miles to travel between gigs. Truly, what was there to complain about?

Mind you, that didn't stop me from asking myself if I would have expected my own band members to live in such conditions during our two months in Germany. I most certainly would not, nor would the clubs' owners. Still, that was then, and this was now. Two entirely different sets of circumstances, which needed to be regarded accordingly. And to be fair, we weren't often asked to play more than the customary two sets per night. Very few rehearsals were called, and those only to brush up on the routines of a few of the band's old warhorses. It did seem a bit odd that so much free time wasn't being made use of to develop new material, but we took it that this was Ian's way of giving us a well-earned breather before starting the grind of touring again in the autumn.

Much as I was enjoying the Arran experience, I had now been away from home for six months, so the highlight of the entire summer season was when Ellie came for a weekend visit.

She was accompanied by my folks (her mother wouldn't have allowed her to make the trip unchaperoned!) and this made the reunion all the more pleasurable. As it does when good things are happening, time flew. Yet I hadn't realised how much I'd missed Ellie until waving her goodbye from Brodick Pier when the Glen Sannox sailed away two days later. I promised that, no matter how busy the band's schedule might be in future, I would find some way of getting back to Scotland to see her without ever having to wait so long again. Even if I believed that parting does make the heart grow fonder, I suspected I'd already put the saying to more rigorous tests than was either fair or prudent!

One evening towards the end of July, and thus the conclusion of the Glasgow Fair fortnight, the boys and I were having a customary pre-gig refreshment in the White House Hotel in Lamlash. Ian, as was his wont, hadn't joined us. Eventually, the topic of breaking attendance records came up. According to Malky and Bill, who had 'done' Arran before, this year's nightly turnouts in all three village halls had outstripped anything they had witnessed previously. Even on relatively quiet nights, the venues had been filled to near-capacity. This led to speculation about how much money was being taken at the door. We knew the admission prices and could fairly accurately estimate the crowd sizes, so it didn't require a great flair for mental arithmetic to calculate what the average nightly take might be. It was impressive. All of this money, minus the modest cost of hall hire, went straight into Ian's pocket. Which, on the face of it, was fair enough, since he had taken the gamble in the first place.

For all that, and human nature being what it is, a consensus was arrived at whereby a bonus ought to be paid to the band members as a reward for our part in consistently attracting such large numbers of paying customers. Tellingly, it was the two senior guys, Malky and Bill, who had been the prime movers of this discussion, and it was they who appointed me as the one best qualified to put the proposition to Ian. 'You bein' an ex-bandleader yersel', so tae speak,' Malky reasoned. 'Aye, just you see what Big Ming says,' agreed Bill. 'You havin' the right patter an' that.'

Suitably persuaded, I did the deed the very next day. 'I hope you don't mind me mentioning this,' I said after exchanging small talk with Ian at his front door, 'but the boys were hoping that, you know, because attendances at the dances have been so good, maybe a wee bonus at the end of the season could be –'

Ian cut my entreaty short with a slow, deliberate shake of his head. 'All that matters is for me to stay solvent. End of story, Pete.'

As with my earlier query regarding the possible addition of a pianist to the line-up, no comment was invited, so none was made.

I duly advised the boys that there would be no bonus, period. The news was greeted with silent shrugs of resignation all round. Only Ian knew his financial state, so we weren't in a position to query it. He paid our wages, and as long as he was able to do so, we had no reason to beef. That was the deal – take it or leave it. And Ian seemed confident that, even if we thought it was all a bluff, we wouldn't call it. All said and done, none of us was so inclined anyway. We respected Big Ming and trusted him. Equally, though, we took a pride in our own work, so would continue to do everything asked of us to help maintain the Clyde Valley Stompers' reputation as Scotland's premier jazz band. And Ian Menzies was well aware of that.

We were due to play our last date of the Arran season on a Friday night, catching the final ferry of the week to Ardrossan the next day. This would allow ample time for us to drive down to London for a club engagement on the Sunday evening. But

Ian told us a few days beforehand that the plans were to be changed. Because the island was still unusually busy, he had decided it would be a good idea to play one extra date – in Brodick on the Saturday night. However, as he had to fly to London for a business meeting that day, it would be necessary for us to play the gig without him. Meanwhile, he'd have taken the bandwagon (with his family on board) over to the mainland on the Saturday ferry, leaving it at Ardrossan for us to pick up when we got there the next morning.

The only snag, he pointed out, was that no ferries sailed on Sundays. Not to worry, though – he had arranged for a private charter vessel to take us over to Ardrossan instead. Problem solved.

Stirred by visions of opulence, we turned up on Brodick pier at seven o'clock on the Sunday morning. And what a beautiful morning it was. The sun was shining in a cloudless sky over the mirror-like waters of the Firth of Clyde. Even the strident cry of the Brodick seagulls sounded uncommonly soothing. Indeed, we couldn't have hoped for a more magical end to our two months on Arran. Then we saw the so-called private charter vessel. It was a twenty-foot lobster boat, open-decked, except for a tiny fibreglass cabin up near the sharp end. We recognised the 'skipper' as the proprietor of a local hotel: a colourful character, better known as a sociable bar host than a seafarer.

'Don't worry lads,' he called out, noting our anxious looks, 'she's a grand wee boatie, so she is, and she's been doing this crossing more years than the Glen Sannox herself. Aye, and we might even beat her sailing time today.' He gestured seawards. 'Flat as a witch's tit. Should be in Ardrossan in under an hour.'

Twenty minutes later, his grand wee boatie was being tossed around like a ping-pong ball in a washing machine. A south-westerly gale had blown up without warning. Not unusual in these waters, according to our skipper. Now he tells us! But we should fear not, he said. We would just go with the wind, so we would, and everything would be fine again in a wee while.

Not quite. The storm whipped the sea into thirty-foot breakers, relentlessly thrusting our boat skyward to topple askew into the deep troughs between the waves.

'Neptune's big dipper ride!' yelled the skipper, his face fixed in a pained grin as he fought the tiller.

With the deck awash and bucking every which way, Bill and Robbie were slithering about in a brave attempt to move the double bass and drum kit into the shelter of the cabin. The rest of us were already in there.

'Leave the bull fiddle and bass drum where they are!' bellowed the skipper. 'There's no life raft, so we might need them yet!'

That's when even those of us not religiously inclined began to pray – into the half bottle of whisky Malky produced from his trumpet case. But matters only got worse. As the storm grew fiercer, someone noticed an object appearing briefly on the crest of a wave ahead of us, only to disappear for a few moments before rising to the summit of the next wind-whipped ridge.

'It's an upturned yacht,' shouted the skipper. 'See, there's a man holding onto the keel!' With that, he wrestled the helm in an attempt to pull alongside the stricken vessel. But to no avail. We were swept past, close enough to see the panic on the sailor's face, but too far off to throw him a line.

'We'll need to turn about,' the skipper yelled through the lashing rain.

Turn about? Even the most unnautical of landlubbers knew that presenting a craft sideways to mountainous seas like these was to invite disaster.

'Ye'll get us all drowned!' Bill shrieked.

'Maybe,' the skipper shouted back, 'but first rule of the sea … must go to the aid of a fellow mariner in distress.'

Jim was now ready to throw up. 'We are *not* fuckin' mariners, man! We're jazz *musicians*!'

'Aye, too true!' Malky gasped between slugs of whisky. 'Leave the yachtie guy where he is, admiral. He's managin' fine on his tod!'

Paying no heed, the skipper swung the boat broadside to the waves. For minutes that seemed a lifetime, we were flung about mercilessly, the sea breaking over us as if daring this puny little tub to stay afloat.

'Maybe we'd better radio the coastguard!' Robbie called out in desperation.

'What radio?' was the skipper's chilling reply.

So, no life raft, not even one Mae West, as far as a panicky rummage through the cabin had been able to establish, and now no radio either. Some private charter vessel! But what its owner lacked in the provision of survival gear, he more than made up for in a sense of succour – or, as it seemed to us at the time, suicidal tendencies.

Call it what you may, he did succeed in turning the boat about, ploughing its bows through the onrushing tide to reach the hapless yachtsman and, unaided, heaving him aboard. He had saved a man's life, and we applauded him for that. However, our admiration quickly turned to censure when, having repeated the highly risky manoeuvre of turning about, he tied a tow rope to the upturned hull and attached it to the stern of his own boat. Our warnings regarding the likely dire outcome of this action fell on deaf ears.

'Second rule of the sea, lads … make the salvaging of a stricken vessel a priority.'

But surely not, we objected en masse, if that risked turning the salvaging vessel into a stricken one as well. Undaunted, our intrepid life-saver allowed the gale to re-set us on our earlier course. Just as we had predicted, every time we descended into a hollow between waves, the yacht's hull would appear at the crest of the following one, to come surfing down at speed into the blunt end of our skipper's pride and joy. We lost count of how often this happened in the two hours we remained at the mercy of the elements. But, knocked about as the back end of our boat had become, we eventually arrived on the mainland in more or less one piece.

'Third rule of the sea, lads … never question the seamanship of your captain.'

There was no answer to that.

As well as trebling the estimated duration of our voyage, the storm had carried us to Largs, eleven miles farther up the Ayrshire coast than intended. Although our overriding reaction was one of thankfulness for having survived a potentially fatal ordeal, I sensed an underlying feeling of resentment too. No-one said as much when we eventually piled into taxis to take us to the bandwagon Ian Menzies had left in Ardrossan the previous day, but I guessed we were all thinking the same thing: we sincerely hoped the income from that extra gig in Brodick last night had been sufficiently vital to the state of his solvency for him to have risked reducing the Clyde Valley Stompers to a trombone-playing one-man band.

* * * * *

CHAPTER TWENTY-SEVEN

'FOLLOW MY LEADER'

In no time, we had become so accustomed to the slog of one-nighters again that it seemed as if those two refreshing months on Arran had never happened. All roads appear the same in the dark, and even in daylight the back end of one lorry looks pretty much like any other. Same goes for hotels: you see one twin-bedded room with a wash basin in the corner and you've seen them all. Even the travelling sales reps you nod to at breakfast time have the same glazed, why-am-I-here? look about them. We probably mirrored it at that ungodly hour. But instead of cold-calling on business folk to try and flog them stuff they really didn't want, at least we had the buzz of playing for appreciative audiences to look forward to. The music – that's what it was all about, and the joy of playing it made everything else seem unimportant.

Having said that, one niggling side-issue of travelling so much was the problem of finding time to look for permanent lodgings in London, especially at an affordable price. Continuing to pay Mrs Curwood for the relative home-from-home comfort of her rooms in Finchley was no longer feasible, given that we'd only occupy them for a few nights every month. On one occasion, we had even taken up an offer from a married couple – old fans of the band – to share two rooms in their Brent council house. But there were five of us, plus four members of the family (two of them teenage daughters!), only one bathroom, and the head of the house was a postman, regularly going out to work when we were coming back in.

In spite of their proximity to Cricklewood, where Ian Menzies still maintained his family home, the Brent digs were never likely to be a long-term solution. Nor were some other accommodation ideas the boys came up with themselves. One even involved dossing down on an old door suspended over the stair well of a cafe in North Finchley. A sure cure for sleepwalking!

Anyhow, against difficult odds, the band's sidemen were doing their utmost to find acceptable places to live in London. But the root of the problem was money, and more critically the equitable apportionment of it. After all, the Clyde Valley Stompers were reputed to be one of the top-earning jazz bands in Britain. This was a thorny subject, and one liable to persist, despite my attempt to broach it being stonewalled back on Arran.

The matter became potentially irrelevant, however, when we were called into the London offices of the band's agent Lyn Dutton only a week or so after the end of the summer season. When Jim, Robbie, Bill and I arrived in the Great Chapel Street premises, Lyn had already been joined by Ian Menzies and, to our surprise, trumpeter Malky Higgins. It was obvious from the tense atmosphere that we were about to be informed of something we might not necessarily like. But this in no way prepared us for what was coming.

Ian was first to speak, and he didn't beat about the bush. In his usual deadpan way, he said he had decided to retire, giving up the band to run a boarding house on the Channel

Island of Jersey. He added that this was something he had been contemplating 'for a wee while now.'

I bet it was! I was immediately struck by the thought that this decision must already have been in the making when I was invited to join the band – and probably long before that. With upmarket Jersey's strict rules on property-purchase, setting-up of businesses and, most crucially, the requisite financial circumstances of would-be 'settlers', such a move could hardly have been prepared and budgeted for in a hurry.

Suddenly, a whole jumble of incongruities began to fall into place: Ian Menzies' decision not to replace the band's singer and pianist; the hurried recording sessions for Pye (the musicians' fees for which would have been trousered by Ian); his sanctioning of the sub-standard taping of the Worthing concert to be released as an LP on Ember (presumably for an advance royalty, also payable to Ian); billeting Robbie, Jim and me in a cramped, airless attic on Arran; arranging for the band to play that one extra gig on the island; putting our lives at risk by not hiring appropriate transportation back to the mainland next day. On top of all those 'savings', he had managed to find the funds to buy himself an expensive car, to lease a comfortable family home in London (while the other married members of his band were obliged to leave their families behind in Glasgow), and even to rent conspicuously superior accommodation for his own family on Arran.

Yet he'd told me the most important thing was to keep *him* solvent. And I, like the other boys, had believed – somewhat naively as it now began to look – that such 'prudent' monetary management was primarily for the long-term good of the band.

Lyn Dutton, a dapper, neatly-built man in his forties, had been watching our reactions to Ian's pronouncement. 'Don't look so worried, boys,' he said through a puff of cigar smoke, 'the Clydes aren't going to fold. I've checked with the main promoters concerned, and they've agreed to honour all engagements currently on the band's date sheet. And before you ask – yes, you'll be on the same wages as at present.'

That was a relief. For a minute, I'd feared we were destined for the dole.

Lyn glanced down at his cigar, rolled it slowly between finger and thumb, smiled at each of us in turn and added, 'On the same wages, for as long as the band keeps up its present level of earning, that's to say.'

He went on to explain that the Clyde Valley Stompers were now a registered company, with himself, Ian Menzies and his wife Janet as its directors. We musicians, from now on, would be employees of the company. With a slightly enquiring note, Lyn then said he presumed we'd find this acceptable, knowing very well that we had little choice. As with Ian's refusal to pay us a bonus on Arran, it was a take-it-or-leave-it situation.

However, there were two other elements to consider now: who would be the new bandleader, and who would play trombone? Before anyone asked, Ian told us that, because Malky was the most senior member of the band, it had been decided that he would assume the leadership. Nods and shrugs of assent exchanged by Jim, Bill, Robbie and me indicated that we were happy with that. Malky, on the other hand, sat staring at the floor, just as he'd been doing since the start of the meeting; and I reckoned I knew why.

Back in the Thirties, the American jazz pianist Jess Stacey was quoted as saying, in relation to his boss Benny Goodman: 'When a guy becomes a bandleader, he automatically becomes a prick. Automatically.' It would be comforting to think that this wasn't *always* so, and it certainly would never have been in Malky Higgins' case. As cheery as he was chubby, Malky didn't have a malicious, selfish or devious bone in his body. Although he originally trained as a painter and decorator, Malky had been born to play music, and as a Dixieland trumpeter he ranked with the best, anywhere, including America. But being a brilliant musician doesn't necessarily qualify you for coping with the responsibilities and hassles of leading a band.

It emerged later that Malky had been summoned to the Dutton office ahead of us, so that the proposition of taking over the band's leadership could be put in circumstances that allowed him to make up his mind without being influenced by the presence of his peers. Fine sentiments, and perhaps they were genuine enough. However, Malky was unashamedly deferential towards Ian Menzies and totally loyal. Even if instinct told him that being a bandleader wasn't for him, he would have felt he was letting Ian, and himself, down by not accepting the offer. Hence his uncharacteristically downcast mien during the meeting.

The four of us who were now to be *his* sidemen realised this and assured Malky we'd back him to the hilt in his new role. Nevertheless, and without prejudging Malky's leadership abilities, we were aware that the band might be heading for choppy waters once again. The best we could do for now was pull together and hope for the best.

*

One unexpected plus to come from Ian's decision to give up was his replacement by trombonist John McGuff, who had played in my own band during our two months in Germany. John, like Jim, had been left in the lurch when I joined the Clydes, so having the opportunity to team up with him again gave me a really good feeling. It was Ian himself who suggested that I should ask John if he wanted the job. Credit where it's due, this was a truly magnanimous gesture on Big Ming's part: proposing to have himself, a fairly run-of-the-mill trombone player, succeeded by one of the best in the business.

And what a difference it made to the sound of the band, not to speak of the sensation John's playing caused when he made his debut on the London jazz scene. At the end of his first gig with the Clydes in Jazzshows club, he was the toast of the Blue Posts pub, hailed by jazz fans and fellow musicians alike. Where, they all wondered, had this twenty-nine-year-old trombone wizard been hiding for so long? John, in his quiet, unassuming way, took it all in his stride. Never having based his playing on anyone in particular (I don't think he'd ever bothered listening to records of the trombone 'greats' all that much), John was a true original, with a flexibility of technique and tone that allowed him be equally at ease playing with the controlled silkiness of Jack Teagarden or the take-no-prisoners aggression of Abe Lincoln.

Putting John McGuff and Malky Higgins together in a Dixieland front line was like setting up a fireworks display. Light the touch paper and stand back! This inspirational spark kindled the rhythm section into producing a new kind of 'heat' as well, even though the lack of a piano continued to deprive it of an essential catalyst – now more than ever. But to counterbalance this, the band was having fun, both in making music with a new-found vitality and in travelling together in the bandwagon again. The schoolmaster had left the room.

Then the reality of being a bandleader hit Malky. Though ever a vivacious and gregarious character on stage, it soon became apparent that Malky's ability to communicate easily with an audience was restricted to his playing. Even announcing numbers made him feel awkward. I knew from my own experience how scary this can be, to such an extent that it takes your mind off the job in hand, which is to concentrate on melding musically with the other guys in the band. But while I'd had the good fortune to learn the ropes in little back-of-beyond places like Longyester Hall, Malky had been thrown straight in at the deep end at some of the country's biggest and most prestigious venues. After adding the headaches that can be involved in everyday chores like mustering the boys for band calls, dealing with promoters, looking after finances on the road, booking hotels, arranging rehearsals, providing advance musical details for broadcasts, and, as a matter of utmost importance, keeping in regular touch with the Lyn Dutton Agency, Malky found himself so far out of his comfort zone that he was left with only one place to go. Just two weeks after Ian Menzies' departure, Malky Higgins announced that he was following suit. He was heading back to Glasgow, to his wife and young family. He was going home.

As if this weren't enough bad news, the Dutton office chose the same day to inform us that Pye Records had decided not to renew the band's contract. All of a sudden, though perhaps not *entirely* out of the blue, the very survival of the Clyde Valley Stompers looked to be at risk.

* * * * *

CHAPTER TWENTY-EIGHT

'A WHIRLWIND
OF CHANGE'

'Health issues' had been the reason for Ian Menzies giving up playing, according to the press release issued by publicist Neville Nisse. Still a few months shy of his thirtieth birthday, Big Ming had never given any indication to the members of his band that he was in any way poorly. Nor did he seem to suffer from 'tour fatigue' any more than the rest of us, even while shouldering the extra weight of being the leader. In any event, he appeared to be as fit as a fiddle when he flew back from sunny Jersey a fortnight into his 'retirement'. He caught up with the band in Bristol, our base during a short tour of the West Country.

After exchanging genial, though brief, greetings with everyone, he suggested that he and I should have a 'wee chat' in private. Lyn Dutton had left a message for me at the hotel's reception desk the night before, informing me that Ian's visit was primarily to talk to me about the band's 'current situation'. It wasn't difficult to guess what was coming, although one particular detail of the proposition *would* catch me unawares.

Gone was the aloofness that was Ian's abiding trait, even when purporting to be 'one of the boys'. Likewise, his usual big-brotherly demeanour had softened to one of almost toady mateyness. I could have been forgiven for treating what followed as the slippery spiel of just another snake oil salesman, but I still admired Ian Menzies for what he had achieved, and I would always be grateful to him for having asked me to join the Clyde Valley Stompers in the first place. He was barely ten years older than me, but when you're twenty, ten years is half a lifetime. I looked up to him.

Ian got straight to the point. Without actually mentioning Malky by name, he said the recent leadership 'experiment' had been undertaken with the best of intentions. No slight against my background as a bandleader had been intended. However, as things hadn't worked out as hoped, it was obvious that the wrong choice had been made. Now, all three of the company's directors were of the opinion that I should take over fronting the band, with immediate effect. 'Assuming,' he added with a teasing smile, which almost succeeded in masking a note of condescension, 'that leading the Clyde Valley Stompers would be something you'd consider doing, Pete?'

We both knew very well, of course, that the only way to maintain a viable continuation of the band's public image would be for one of the remaining members to take Malky's place at the helm. And I just happened to be the one who had enough experience, albeit debatably, to assume responsibility for getting a rapidly listing ship back on an even keel. Some might have substituted 'foolhardiness' for 'experience', and not without justification. But what choice did I have? If I baulked at this challenge, I'd risk putting myself back on the same scrapheap that joining the Clydes had rescued me from, *and* I'd be failing the other lads – for the second time, in the case of Jim Douglas and John McGuff.

While I shared Ian Menzies' desire to save the Clyde Valley Stompers' name from extinction, safeguarding the livelihood of those of us now about to be charged with the undertaking was of equal importance. So, since one objective could not be achieved without the other, I had no hesitation in taking up the gauntlet, though with a considerable degree of trepidation, which I tried hard not to reveal to Ian.

His usual self-assurance swiftly regained, he then informed me he had decided to sell *his* bandwagon, as it was now 'getting too old to be reliable'. In any case, he thought it better for the band to travel in two separate vehicles, just as it had done in the final months of his leadership. I had never quite grasped the logic of this, and I was about to say so, when Ian came out with a suggestion that both cut me off at the pass and took me completely by surprise.

He and his fellow directors had devised a plan which would provide me with the security of a personal asset, while also allowing the Clyde Valley Stompers 'company' to manage its finances in the most efficient way: I would buy a car, which the company would rent from me, for a weekly sum that would cover my hire purchase payments *and* provide me with a mileage allowance to take care of wear-and-tear. At the same time, the company would purchase a small van to replace the old minibus as a means of transporting the band's instruments and baggage.

I couldn't see any more sense in this arrangement than the one it was emulating, but Big Ming Menzies hadn't gained a reputation for being the most persuasive of characters without good reason. Not being a particularly talented player, cajolery had probably been his most effective stock-in-trade as a leader of sidemen who, in notable instances over the years, had possessed more musical ability than he did himself.

Be that as it may, he certainly succeeded in talking me into buying a car I neither could afford nor actually needed. By the time he left for Jersey later that same day (which would turn out to be the last time I'd ever see or have any contact with Ian Menzies), I was the owner of a nearly-new Ford Zephyr Six saloon – or, more accurately, the signatory to a three-year hire-purchase agreement on said vehicle. Once my head had stopped spinning, my immediate summing-up of the situation was that Ian had seen this as a way of tying me to the band, at least for the immediate future. But a few more moments of thought pooh-poohed that idea.

For where was I likely to go, even without the millstone of car payments round my neck? I didn't kid myself that Ian really believed I'd have any better offers than the one he'd just made me. So, there had to be another reason for his sweet-talking me into buying this car. When the penny finally dropped, I tried to convince myself I hadn't been sold a large bottle of snake oil after all. Yet it seemed the most likely explanation. Big Ming realised there was a very good chance the band might not survive its current state of turmoil. If promoters and fans took exception to yet another change in personnel and leadership, the Clyde Valley Stompers would be finished. And who would be left burdened with any debt still outstanding on the Ford Zephyr Six?

No, I told myself, no-one could be devious enough to dream up such a dodge. Then I saw what had been bought as a replacement for the band's minibus. It was a little Hillman Minx Estate Car, at *least* as long in the tooth as the 'old' bandwagon, in no better condition and, with only a comparatively small motor under the bonnet, less well equipped for the long and arduous journeys it was intended for tackling. If the minibus had been traded in for this without a financial inducement in Ian's favour, he had been taken for a mug. But, as was becoming ever more apparent, Ian Menzies protected his pennies too jealously for there to have been much likelihood of that happening.

*

Stepping into Malky Higgins' shoes was always going to be difficult for any trumpet player, and it seemed for a while that, despite the Dutton Agency's best efforts, none capable was going to be found. The first given the opportunity was George Patterson. He hailed from Glasgow, which the company believed, understandably, to be a Clyde Valley Stompers link worth prioritising. No-one could fault George's musicianship, but in a touring band social compatibility is just as important as musical competence. George was destined not to last.

Then there were a couple of trumpeters whose names I forget, but who, for all they knew about the Clydes and the type of music we played, might just as well have been picked from a line in Archer Street, the time-honoured Soho hang-out of musicians touting for work. One, when asked what jazz tunes he knew, said, 'Well, er ... there's *Tangerine*,' while the other replied, 'I, uhm, can just about handle *Perdido*.' Both of these numbers are about as far removed from the traditional jazz idiom as *Handel's Largo*. But the guys meant well, did their best and we made it surprisingly painlessly through the few gigs they were involved in. On the whole, in fact, we had a fair amount of fun trying out replacements for Malky Higgins.

The one seriously negative experience encountered was when, during the interval at a dance engagement in London's Brunel College, we returned to the band room and found the current try-out trumpeter going through the pockets of our street clothes, swiping money from wage packets delivered by the Dutton Agency before the start of the gig. Musicians are not usually noted for their propensity to physical violence, but I can honestly say the boys and I had to muster every ounce of our self-restraint to avoid sending that chancer away with his teeth in his hands. (He wore dentures, as I recall.)

Only much later did we find out he was known in his home town as 'Dipper'.

*

Wisely, the Dutton office had decided not to repeat the publicity blitz they'd organised to announce Malky Higgins taking over leadership of the Clydes. For fear of the main promoters taking fright and cancelling en bloc those engagements already confirmed for months ahead, the agency's ploy was to let news of the latest change spread as unobtrusively as possible. But it was a forlorn hope. Tongues were soon wagging, and not necessarily in the most positive of ways. Not long after Malky's departure, we turned up for a jazz club gig at the Wooden Bridge roadhouse in Guildford to be informed by promoter Jack Stokes that veteran bassist Micky Ashman, whose band had played there immediately before us, had advised the audience of our forthcoming appearance with the somewhat snide aside: 'Yeah, and I wonder who'll be leading 'em *this* week!'

Fortunately, Jack Stokes turned out to be just one of the many promoters who believed this new Clyde Valley Stompers incarnation deserved a chance to prove its worth without prejudgement, to let the fans decide whether or not the band earned the right to survive, irrespective of who was fronting it. And it's to the credit of all those people that our efforts were never subjected to the type of summary dismissal Micky Ashman had meted out. For my own part, all he had done was make me more determined than ever to prove such doubters wrong.

Throughout this testing period, our most significant saving grace was the ability to see the bright side of difficulties that came our way. Playing jazz is fun, and we weren't about to let matters beyond our control get in the way of that. In retrospect, it was probably the communication of this positive mood to the public that contributed more than anything to the band's survival.

But survival wasn't enough. The band had to be transformed from the glorified pick-up group that, by necessity, it had become. Building a stable and musically distinctive line-up around the remaining nucleus had to be done while the support of promoters and fans lasted. Time was of the essence. Although finding an adequate and permanent replacement for Malky Higgins remained a priority, the addition of a piano to the rhythm section was absolutely essential to supporting the beefy, free-swinging sound the band was now capable of creating. I made a point of saying this to Lyn Dutton at the first opportunity.

Lyn was absolutely unequivocal in his reply: 'Can't budget for that unless we lose somebody from the payroll.'

I was equally frank in my response: 'Well, cutting back on the number of musicians would be a step in the wrong direction, and there's *no*-one else on the payroll … that I'm aware of anyway?'

Gazing down at his cigar, Lyn rolled it between middle finger and thumb in his usual pensive way. 'There's your publicist,' he said, looking up with one eyebrow raised.

'Neville Nisse?'

Lyn obviously gathered from my tone that I thought he'd hit on a possible solution. 'He's done some pretty good things for the Clydes in the past, though, you know.'

I was about to say that 'producing' a horrific live album at Worthing wasn't one of them, but decided against it. No point in opening *that* can of worms at this stage of the game.

'You mean *he*'s on the same wages as the *boys*?'

Lyn nodded his head behind a billow of cigar smoke. 'More or less.'

That clinched it for me. 'Time enough to hire a PR man when the band's ready for publicising. And getting it into that state means spending any available money on the right musicians.' I looked Lyn squarely in the eye. 'We need to hire a piano player.'

He pulled an impassive shrug. 'OK, if that's what you want, I'll let Neville know, and we'll cast the net for a pianist.'

After leaving Dutton's Great Chapel Street office, I had only walked a few yards towards Tottenham Court Road tube station, when I was tapped roughly on the shoulder.

'You're a fucking schmuck! A fucking Scotch schmendrick!'

Although not a Yiddish speaker myself, I could tell that Neville Nisse wasn't paying me any compliments.

'Bad news travels fast,' I said.

'I was in the room next to Lyn's, so it didn't have to travel far, you back-stabbing Jock schmo!'

I was being insulted fairly vehemently, and without due reason, in my considered opinion. My instinct was to ask this foaming-at-the-mouth candidate for a heart attack if being obnoxious came naturally to him, or if he got up early and practiced. However, he was twice my age, and showing respect for my elders – even those who didn't deserve it – was a principle I hadn't abandoned.

'Lang may yer lum reek wi' ither folk's coal,' I smiled. 'That's *Scotch* for "good luck", by the way.'

While Neville continued to pollute the Oxford Street air with Old Testament curses, I offered him my hand – which he rejected – then went on my way. Lesson learned? Hell hath no fury like a PR man scorned. But all I really cared about right then was that PR men were a lot thicker on the ground than good jazz pianists. I could live with being a fucking Scotch schmuck.

* * * * *

CHAPTER TWENTY-NINE

'CLYDE VALLEY, I PRESUME?'

Ellie and I got engaged while sitting on a wall overlooking the seal enclosure at Edinburgh Zoo. It was feeding time.

'Anything for a round of applause,' quipped Ellie, as I opened the little velvet box.

'Nah, I've never had a reception like this – ever.'

'Maybe you should try throwing dead fish to your fans as well, then.'

'I do. They're called clarinet solos ... it's been said they smell just as bad.'

Ellie smiled, but declined to comment, her attention now fully focused on the modest but elegant curve of diamonds sparkling on the third finger of her left hand.

It was early November 1961, and the band was on a mini tour of Scotland, the first time we'd been back on home turf since the end of our summer season on Arran, some two months earlier. We had driven 540 miles up from London the day before to play at the Two Red Shoes in Elgin for our old promoter chum Albert Bonici. On arrival, we'd crossed paths with an up-and-coming trio called the Springfields, their girl singer Dusty looking surprisingly effervescent in the midst of what they told us was a 'bloody knackering slog of one-nighters.' Tell us about it! Four nights later we'd be back in London, having crammed in a TV appearance and three more whistle-stop gigs en route.

And now, here I was, cramming in yet another engagement, albeit of a more personal nature. Since the day I'd left for Germany almost a year earlier, my courtship with Ellie had been conducted mainly by letter. She had limited access to a phone in the nurses' residence at the hospital, and I was nearly always on the move. So, if we wanted to hear each other's voice, it was a case of my finding a convenient call box at a time when Ellie *might* be off duty. The two conditions didn't coincide all that often. Nevertheless, our relationship grew stronger. Although we were very young – Ellie still just eighteen and I not yet twenty-one – making a formal commitment to tying the knot some day seemed the natural thing to do. It hadn't even taken much talking about. And both sets of parents, while perhaps more apprehensive than surprised, gave our decision their blessing.

Why choose Edinburgh Zoo for the big occasion? We had bought the ring a little earlier in a jeweller's shop near the famous Greyfriar's Bobby statue in Edinburgh, stopping off there en route to Glasgow, where the band was due to play at a students' ball that night. Edinburgh Zoo is located on the Glasgow road out of Edinburgh, and it caught the eye in passing as a place with enough space to afford us a reasonable measure of privacy. It served the purpose, that round of applause from the seals aside.

*

'Don't worry, Pete, ye've still got time to leave the country!' So advised trombonist John McGuff on the bandstand at Glasgow Uni. We were in the middle of playing a sprightly number to a packed dance floor, when Ellie and John's wife Janet came shimmying past the front of the stage. They were plastered.

'Babycham!' beamed Ellie, pie-eyed. She was waving her hands above her head. 'Blabyslam! Been – *burp*! – jinking it wiz Dranet!'

'Proper champers too!' Janet put in, waving the evidence above *her* head. 'Sum'dy gave us ziz borrle!'

I knew Ellie didn't drink, at all. I also knew that Janet did, quite fluently when the occasion warranted, as the occasion of Ellie's betrothal patently had. It followed that, students being students, the sight of bubbly being quaffed in their bar gave the clue to something being celebrated. And, Glasgow students being Glasgow students, the two celebrators had soon been joined by a group of warm-hearted supporters. The result was grinning vacantly up at me as Jim Douglas belted out the last chorus of, ironically, *I Want A Gal Just Like The Gal That Married Dear Old Dad*.

'Aye, head for the coast, Pete,' John McGuff shouted in my ear, 'and don't look back!'

If John and Janet hadn't been the happiest of couples (in or out of their cups), I might have taken him seriously. Instead, as with all the other unforeseen happenings that had been sent to try me of late, I tried to see the bright side of this one.

'Never again,' Ellie moaned, opening the car window as I drove homeward at the end of the gig. 'Never, *ever* again!'

I remembered having sworn that very oath myself after throwing up over her mothers' fence at Hogmanay two years earlier. Ellie now switched the order of the same routine by puking out of the window, the car's slipstream carrying the aftermath of what should have been the most romantic day of her life into swirling oblivion. The seeds of a lifetime of sobriety had been sown.

*

Every time the band arrived at a venue, we realised we had been booked to play there on the strength of the reputation gained by the Clyde Valley Stompers before any of us, with the exception of bassist Bill Bain, had become members. We were depending on the good will of promoters in the first instance, followed by the positive response of whatever customers decided to come and hear us. It seemed we had made a pretty good account of ourselves so far, with turn-outs and audience reaction always favourable, the promise of return bookings the norm. But one aspect not to be ignored amid all these positive vibes was that the current 'Trad Boom' was still in full swing, and we were just one of many bands benefitting from the keen appetite prevailing for what was, broadly speaking, 'our type of music'. Being tagged *Scotland's Premier Jazz Band* didn't mean all that much now that we were based in London, so our ability to consolidate the Clydes' place among the elite of Britain's jazz bands was by no means a foregone conclusion. Which is where being represented by a top agency showed its worth.

*

Border Television was a relatively new addition to the network of regional Independent TV stations being established in Britain. It was also rated as one of the smallest, beaming programmes from its Carlisle studios to largely rural areas in northern England and southern Scotland; thus all too easily ignored by London booking agents. Not so Lyn Dutton, who offered the Clydes to Border TV for a guest appearance on their early-evening *Lookaround* magazine programme on our way back south from that brief Scottish tour. And a shrewd move it proved to be. It gave us valuable experience in how to present ourselves on live television and, in one three-minute spot, provided a much wider shop window for our wares than would weeks of one-night stands throughout the entire region.

This also set a precedent for the Dutton office to book us, often with little notice, onto similar TV magazine programmes during our travels in other parts of the country. The next would be in Southampton, on Southern TV's *Day by Day* local news and current affairs programme, which was also transmitted live during the peak 'teatime' viewing slot. We had just finished setting up our gear for rehearsals when the studio doors swung open and in swept a fellow of histrionic mien. Velvet jacket draped over his shoulders, he made straight for me.

'Ah, young Mr Valley,' he gushed, 'I recognised you from the pics your agent sent.' He extended his hand, limply. 'I'm Nige, your producer today. *So* pleased to meet you, Clyde!'

'No, no, don't call me Clyde, for Christ's sake!' I spluttered. 'Ian Menzies probably owns the copyright!' And I was only half kidding.

Nige was too busy eyeing up the boys to bother. 'And, uhm-ah, I take it you all wear the kilt, do you?'

I told him we didn't. 'In fact,' I said, 'we don't even wear tartan jackets any more. Too much like Bill Haley and the Comets these days … for a jazz band.'

'Balmoral bonnets, then? Tam o' Shanters? Hairy sporrans are always *very* fetching, I feel.'

No, I confessed, we didn't wear funny hats, or any other fancy-dress gimmicks currently in vogue on the trad scene. Just smart mohair suits – mid-blue with a discreet glimpse of tartan on the lapels. While Nige pursed his lips, visualising, I moved swiftly on to musical matters:

'So, did you get the bar breakdowns I sent you?'

'Bar? *Break*downs?'

'Yeah, you know – the bar-by-bar routines for the tunes we're playing on the show tonight?'

Nige's face lit up. '*Oh*! Yes, yes – I have them right here!' He pulled a folder from under his arm. 'Great idea!' He gave me a nudge and a wink. 'Absolutely *bona*, Clyde! Gonna save *so* much hassle!'

Comparing producers of local TV magazine programmes with Ted Heath (the government minister, not the bandleader) was a flash-back to my civil service experiences, which came to me a few days before the Border Television date. The chances were, I figured, that the background of these particular TV guys would be more journalistic than musical, just as Ted Heath's was more – well, *some*thing than Ministry of Labour. It would make sense, therefore, to treat the telly boys the same way as I'd treated Ted every month, by providing them in advance with a brief, easy-to-understand summary of what was at stake.

So, I'd jot down the musical arrangement as, for example:

Four bars drum intro –
Sixteen bars ensemble –
Eight bars trombone solo –
Eight bars ensemble ... and so on.

No need to read music, just the ability to count four beats to the bar.

It had worked well at Border TV, and Nige was sure the same would apply here.

'Got all the camera shots worked out already, Clyde,' he beamed. 'Gonna save *so* much rehearsal time!' Snatching a sidelong glance at Bill Bain's buttocks, he pouted again. 'Hmm, just a pity about the kilts, though...'

*

Without a current record deal, we hadn't anything specific to plug on telly. We chose evergreen jazz standards instead: nothing too hackneyed, but catchy, cheerful tunes intended to appeal to the wide range of age groups likely to be watching a general interest programme at that time of day. The integral newscasts were never liable to be without *some* doomy content, so we made a point of keeping our input light. Likewise, our approach to those feet-finding regional TV appearances was straightforward. We turned up on time; our chosen material was well prepared; we were always cooperative, no matter how travel-weary; and we made sure we were immaculately turned-out at transmission time.

It was a simple policy that paid surprisingly quick dividends.

'Fixed you a couple of network TV spots,' said Lyn Dutton a few days later. I was paying his office one of my regular visits to hand over the takings from our latest tour. 'First one's a Danny Williams special on 28th November – that's here in London. Also on the bill is Cleo Laine, branching out on her own from Johnny Dankworth's outfit. Big things are predicted for her as a solo act, so you're in good company.' Lyn's manner was so matter-of-fact he might just as well have been reading his wife's shopping list. 'Next telly date,' he went on, 'is up near Glasgow – Olympia Ballroom, East Kilbride – Scottish Television's *Hogmanay Show* on 31st December. Usual haggis-and-heather stuff, plus you guys.'

Danny Williams was a nineteen-year-old black South African singer, whose recording of *Moon River* was about to top the UK pop charts and establish him as a major international recording artist. Securing a spot for us on his special was a clever piece of business on Lyn Dutton's part. No less so was our inclusion on STV's *Hogmanay Show*, which would be beamed live throughout the country at midnight on New Year's Eve, one of the peak viewing slots of the year.

'Now, here's the Danny Williams angle,' Lyn Dutton continued, raising a conspiratorial eyebrow behind a haze of cigar smoke. 'It's scheduled for 28th November, which is…?

I thought for a few seconds. 'Well, it's my birthday, but I don't suppose that makes any diff–'

'It's your *twenty-first* birthday,' Lynn interrupted, 'and that makes *all* the difference! Think about it… Special announcement by Danny after the band's spot. Birthday congrats to you. An extra bow for the Clydes. All on prime-time telly. Would cost a fortune to *buy* that kind of exposure, you know.'

I was impressed.

But Lyn hadn't finished. Rubbing his hands together, he leaned forward over his desk. 'Right then, Pete, what kind of celebration can we tie in with the Scottish Television *Hogmanay Show* ... hmm?'

* * * * *

CHAPTER THIRTY

'FOR RICHER, FOR POORER – FOR BETTER OR FOR WORSE'

Ellie and I were married on 1st January 1962. I'd celebrated my twenty-first birthday just over a month earlier; Ellie her nineteenth a fortnight later. Our wedding took place twelve hours after the end of STV's *Hogmanay Show*, and on the first of the band's only two days off for the coming couple of months.

'I hope you don't *have* to get married,' the hospital matron had said to Ellie on the day she handed in her notice.

Ellie replied with due respect that, if what the matron was implying came to pass, she would change her name to Mary and wrap the baby in swaddling clothes.

In fairness to the matron, she had been genuinely disappointed that Ellie was giving up her nurse's training prematurely, and her response may well have been the result of past experience. But it was a clumsy approach, to which Ellie took exception.

The sense of rectitude drummed into her by her mother had been strictly observed, so the matron should save such aspersions for those who deserved it – or words to that effect. End of conversation.

And it wasn't as if Ellie had stars in her eyes either. She was level headed enough to know that life in London for the wife of a touring jazz musician would not be all glitz and glamour. More likely the reverse. Essentially a small-town girl, she would be leaving her home, friends and everything familiar to live, often alone, in a big-city environment not always noted for its warmth towards strangers. This was a source of concern for me, as was Ellie's sacrificing the independence that completing her nursing exams would have given her. But I knew her well enough to suspect that these decisions had been made because she sensed I needed her support at this crucial time in my life. Also, she was showing that she shared my spirit of now-or-never, even if it bordered on recklessness in the eyes of those with a more 'circumspect' outlook on life. We would accept the cards fate dealt us, and would play them with the dogged optimism of youth ... win or lose, for better or for worse.

I've often wondered how long we would have waited to tie the knot had Lyn Dutton not pressed me to think of a celebratory 'angle' to highlight the Clydes' appearance on that New Year's Eve television show. All I can say is that, while we certainly didn't fix the date to satisfy the promotional machinations of the band's agent, it did seem that providence had presented us with an opportunity which was ours for the taking. And Lyn's hankered-after 'angle' did also materialise, by way of the show's host, veteran broadcaster Jack House, presenting me, on-camera, with a bottle of champagne after the band's final feature.

'Congratulations, son,' he said, shaking my hand. 'Please accept this wee gift from Scottish Television, and may your married life be long, prosperous and happy.'

Old Jack kept a tight grip of my hand while the studio audience applauded. He also kept a tight grip of the bottle of bubbly, which he snatched back the moment the cameras panned away.

'Just a prop, son,' he whispered, winking. 'Gotta put it back in the stores – know what I mean?'

Later, sounds of the 'prop' popping, glasses clinking and Jack laughing heartily rang out through a dressing room window as we lugged our gear into the East Kilbride night.

'Never mind,' I told the boys, 'the champers served its purpose. In the words of our agent, it would cost a fortune to *buy* that kind of exposure!'

*

Naturally, Ellie had wanted a white wedding, and she got it – in more ways than one. The snow, which had started to fall as I drove the sixty miles back to my parents' house in the middle of the night, was covering the landscape in a crisp blanket of white by the time I got out of bed after a few hours of much-needed sleep. The ancient grounds of St Mary's Parish Church in Haddington had the appearance of a Christmas card when I arrived with Jim Douglas, who, as my best man, had helped prepare me for the coming 'performance' with a couple of nerve-settling shots of vodka. My knees were still knocking, though, and they came close to giving way altogether when Ellie arrived by my side at the altar. She looked absolutely stunning.

I don't remember much of the service, which seemed to pass in a kind of detached blur. Suddenly, Ellie and I were outside, standing with the rest of the wedding party in the arched doorway of the kirk, photographers snapping away, a group of well-wishers shouting their congratulations while showering us with confetti. The sun was shining, the snow glistening, God was in His heaven, and all was right with the world. Well, our world, for the time being, at any rate.

The wedding reception was held nearby, in the centuries-old Tyne House Hotel, which sits by the banks of the river, a mere stone's throw from Tynepark corrective school for girls, the old mansion where Jim and I had once played for the 'students' with our first band, the Hidden Town Dixielanders. Much water had passed under the River Tyne's bridges in the three intervening years. At the same time, much more than we could have imagined had happened for us as musicians, and, undaunted by the few setbacks we'd encountered along the way, we had high hopes for even better things to come.

But today was Ellie's day. She was the belle of the ball: her very own ball. In her white satin wedding dress, she looked every inch the fairy-tale princess. A princess for a day – or rather for the two hours we could afford to spend at the reception. London beckoned, with another long stretch of back-to-back engagements for the Clyde Valley Stompers due to kick off soon after we got there.

For our one-night honeymoon, I had booked a room in Yorkshire's famous Scotch Corner Hotel. Although the establishment enjoyed a good reputation for comfort and service, the choice had been made for mainly practical reasons. Scotch Corner, little more than a junction of major trunk routes on the Great North Road, may not be noted for its romantic surroundings, but it does lie approximately one-third of the way between Haddington and London, and I'd calculated that those 130 miles would be about right for the first leg of our journey.

But my plans, best-laid as they were, were soon ditched. We didn't even make it a third of the way to Scotch Corner. And it wasn't because we couldn't wait any longer to put an end to Ellie's mother's insistence on her daughter's adherence to chastity-before-marriage. Although the weather had remained unseasonably sunny all afternoon, the snow started to fall again a few minutes into our long drive south. By the time we reached the outskirts of Berwick-upon-Tweed, some forty miles from Haddington, we were unable to see anything in the beam of the car's headlights but driving snow. Then, shimmering through the white-out, there appeared an illuminated sign – *The Castle Hotel*.

I pulled over, my knuckles the colour of the snowflakes now fighting a winning battle with the windscreen wipers. 'I've had enough of this, Ellie,' I gasped. 'If there's a room available in this place – even a henhouse out the back – that'll be your bridal suite for tonight!'

Ellie gave a stoical little smile. 'I'm game … if the hens are.'

*

We arrived on the outskirts of London the following night to find that, even this far south, the streets were covered in a mantle of snow. It was Ellie's first time in the capital, and while she didn't say anything as we drove on and on through the suburbs, I imagined her feelings of adventure must have been tempered by a sizable measure of trepidation. What had she let herself in for, coming all this way to settle in a vast metropolis without knowing a solitary soul? Except, of course, her high school sweetheart, now her *husband*. And he would be away on the road for days, sometimes weeks, at a time. She'd be all by herself, lonely, and probably homesick. That, anyhow, is what I imagined she'd be thinking, but time would show me she was made of sterner stuff. And just as well too.

Collingwood Avenue in East Finchley looked pretty much the same as countless other streets that constituted the Victorian era's contribution to the urban sprawl of London: a neat, tree-lined thoroughfare of neat little terraced houses, with neat little front gardens, net-curtained bay windows and a pervading air of lower-middle-class respectability. It was the type of street where front doors would open at seven-thirty sharp every morning, and bowler-hatted clerks, rolled umbrellas and brief cases to the fore, would emerge and march off in line to take the tube to the City. Collingwood Avenue exemplified the kind of 'safe' environment in which I'd feel comfortable about leaving Ellie when I was away. So, even though the rent for the ground-floor flat I'd found for us wasn't cheap, I considered it worth every penny.

While I brought our things in from the car, I left Ellie to explore her new home. Not that there was much to explore: a living room, one bedroom, and a galley kitchen, with a worktop which could be removed to reveal a small hip bath. A toilet led directly off the kitchen. Neither of these latter two features would be permitted under hygiene regulations now, and for all I knew they may not have been then. But in London on a limited budget, you have to accept compromises.

I had already told Ellie about the kitchen-cum-bathroom quirk, and she didn't see it as a problem. Just a matter of organisation, she'd reasoned. No taking a bath when vegetables needed chopping, for instance. And anyhow, she'd be in the flat on her own much of the time, so everything would work out fine.

'Well, how do you like the pad?' I asked after I'd carried in the last of our bags.

Ellie was already rearranging some pots and pans on a shelf in the kitchen. 'Great!' she smiled. 'Yes, I'll make a home out of this all right.' Then, with a flutter of her eyelashes, she took me by the hand and led me towards the bedroom.

I made a token show of resistance. 'Don't you think we should wait until we've unpacked?'

'Would it make any difference?' she said. 'Look.'

I couldn't believe my eyes.

Ellie was trying to stifle a giggle.

'It's not funny, Ellie! There *was* a bed in here when I agreed to take the place … honest! That lousy landlord,' I muttered.

'And I paid him three months rent in advance too – *plus* fifty bloody quid damage deposit!'

Ellie was in stitches.

I was livid. 'He's not getting away with this! I'm going to phone the bugger right now!'

Unfortunately, there wasn't a phone in the flat, so I had to keep my anger on the boil while I trudged through swathes of slush to a phone box at the corner of the street. The landlord couldn't have been more apologetic, citing a wrong entry in his diary for the blunder.

'Not my problem!' I retorted. 'I rented the flat fully furnished – entry date yesterday. Now, a day later, I drive nearly five hundred miles to find you've nicked the damned kip! And me just married too!'

'Please, Mr Kerr – what can I say? I'm mortified. Look, tell you what – you and your wife can stay here at my place tonight – it isn't far – and I'll get a bed delivered as soon as –'

'Not good enough!' I barked. 'You'll be hearing from my lawyer in the morning! Goodnight!' In my present mood, the fact that I didn't have a lawyer was neither here nor there. I had put a flea in this arsehole's ear, so screw him and all thieving landlords like him. I was still mumbling curses when I got back to the flat.

Ellie was in bed – or in the next best thing, under the circumstances. She was reclining at floor level on top of what she revealed were cushions from the living room's three-piece suite. A rummage in a cupboard had produced a couple of spare sheets, pillows and a blanket. *Et voila*! Ellie was patently pleased with herself. 'Make do and mend!' she chirped.

'The story of my life,' I replied, spirits ascending. 'Welcome to the club.'

'There weren't any more cushions,' Ellie told me as I started to undress, 'so it's a bit narrow.'

'All the better for that,' I came back, my mood lightening by the second.

'Hmm, and at least it's better than a henhouse in Berwick.'

'Good attitude!' I grunted, pulling my socks off with some urgency. Then a sobering thought crossed my mind. Much as I admired Ellie's pluck, I couldn't help recalling the benediction my grandfather said farm labourers offered their wives in the bad-old days of yore: 'Blessed are they who expect nothing, for they shall not be disappointed.'

Fortunately, this fleeting rush of negativity appeared to have gone unnoticed by Ellie. 'So, how did your phone call to the landlord go?'

'Oh, *him*?' I scoffed. 'Well, I just told the old bandit straight I'd be on his case in the morning. Taking me for a mug like that...'

Ellie uttered a seductive little growl. 'Go get 'em, tiger!'

Bravado and libido duly boosted, I snuggled down beside her. 'Mmm, right enough,' I crooned, 'it is a wee bit narrow in here, isn't it?'

'All the better for that,' Ellie purred.

'Good attitude!' I murmured, this time unmolested by any restraining thoughts.

On this night of all nights, however, Cupid had decided to arm himself with mischief-tipped arrows. Just as we were about to pick up the pieces of our fractured honeymoon, a knock came to the front door. Mumbling a fresh selection of curses, I hauled on my trousers and stumbled into the hallway.

'*YES*! Who the hell is it at *this* time of night?'

'Finchley Removals, mate. Got a double bed 'ere for ya. Geezer said it was urgent.'

Cascades of giggling flowed from the bedroom as I opened the front door.

Outside, it had started to snow again.

* * * * *

CHAPTER THIRTY-ONE

'PROKOFIEV SWINGS!'

For the perpetually-itinerant Clyde Valley Stompers, those hazardous driving conditions at the start of 1962 actually resulted in life becoming easier, in a perverse kind of way. We were still travelling in two vehicles: John and Jim with the band's gear in the little Hillman estate car, the rest of the boys with me in the Ford Zephyr saloon. One late-January morning, after playing Redcar Jazz Club in the north-east of England, we set out for Kidderminster, an awkward two hundred miles to the south. The journey involved crossing the Pennines, that long upland chain which forms the 'backbone' of England and is justly famed for its scenic beauty – in summer. We knew from experience, though, that it could be a very different matter in winter, when, with little warning, roads through the high passes can be swept by blizzards. Which is precisely what happened on this occasion.

Despite our best efforts to stay in tandem, our two cars became separated. By the time the boys and I cleared the far side of the Pennines, we had no idea whether John and Jim were ahead of us, behind us, or even still on the same road. In those days before mobile phones, there was nothing else for it but to press on and hope that both segments of the band would arrive at the venue in time for the gig. Up to then, the outcome had always been positive, but this was to prove the exception to what I'd always seen as a pointlessly risk-laden rule. Unduly extravagant as well. Why be saddled with two bills for fuel, road tax, vehicle maintenance and insurance?

The scheduled end of the dance at Kidderminster had come and gone (as had several hundred dancers) before John managed to get a call through to the ballroom. He was still a hundred miles away, having been stuck for several hours in a snowbound traffic jam somewhere in the hills. Meanwhile, the ballroom manager had been going nuts about having to forfeit a whole night's takings, while the boys and I had been worried sick about what might have befallen our two chums.

'We really will have to start travelling in one bandwagon again,' I said to Lyn Dutton in his office the following day. 'It's bad enough not knowing where our mates are or whether they're alive or dead, but the band getting a reputation for not turning up for engagements is the kiss of death.'

'Hasn't happened before,' Lyn shrugged.

'No, but it'll happen again.'

'Isn't a problem for other bands on my books.'

'Yeah, but just look at the amount of time *we* spend on the road – distances between gigs too.' I tactfully added that we had no beef about the volume of work the agency put our way. It was just that I wanted our travelling arrangements to be set on a *sensible* footing, that was all.

Clearly, my forthright manner had taken Lyn by surprise. With a wry smile, he looked at me, nodding his head slowly. 'It's all a question of finance – you realise that, don't you?'

'The boys and I work hard to create the band's finances, Lyn, but it's for you to put them to best use – for all of us.'

'Meaning?'

'Meaning that keeping the boys' morale up is paramount, and creating unnecessary hassles during journeys has exactly the opposite effect. That's one reason why we need to start travelling together again – and the sooner the better!'

'And if Clyde Valley Stompers, the company, can't afford it?'

'Can't afford cutting travelling costs by half?' Now *I* gave a wry smile. 'Look, I'm not privy to details of where the band's earnings go, Lyn – all I know is what I collect in fees at the end of some gigs.' As soon as I'd said that, Lyn's expression told me I'd touched a nerve.

Yet his reaction suggested he was was more sympathetic than hostile. 'OK, Pete,' he smiled, 'you've made your point, and I'll see what can be done.'

Two days later, I was at a commercial vehicles depot in London's Ladbroke Grove, collecting the brand new Commer FC Minibus the company had hired on a fixed-term contract for the exclusive use of the band. So, my frank tête-à-tête with Lyn Dutton could hardly have had a more gratifying conclusion. All the same, the speed and relative ease with which it had been achieved surprised me. I wondered if, until now, Dutton had simply been exercising the company's authority on behalf of the other two directors, for no better reason than to remind us who 'owned' the band. This, in turn, got me thinking about whether the boys and I were getting a fair cut of the healthy income our efforts had generated since Ian Menzies' departure. But that, I judged, would be a subject for a tête-à-tête best left for another day. In the meantime, I set about finding a buyer for the Ford Zephyr.

*

Things were taking a turn for the better, and they didn't stop with the resolution of the bandwagon issue.

Tyne Tees Television in Newcastle-upon-Tyne were planning to revive a series of live music programmes they had first produced for the ITV network in 1960. While the first *Young at Heart* show had catered for a mainly teenage audience, this new version would be aimed at a slightly wider viewing target. The content would still be predominantly pop-orientated, but with a regular jazz slot, which the Clydes were invited to fill. So, for several weeks, we'd catch the Tuesday-night sleeper train from London to Newcastle, grab taxis to the TV studios in City Road, spend the day 'in rehearsal' (mostly sitting around waiting to take our turn for sound checks and dry runs), before doing our stuff live on the early-evening transmission.

It was a slickly-presented show, featuring an impressive array of current hit-makers from both sides of the Atlantic. Brenda Lee, Shirley Bassey, Bobby Vee and (once more) Danny Williams were typical of the 'names' appearing on the bill each week. Even if not on the same musical wavelength as the popsters, we were extremely grateful to be watched by the millions of viewers *they* attracted, and acutely aware that our inclusion on this peak-time programme would do more in a few weeks to raise the Clyde's profile with the general public than years of playing in clubs and dance halls had done.

The educational aspect of those visits to Newcastle was also valuable – in a slightly masochistic way. The members of Tyne Tees TV's own big band, which backed the guest singers on *Young at Heart*, were a fine bunch, both musically and socially. As we had over three hours to kill before catching the Wednesday-night sleeper back to London, a few of the Tyne Tees staff musicians always made a point of taking us for a post-show refreshment in the Egypt Cottage pub, which was conveniently located right next door to the studios. There, they would tutor us on how to acquire a taste for what they called 'The Broon', alias Newcastle Brown Ale, or 'Madhouse Brew', as more judicious Geordies dubbed it. The required acquired taste was gained by drinking progressively more of 'The Broon' with each visit to the Egypt Cottage. The results were predictable, though progressively less recallable. One image which does linger, though, is that of drummer Robbie Winter, loading his treasured new Pearl drum kit onto the train with all the studied care of the seriously stoned. While we looked on from a safe distance, he eventually managed to slide the last of his five cases into the guard's van. Turning to us with an approval-seeking grin, he then stumbled backwards and disappeared arse-over-tit between platform and train. We managed to haul him out before whistle time, grubby but relatively unscathed ... and still grinning.

*

True to his word, Lyn Dutton had cast the net for a suitable pianist, and in mid-February he, or rather the agency's scouts, succeeded in making the ideal catch. Thirty-year-old Bert Murray hailed from Kirkcaldy in the Scottish county of Fife, moving south in the mid-1950s to establish himself as one of the most sought-after piano players on the London traditional jazz scene. Prior to joining the Clydes, he had played in bands led by such notables as Lennie Hastings, Al Fairweather, Cy Laurie, Alan Elsden, Freddie Randall, Wally Fawkes and Nat Gonella. The Dutton office had done us proud.

Compactly built and bespectacled, Bert had a slightly undershot jaw, which lent him a curmudgeonly appearance at times. And Bert could indeed be grouchy – abrasive too. On occasions, his blunt manner was deliberately cutting, while at other times it merely masked a wicked sense of humour. Trouble was, it was difficult to tell whether Bert was kidding or not. He was one of nature's more cryptic characters: a walking conundrum.

Bert had been with the band for only a few days when I found myself on the receiving end of a typically-acerbic Murray gibe. We were playing an all-night jazz band jamboree in Leicester's De Montfort Hall, sharing the bill and dressing room with half a dozen other bands. As we prepared to go on stage for our first set, I noticed that the tip of my clarinet reed was slightly frayed. Not a problem. It could easily be put right by burning off the offending 'frills' with a match, while holding a penny against the curve of the tip to act as a template. The only snag was that I didn't have any change handy.

'Anybody got a penny?' I called out. 'I need to burn the end off this reed.'

Bert dipped into his pocket. 'Here!' he grunted. 'Take this two-bob bit. Burn the whole fuckin' instrument!'

Even if Bert hadn't been joking, I could take comfort from the knowledge that he had insulted many better musicians than me in his time. But that didn't stop a rumble of chuckles from rippling round the room. Jazzmen liked Bert's sense of humour. And I was no exception, especially when someone else was the butt of it. Anyway, I chuckled along and, after fixing my reed, I pocketed Bert's two-bob bit, which drew even more chuckles from the assembled musicians. All but Bert, that is.

Still, Bert Murray and I soon established a rapport, of kinds. Maybe it was because I never showed any outward sign of taking his grumpiness seriously (even when I did), or perhaps he felt slightly protective towards me, having been around the scene much longer and realising I was just a young guy trying hard to help establish a fresh reputation for a band that had been on the brink of collapse six months ago.

While Bert's hard-boiled manner, contrived or otherwise, would never have allowed him to let anyone in the band think he had taken me under his wing, he was never slow to offer me a nugget of worldly advice (out of the corner of his mouth) whenever he thought it might be useful. Also, no sooner had he learned that I had a young wife without social contacts in London than he invited Ellie and me to meet his own wife in their basement flat near the old Arsenal football ground in Highbury.

Marion Murray was everything Bert was not, except in height. Petite, pretty and with a ready smile, she was shy,

288

retiring, warm-hearted and gave the impression that she saw the best in everyone. Bert and Marion were an unlikely couple, but all the more likeable for it. That said, they didn't seem to have many friends, although their little poodle Heather clearly thought the world of them both. And Bert openly reciprocated this feeling of domestic harmony – towards the dog, at any rate.

Ellie and Marion hit it off right away, both clearly welcoming the prospect of being able to enjoy each other's company from time to time. Presumably, this was an outcome that Bert had foreseen, as only someone married to a 'jazz widow' could. It appeared, then, that somewhere deep beneath the tough Murray shell a soft centre lurked.

It wouldn't be long before Bert revealed a similarly benevolent attitude towards the band. The presence of his piano had already provided the essential fullness the Clydes' rhythm section had been lacking, while the assertive side of Bert's nature, so evident in his playing, gave the entire line-up a tremendous boot. However, as an unforeseen bonus, his addition to the payroll was destined to boost the fortunes of the Clyde Valley Stompers much more than even a PR man of Neville Nisse's reputed clout could ever have done.

A month or so after Bert joined the band, the Dutton Agency finally found us an adequate and, we hoped, permanent replacement for trumpeter Malky Higgins. In actual fact, though, describing wee Joe McIntyre as merely adequate would have been to do him a gross injustice. Irish by birth and perky as a leprechaun, Joe was a member of one of the Emerald Isle's most respected musical families, having cut his professional teeth at just seventeen with his cousin Gay McIntyre's showband. Since moving to London a year later, Joe's trumpeting talents had been employed by such famous bandleaders as Harry and Laurie Gold, Vic Lewis, Teddy Foster and, latterly, Sid Phillips. Still only twenty-seven, he had a tone and delivery as warm and lusty as a shot of Old Bushmills, and, when the music called for it, could deliver a kick like a Connemara pony – yet always with impeccable taste.

The incorporation of Joe McIntyre into the Clydes' front line was a rare treat indeed for John McGuff and me. Just as it's inherent for a jazz band to have a trumpet 'lead', it's normal for the trumpet player to assume that the trombonist and clarinettist will do the necessary weaving through, above and below the 'melodic' framework laid down by him. But Joe possessed an extraordinary ability to produce a clean, punchy lead while also contributing to the improvised ornaments being created around him.

It was a privilege to have such a gifted jazz musician in our ranks. And none of us was more appreciative than Bert Murray, who, though never flaunting the fact, had played with some of the best. We had gathered in the Finchley church hall we used for rehearsal purposes, primarily on this occasion to familiarise Joe with some things in our repertoire he might not have come across before. Everyone was feeling good, enjoying the new textures Joe's horn playing lent the band's sound, when, at the end of one of the numbers, Bert swung round on the piano stool, his normally glum features wreathed in smiles.

'At last,' he beamed, 'a jazz band fit to play Prokofiev!'

Bert broke the stunned silence which followed by revealing that he had been carrying around in his head for years a conviction that one of the great Russian composer's most popular works was well suited for jazzing up – in a commercial way, of course. The word 'commercial' sounded strange, coming from such a jazz-for-jazz's-sake diehard as Bert; almost as strange as the suggestion that *any* music by such a serious long-hair as Prokofiev would lend itself to being knocked about by a bunch of jazzers.

'I'm talkin' about a sure-fire hit here,' Bert continued, his enthusiasm undampened by the confusion in the six pairs of eyes staring at him. 'Tellin' ye, given the right treatment, this one'll zoom up the charts – make us a mint!'

Six pairs of ears pricked up.

'So, uh, which particular Profuckioff piece did ye have in mind?' drummer Robbie enquired, his interpretation of the composer's name indicating that he was about as familiar with contemporary classical music as the rest of us.

Bert scanned our blank expressions, then muttered, 'Bunch o' bloody Philistines!'

'Nah, never heard that one,' said Robbie, scratching his head. 'But, hey, no sweat, man – just hum it and we'll all join in.'

Once the groans and hisses which greeted that corny old wisecrack had died down, Bert proceeded to enlighten us. *Peter and the Wolf* was, he said, a children's story about a boy called Peter, who dreams of catching a wolf, with different instruments of the orchestra symbolising the various characters and animals in the narrative. But, Bert advised, he reckoned that only the two best-known themes need be employed for our purpose: the main orchestral one, which represents Peter, and the other, played by solo clarinet, which depicts a cat.

As he plonked out the two melodies on the piano, eureka bulbs lit up in our heads. We all recalled those tunes from somewhere in childhood, and, no doubt about it, they were ripe for a Dixieland-style reworking and sufficiently catchy to grab Joe Public's ear – given, as Bert had cautioned, the right treatment.

Within an hour, we had it nailed. All we needed now was a recording contract.

* * * * *

CHAPTER THIRTY-TWO

'FROM ABBEY ROAD TO LAND'S END'

Our arrangement of *Peter and the Wolf* all but created itself. Everyone in the band chipped in with ideas for an intro and coda, then we filled the spaces in between with statements of the two themes delivered by each of the front-line instruments. Well-tried devices like playing in unison an octave apart, employing uncomplicated harmonies and throwing in a couple of key changes completed the framework, which also left ample scope for improvisation. Deliberately commercial though the arrangement was, jazz remained a prominent element. As a result, we left the church hall that afternoon sharing a feeling that we had come up with something a bit special. And the simple arranging structure born of *Peter and the Wolf* had also inspired us to think up a handful of other well-known but unlikely pieces of music that could be given a similar treatment. Bert Murray, we were sure, had set us on a roll.

This hunch was endorsed by Lyn Dutton when I told him about our 'borrowing' from the music of Prokofiev. Purely on my verbal description of what we had hatched, he said this could be just what an up-and-coming A&R man at EMI Records had been looking for. George Martin, a staff producer for the Parlophone label, had been specialising in comedy and novelty recordings by the likes of Peter Ustinov, Flanders and Swann, Spike Milligan, Peter Sellers, Peter Cook and Dudley Moore, but now wanted to dip his toe into the mainstream of popular music, where traditional jazz was still in the swim.

Lyn Dutton's intuition proved to be sound. A week later, George Martin sent his assistant Ron Richards to the Finchley church hall to check out our version of *Peter and the Wolf*. A few days before that, however, Lyn had presented me with a completely different arrangement which, without our knowledge, he had commissioned from Kenny Graham, one of the UK's top big-band arrangers. And Lyn still hadn't even listened to *our* arrangement! Taken aback as we were, we gave Kenny's score a fair appraisal and duly rejected it. We meant no disrespect to the man, whose arranging credentials were second to none, but he had never heard the Clydes play, therefore knew nothing of our individual and collective characteristics. His interpretation of *Peter and the Wolf* was, predictably, no different from what he might have come up with for a 'Dixie splinter group' drawn from the sections of, say, the Ted Heath Orchestra, with which, coincidentally, both he and the Dutton office had historical ties. Our own arrangement, on the other hand, was tailor made by us for us, and it showed. No contest. Ours was the version we would play for Ron Richards.

'Fantastic!' Ron beamed after hearing it just once. 'A great A-side – all the makings of a hit – no changes needed. I'll report back to George and we'll book a session at Abbey Road for the first available date.'

We took an instant liking to Ron, and not just because he was sold on our idea for a single. He seemed a genuinely nice guy: affable, enthusiastic, down-to-earth and clearly devoted to music – though perhaps not entirely familiar with the line most jazz musicians would refuse to cross in pursuit of commercial success.

'You know,' he said as he was about to leave the hall, 'that Prokofiev adaptation of yours has got me thinking. And I'm thinking Gilbert and Sullivan, you know?'

Silence.

'Yes indeed,' Ron went on, '*The Mikado* … *Three Little Maids from School Are We*. Know that one?'

Those of us who didn't remained silent. Those of us who did followed suit.

'Anyway,' Ron smiled, 'have a think about it, boys. I'm sure you could work your magic on it.'

'Thanks, Ron – good idea,' I lied. 'We'll certainly put our minds to that one.'

We never would in a million years, of course. Even if the tune had been suitable for jazzing up, which we thought it wasn't, its title ruled it out for any band of self-respecting heteros, which we knew we were.

*

In April 1962, EMI's Abbey Road Studios had still to achieve the iconic status ultimately bestowed upon them by an as-yet little-known beat group from Liverpool. From the outside, the building looked no different from countless other Georgian townhouses in leafy St John's Wood. Once through the front door, however, you were presented with an impression of surprising space. Even Studio Two, where we had been told to report, was big enough to accommodate a fifty-piece orchestra, so we felt somewhat dwarfed and, for a jazz band, alien in so cavernous a 'room'. But George Martin soon had us in relaxed mood and feeling just as at home as we would have been in the cosy confines of the average jazz club. Tall, slim and gentlemanly, George possessed the same friendly, unassuming and enthusiastic qualities as his colleague Ron Richards. He was a no-nonsense professional who, by reputation, expected whoever he was recording to turn up well prepared and capable of making the most of valuable studio time. We were already in the habit of complying with such preconditions for TV appearances, and we had made doubly sure they'd be upheld here.

George explained that, since the use of multi-track tape machines had yet to become the norm at Abbey Road, no post-session remixing would be possible. Whatever went down on tape would be what came out on record. As we had known nothing else, I assured him this wouldn't be a problem. We were fully rehearsed and ready to roll.

'OK,' he said, 'just give me a couple of run-throughs to set the balance, and we'll go for it.'

Two run-throughs and one take later later, George called us up to the control booth to hear how our version of *Peter and the Wolf* sounded. We were relieved to see a smile on his face, and pleasantly surprised when we listened to the playback. The balance George had created was spot-on, the recorded sound vibrant, and the nods of approval exchanged by the boys confirmed that we were happy with our contribution as well. But with one reservation…

'I made a squeak on the clarinet in the last chorus,' I confessed. 'Sorry about that – it was a good take otherwise.'

George Martin merely laughed. 'It was a *great* take, and nobody's going to notice your little fluff. I didn't!' He gave me a reassuring pat on the shoulder. 'Right, Pete, that's the A-side safely in the can, so let's hear what you've brought along to back it up.'

We had arranged *Loch Lomond* with the same blend of clearly stated melody and easy-on-the-ear harmonies as *Peter and the Wolf*, maintaining once again a respectable jazz content without being self-indulgent. The object of the exercise, after all, was to make a record that would appeal to as wide an audience as possible, and B-sides had been known to come out on top before.

George caught our drift. 'Been keeping an ace up your sleeves there, haven't you?' he grinned, stroking his chin. 'Hmm, could be tempting to make this a double A-side.' He thought for a moment. 'But no, I think the surprise element of Prokofiev will open more doors, so we'll go with *Peter and the Wolf*.' With that, he thanked us for our efforts, assured us we had been a pleasure to work with ('Like shelling peas for me,' were his exact words), then said he was sure we'd be back at Abbey Road making a follow-up to our first hit single before too long.

We walked on air all the way to the nearest pub. No more than half of our allotted studio time had been needed, which allowed us to take an unexpected break before embarking on a thity-five-mile drive north for the jazz club gig we had been booked to play in Hitchin that evening. Time-consuming and taxing as our recording date *might* have been, the wheels of our new bandwagon weren't being allowed to gather moss for any longer than was absolutely necessary!

Like all jazzmen, the current members of the Clydes were motivated by an urge to play at every opportunity, yet I couldn't help but wonder how long they would continue to accept that being worked so hard was a worthwhile means towards this end. Still, I guessed the boys' immediate thoughts, following such a satisfying recording session, would be drawn more to George Martin's use of the word 'hit' than any concerns they might have had about the agency saddling us with too many engagements. Even so, being justly rewarded for their efforts was also a priority, and, as Bert Murray had suggested when first introducing us to *Peter and the Wolf*, it had the potential, given the right treatment, to make the band a mint.

'Aye, that George Martin lad knows his stuff,' Bert said over a pint in the Clifton Pub along the road from the studios.

'Got "hit" written all over it, that Prokofiev thing.' He took a slurp of his beer and cast me a sideways glance. 'Let's hope yer man Dutton remembers who came up wi' the idea when the royalties start comin' in!'

'Yeah,' I agreed, fingers crossed behind my back, 'let's hope so, Bert.'

*

Adding a personal dimension to this new air of expectancy was Ellie's announcement that she was pregnant, the happy event due, she calculated, around the middle of October.

'Should've bolted the course before ye got hitched, like I said,' quipped trombonist John. 'Now ye'll find out the truth about three livin' as cheap as one!'

While I took this to be nothing but a piece of typical McGuff drollery, I knew there was also a fair amount of truth in what he said. For a start, I would have to find somewhere else for my extended family to live; it was clearly stated in the rental conditions of our Collingwood Avenue flat that no dogs, cats or children were allowed. Inevitably, this would lead to stretching our already strained budget to breaking point. But, what the hell? – I'd tackle that problem in good time. For the present, there would be enough to think about in the day-to-day business of leading the band, since our workload was likely to be subjected to even more weight in the run-up to the launch of our new single.

EMI Records London offices were located in fashionable Manchester Square, a couple of blocks behind Oxford Street. Part of the building's basement was fitted out as a studio, in which 'audio showcases' plugging the company's latest releases were taped. Our rendition of *Peter and the Wolf* was slotted in between spots featuring such diverse performers as Bernard *Hole in the Ground* Cribbins, Frank *I Remember You* Ifield, Helen *Walking Back to Happiness* Shapiro and a hardboard-wobbling guy with a beard who waxed lyrical about tying down a kangaroo. As Bert Murray mumbled after watching this latter act, 'We're only a few hundred yards from Jazzshows, man, but it seems like we're on another fuckin' planet!'

Maybe so, but we were now subjects of EMI's powerful promotional machine, and would be pushed into the same limelight as many of the pop artists Bert considered to be Martians. This would be a price we'd have to pay if we wanted to reap the benefits of a hit single, and the prospect of raking off a personal reward for his contribution was sufficient to help Bert resist making any more complaints – for the time being at least.

As the record's release date approached, we were booked onto the BBC Light Programme's *Saturday Club* and its Sunday morning counterpart *Easy Beat*, both shows compèred by the now legendary Brian Matthew. These were the UK's first network radio programmes dedicated to the popular music of the day, and aimed squarely at a youthful audience. A plug for a new single on either of these shows was regarded as gold dust. That didn't ease Bert's discomfort at being involved, but at least all the 'live' input to *Saturday Club* was individually pre-recorded, so he was spared the risk of rubbing shoulders with the likes of Jerry Lee Lewis, Cliff Richard and the Shadows, Little Eva, the Everly Brothers and that freaky wobble-board bloke who sang about indulging in bondage with a marsupial.

To target a potentially wider 'family' market, EMI and the Dutton Agency combined their considerable influence to net a spot for us on *Val Parnell's Startime*, one of the most popular TV programmes in the country. We were on the same bill as every mum's favourite piano player, the develishly smiling Russ Conway, and every dad's favourite bundle of singing curves, Jill Day. Without taking anything away from those involved in securing such invaluable national exposure for the record, it has to be acknowledged that it was our choice of material, and treatment of it, that made the individual programme producers sit up and take notice in the first place. In that respect, George Martin's forecast had been absolutely correct. And the general pre-release buzz about the record suggested that Bert Murray's make-us-a-mint prediction might also be proved right.

We were playing a double-header with the Kenny Ball Band in Nottingham's Mecca Ballroom a few days after our latest TV appearance. Kenny already had a handful of big-selling singles to his credit, the most successful being *Midnight in Moscow*, which had recently reached No. 2 in the UK charts. He knew what it took to make a hit.

'Caught that Russian geezer's number you guys played on telly the other night,' he grinned as he walked into the dressing room. 'Great! Yeah, I'd've given my right bollock to have thought that one up!'

I glanced at Bert, who was glaring at me in a pointedly told-you-so sort of way.

Kenny, meanwhile, flipped open his trumpet case and, as was his wont, started passing round his collection of dirty postcards. 'Check the gazungas on *that*!' Subject changed.

*

The enlistment of a trumpet player of Joe McIntyre's calibre had proved to be worth the wait in more respects than one. He added a distinctive quality all his own to the band's sound, and he also fitted in well on a social level, an essential within the often testing confines of a touring band. But Joe was also a confirmed home bird, which created a tricky balance for a member of touring band to strike. He lived with his young Irish wife Maireadh in the north-London Irish enclave of Kilburn. Both Joe and Maireadh were what might fairly be described as pocket-sized, so the modest dimensions of their tenement flat posed them no particular problem. The same couldn't always be said for the shared toilet on the landing, which I guessed was one reason why Joe had opted to take to the road with the Clydes. Earning more than he had with Sid Phillips might ultimately facilitate a move to a slightly more 'opulent' pad.

In the meantime, I was glad Ellie had another girl friend to call on when I was away, and it was obvious Joe was equally happy on Maireadh's behalf. For all that he would rather have been returning home to her every night, he was always cheery on our travels, admitting he enjoyed the 'freedom' that came with being a member of an out-and-out jazz band. Although veteran clarinettist Sid Phillips had been associated with playing Dixieland music for longer than any other British bandleader, his tightly scored arrangements left little scope for improvisation. Joe revealed that Sid even preferred his sidemen's ostensibly ad-lib solos to be played exactly the same every time. He laughed as he recalled one occasion when the Phillips outfit arrived early for an engagement, and the steadfastly conservative leader suggested, for the first time that even his longest-serving musicians could remember, that he and the boys should repair to a pub for a pint, 'like real jazzers.'

But Joe also had a refreshingly self-deprecating sense of humour, as witness his chosen feature number, *Yes! We Have No Bananas*, complete with vocal refrain. For delivery of this, he temporarily abandoned his impeccable musical taste. Yet, easy-going as he was, Joe didn't lack a readiness to bluntly speak his mind when he thought fit. This was revealed to me towards the end of one particularly gruelling tour, which had involved a ninety-mile ferry voyage from Liverpool to play on the Isle of Man, followed by a cross-country trek to Durham University, and eventually – via jobs at the Hen & Chickens Roadhouse at Oldbury in the West Midlands and the so-called 'Chinese' Jazz Club in Swindon – to a holiday village at Redruth near Land's End. Fifteen hundred map-spanning miles and five gigs in as many days.

'Ye're all mad!' Joe panted as he collapsed on his bed in the room he was sharing with me.

The owner of the Redruth complex was proud of his collection of rare Scotch whiskies, which he had insisted we should sample comprehensively at the end of the gig. How often, after all, would he get an opportunity to show off his stash to a bunch of musicians who hailed from 'the source' and would, therefore, fully appreciate the subtleties of the various blends and single malts?

Joe was no more a whisky aficionado than I was. In fact, neither of us particularly liked the stuff. Nevertheless, manners are manners, and the last thing we'd wanted to do was insult the man by declining his invitation.

'Yeah, completely damn mad!' Joe groaned, and pressed a hand to his forehead.

I was in no condition to argue. 'That's right,' I muttered, flopping down on my own bed.

'Why the hell do you do it?' said Joe, his voice quavering now. 'Livin' like bloody nomads!'

Sleep began to overcome me while Joe ranted on about how crazy we were to allow ourselves to be flogged like this. And, he stressed, *I* was the biggest stooge of all. Jeez, the way I drove myself, anybody would think it was *my* band. The last thing I remember him saying was, 'What do ye expect to get, Pete – a goddam medal?'

I woke up in the middle of the night standing three feet off the floor in the wash-hand basin.

'That's the Glenmorangie for ye,' I heard Joe mutter into his pillow.

In the morning, he told me he was handing in his notice. And I knew it wasn't the whisky talking.

Less than three months after joining us, Joe McIntyre returned to the Sid Phillips Band, to its uneventful round of society hops in the Home Counties, and the comfort of his own pad every night – shared toilet and all.

* * * * *

CHAPTER THIRTY-THREE

'DEMONSTRATIONS AND CELEBRATIONS'

Malky Higgins' devotion to the Clyde Valley Stompers had never been in doubt. All of us knew his departure ten months earlier had been due to an attack of homesickness, exacerbated (or perhaps even caused) by having the burden of bandleading thrust upon his willing but unaccustomed shoulders. He didn't have to be asked twice to return to the fold, though no doubt to the dismay of his long-suffering wife Nancy, who might have assumed (or at least hoped) that his wandering-minstrel days were over.

He arrived in London in early July 1962, happy to be a Clydes sideman again, and just in time to join us on a trek back north to Liverpool, where, as related at the start of this story, I would have my credentials queried by a domineering doorman outside the Cavern Club. The following morning, we flew from Liverpool to Belfast, for the start of a tour which, as chance would have it, was scheduled to take us the length and breadth of Joe McIntyre's home turf.

The first venue on the itinerary was Belfast's Plaza Ballroom, where we headed straight from the airport. Our minibus driver had said a group of local musicians would be waiting to welcome us. We assumed the little giggle that followed his announcement was merely a mannerism. Then we saw the reception party...

Two dozen placard-toting, slogan-shouting pickets were blocking the entrance to the ballroom. It was difficult to make out the exact words they began hurling at us, but the looks on the faces of the hurlers left us in no doubt they weren't words of welcome. Anyway, there was only one way to find out what all the excitement was about, so, loins girded, I got out of the bus and approached the guy who appeared to be leading the demo.

This was a show of solidarity by local musicians, he barked at me: an official, union-backed protest against 'overseas' bands making hit-and-run invasions and being paid more than the Irish boys. When I asked him if he knew what the Clydes' wages were, he admitted he didn't. How then, I went on, could he tell we were earning more than his members? His response was to ask me if I thought his head buttoned up the back. While yelled invitations for us to go back where we came from were chanted by the pickets, their spokesman informed me that the ballroom's house band had withdrawn its labour and, consequently, would not be playing opposite us. Furthermore, we would not even be allowed to enter the building until his union's grievances had been satisfactorily addressed. The management of the ballroom had been advised accordingly. Discussion over.

As well as being a practising capitalist, Lyn Dutton was a professed socialist – an understandable enough paradox of principles for any effective band agent to operate under. He was in a meeting when I phoned from our Belfast hotel.

'Ask him what he suggests we do now?' I said to his right-hand man Colin Hogg.

After a couple of minutes Colin rang back. 'Lyn says to abide by the instructions of the Irish Federation of Musicians at all times.'

'Tell him they've instructed us to leave the country.'

A few more minutes later Colin came on the phone again. 'He says to abide by all the Federation's instructions *except* that one.'

'But we're not being allowed to work!'

'Yeah, well ... we'll, uhm, have to get back to you on that.'

Following an unexpected (and unpaid!) night off, I emerged next morning onto the balcony of our hotel and inhaled the smell of the sea wafting up from Belfast Lough. Unlike the attitude of the local musicians' union, I found it refreshing.

'Mud flats and seagull shite!'

I recognised the voice, and the cynicism. ''Morning, Bert,' I said to our pianist, who had appeared at my side and was surveying the urban scene spread out before us. 'Looks a nice enough wee city,' I suggested. 'Got a kinda positive feel about it too, eh?'

'Matter of opinion,' Bert grunted. 'This is where they built the *Titanic*, ye know.'

Just then, the sound of music drifted in from a few streets away. Rousing, assertive music, being played by flutes and driven by the thump, thump, thump of drums.

I sensed Bert tensing. He nodded towards the crowds that had started to line the pavements in front of the hotel. 'I don't like the look of this, man!' he muttered. 'Nah, I'm gettin' the hell outta here!' Without resort to explanation, he retreated indoors.

The Twelfth of July Parades in Northern Ireland meant nothing to me. Even as the flute bands and rank after rank of flag-bearing, banner-carrying men wearing bowler hats and orange sashes marched past, I assumed it was all just part of some local festival. Perhaps the Belfast equivalent of the fun-filled miners' galas celebrated in parts of mainland Britain, or maybe the preamble to some sort of flute-players' convention. Only when another hotel guest told me that this annual pageant marked the victory of Protestant King William of Orange over Catholic King James II at the 1690 Battle of the Boyne on the east coast of Ireland did it dawn on me why Bert had made himself scarce. Though unknown to me before then, Bert was a Roman Catholic, and his disquiet about the public goings-on in Belfast that morning presaged the 'Troubles' which, later in the decade, would engulf the entire province in a bloody politico-religious conflict destined to last for the next thirty years.

But right now we had our own troubles to contend with – or, rather, the Dutton office had. There was nothing I could do about our dilemma, other than sit by the phone waiting for news regarding some sort of settlement of the industrial dispute we'd innocently become embroiled in. That news came from Lyn Dutton himself on the second day of the impasse.

'Problem solved,' he said. 'Been talking to my man at the UK Musicians Union HQ here in London, and he's persuaded his Northern Irish counterpart to come to a compromise. The ban on employing the Clydes will now only apply to venues that come under the jurisdiction of the union's Belfast lodge. You can play anywhere else in the province, so get the boys ready to hit the road!'

Clearly, Lyn knew when to wear his socialist hat in preference to his capitalist one. I suspected, however, that he had been wearing both at once on this occasion. As he said before hanging up, 'It could only happen in Ireland!' He might have added, 'But you ain't seen nothin' yet!'

Our next gig was in a typical 'out-of-town' Irish dance hall, or, more specifically, a large shed in the sticks. This one made the environs of Longyester Hall back in Scotland seem like Piccadilly Circus in comparison. It was located at a crossroads somewhere in the hinterland of Ballymena or Ballymoney.

Then again, it might have been Ballyclare or Ballybogey. Only the driver of our minibus, a Northern Irishman himself, knew for sure. He also knew the local showband supporting us, and he was sure we'd be impressed by their cover versions of all the new pop hits.

'Second-hand crap stinks even worse than fresh crap!' Bert Murray informed him.

But the rest of us *were* impressed, even if we didn't particularly like the material being replicated. This nine-piece combo, sharply suited in drape jackets, drainpipe trousers and winkle-picker shoes, also featured three vocalists. They had the current charts stuff off pat, and the crowd lapped up every carefully copied note.

During one of our breaks, we found the secret of this ultra-accurate performance. If the customers thought what they were hearing sounded exactly like the real thing, it was because it actually was. Strategically seated behind the stage, a roadie was hunched over a tape recorder, its output patched into the band's PA system. When he saw us gaping at him, instead of trying to disguise what he was up to, he merely winked and gave us a 'well, we have the technology' kind of shrug.

Out in the car park, the showband's bus had a sticker on its back window, with the slogan *KEEP MUSIC LIVE!* emblazoned under the official logo of the Musicians Union. When our driver saw us gaping at it, he merely echoed Lyn Dutton's words: 'It could only happen in Ireland.' We said amen to that.

*

Back on the other side of the Irish Sea, late July found us settled into a welcome break from travelling, thanks to a two-week residency in the most popular seaside resort in the UK. A fitting monument to Victorian opulence, the Empress Ballroom in Blackpool's Winter Gardens complex was a world apart from the village halls we had been playing on the island of Arran the previous summer. Said to be the biggest ballroom in the world when built in 1896, the Empress boasted a parquet dance floor covering one third the area of a football pitch. Yet what made it really unique was its decor. Chandeliers hung like diamond encrusted stalactites from a high, barrel-vaulted ceiling embossed with ornate plasterwork, while rows of theatre-box balconies extended all around.

'Hardly up to British Legion Hall standards,' Jim joked the first time he and I entered the ballroom. And our circumstances certainly had changed in a way we could never have imagined after that first faltering gig with the Hidden Town Dixielanders three-and-a-half years earlier.

My eyes were on sticks. 'Yeah, I wonder how many budgie-breeding quickstep champs we'll come across in a dump like this!'

Jesting aside, we considered ourselves privileged to be playing in such sumptuous surroundings, flattered to be 'supported' by such a fine group of musicians as the resident dance orchestra, and tickled to be part of a presentation that maintained the renowned Blackpool tradition of having intermission music played on a 'mighty' Wurlitzer organ. As seasoned, one-night-stand vagabonds, we felt almost guilty to have it so good. We were also learning a valuable lesson about what had made Blackpool *the* mecca for so many generations of British holidaymakers. While comedian Ken Dodd headlined a family-targeted variety show in the three-thousand-seater Opera House next door every night, the Empress Ballroom's management were reaping the rewards of catering for a more eclectic dancing clientele than might have been deemed viable anywhere but Blackpool. There was something for everyone, from jive monkeys to wedding-reception-style shufflers, serious ballroom dancers (budgie-breeding and pigeon-fancying factions especially welcome), and even sit-and-watch-the-passing-show clusters of blue-rinse matrons. All of this within an atmosphere of generation-spanning bonhomie. Wonderful.

*

The buzz we'd felt on the recent release of our *Peter and the Wolf* single had been tempered somewhat by Kenny Graham being credited on the label as musical arranger. Not one iota of the arrangement Lyn Dutton had commissioned him to write (at the band's expense, but without our say-so) had been used on the recording session. Lyn duly apologised for the mistake, saying a simple clerical cock-up had been responsible. We had no reason to doubt that. Nonetheless, it was a careless error to have made, and those of us who had actually been responsible for the arrangement were entitled to be a tad peeved.

It wasn't that we were expecting any arranger's royalties to come our way; we knew that *Peter and the Wolf* was still under copyright, with all related earnings payable to the late composer's estate. But there was a principle involved here, particularly as the B-side, *Loch Lomond*, was a traditional tune, with the equivalent of the composer's royalties payable to the arranger – in this case, the band. Although there was no cause to suspect impropriety, I'd still be keeping an eye on whose bonnie banks the sun was eventually going to shine!

For the moment, though, our main interest was in whether the record would make even the lower reaches of the best-sellers lists. We were tempted to believe that air plays so far generated were helping attract at least some of the customers who crowded into the Empress Ballroom every evening, but the only true measure of how the disc was selling would be how it featured, if at all, on the national singles chart. Breaking into the official Top Thirty was the accepted yardstick of impending hit status. *Peter and the Wolf* did just that on 5th August 1962.

The boys and I were sitting in a cafe on Blackpool seafront, listening intently to the chart show on the radio when it was announced. Even the news, a few minutes later, of Marilyn Monroe's tragic death failed to drag us back down from cloud nine. George Martin's prediction looked as if it might just turn out to be accurate. But even if the record climbed no further up the 'hit parade', it would have achieved success far in excess of any other single in the Clydes' history. The following week it reached No 25, a position matched by no other British jazz band, bar Humphrey Lyttelton's (*Bad Penny Blues* – 1956) and those of the undisputed leaders of the current pack – Chris Barber (*Petite Fleur* – 1959), Kenny Ball (*Samantha* et al – 1961) and Acker Bilk (*Summer Set* et al – 1960/61).

'This calls for a celebration, chaps!' said the Dutton Agency's Colin Hogg on our return to London a few days later. Colin, a portly fellow of cheerful mien and a former Ted Heath road manager, had joined us in the Blue Posts pub following a Jazzshows gig we had just finished. 'Whiskies for the lads!' Colin called to the barman.

We didn't know it at the time, but those nips (just one each) would prove to be the only benefit we'd ever derive directly from the Clyde Valley Stompers' biggest hit. In the meantime, our new-found success was set to breed even more of the same, and we were ready to commit ourselves wholeheartedly to making the most of whatever opportunities this might present. The first was an appearance on the *Morecambe and Wise 'Two of a Kind'* TV show, compulsive Saturday-night viewing for just about every household in the UK. Even Bert Murray conceded that blanket exposure didn't come any better than this. He showed his resigned acceptance of the price to be paid by giving a nod and a wink in passing to our co-guests, the eminently unhip Beverley Sisters.

* * * * *

CHAPTER THIRTY-FOUR

'SUCCESS BREEDS UNREST'

Although Ian Menzies hadn't made contact since talking me into buying the Ford Zephyr ten months earlier, I thought it strange he didn't get in touch to congratulate us on taking the band into the UK singles chart for the very first time. I had assumed he would have been pleased that *his* Clyde Valley Stompers, teetering so recently on the verge of collapse, had not only survived but were now attracting a wider following than ever before. This had also ensured the continuation of his source of income as a director of 'the company'. Anyhow, I had neither the time nor inclination to ponder the reasons for his apparent indifference. All things considered, it was best that Big Ming concentrated on running his boarding house business in Jersey, while I got on with the business of leading the Clydes.

I also had to attend to the matter of finding a permanent home. With just two months of Ellie's pregnancy to go, the landlord of our Collingwood Avenue flat was now pressing us to vacate the place. In my absence, Ellie had been doing the rounds of letting agencies and scouring the cards in newsagents' windows, but had been unable to find a baby-friendly flat to rent within our price range. In desperation, I went back to Moss Hall Crescent in North Finchley and told our tale woe to Mrs Curwood, my very first London landlady. Kindly old soul that she was, she immediately offered us a room, but on the strict understanding we would be gone before the 'happy day'. Baby noises wouldn't go down at all well with the travelling salesmen who were her regular clients.

Mrs Curwood had referred to our new accommodation as a ground-floor bedsit. And it conformed to that description in as much as it had a couple of armchairs to sit on and a double bed that folded down from the wall. It also had a self-contained kitchen, or rather a walk-in cupboard with a sink and a little electric hotplate. A bathroom on the first-floor was shared with the other 'guests'. I had a sinking feeling when Ellie first walked in that her stoicism was about to be tested to breaking point. But she said she really liked the room. It had a homely feeling about it, she said, and she thought Mrs Curwood was a lovely old lady. She'd get on just fine with her. Besides, she liked what she'd seen of the area so far: nice and quiet, with nice trees outside the house, and a nice selection of shops just along the road. Yes, she smiled, she'd be happy living here all right.

I breathed a sigh of relief, telling myself how fortunate I was to have such an understanding wife. Now all I had to do was find a home worthy of her enduring support – and soon! Yet, despite my best efforts to remain optimistic, I couldn't help thinking again of the old farmhands' nugget of advice to their wives that my grandfather had once told me: 'Blessed are they who expect nothing, for they shall not be disappointed.'

On a more positive note, at least I had access to a telephone in Mrs Curwood's front hall. During all our time at Collingwood Avenue, I must have been unique among leaders of the country's busiest bands by having to keep in touch with our agent, as well as discuss programme details with radio and TV producers, via a call box at the end of the street. It had reminded me of a Glasgow promoter called Andy Daisley, who conducted the telephone side of his business from a public booth near his house. Andy actually went so far as to employ a gang of small boys to take turns, at a few pennies a time, to knock on his front door whenever the phone rang. Even if I'd decided to adopt the Daisley system, chances were that the small boys of Collingwood Avenue wouldn't have been that skint.

*

The popularity of *Peter and the Wolf* soon resulted in more radio and television dates being squeezed into our already crowded schedule. But we were thankful for the exposure and took the extra workload in our stride. One of the pioneering pop-music TV programmes back then was an off-shoot of Radio Luxembourg's *Cool for Cats* called *Discs a Go-go*, produced in Bristol and Cardiff by Television Wales and the West (TWW). The host was the cool and personable Kent Walton, a disc jockey with a mid-Atlantic accent, perhaps better known as the voice of Britain's all-in-wrestling television extravaganzas. To keep the cost of hiring live bands to a minimum, the show featured a troupe of girl dancers (hence the *Go-go* handle), who became forerunners of Pan's People on the legendary *Top of the Pops* BBC series. We played on a few of those programmes, which had an easy-going party atmosphere and were always good fun.

Then, in mid September, it was back to the more formal variety-show format of ATV's *Melody and Rhythm*, with Danny Williams topping a bill that included Susan *Bobby's Girl* Maughan and, performing their new single *Island of Dreams*, the Springfields, whose girl singer recalled our one-

313

night-stand paths crossing at the Two Red Shoes dance hall up in Elgin less than a year before. 'You guys looked about as knackered as we felt,' she laughed. Dusty was on the cusp of becoming an international superstar in her own right, but still very much 'one of the boys'.

Being busy can be a breeze, as long as everything's running smoothly, but it doesn't take much to turn a breeze into a hurricane. And ill winds have a habit of not turning up singly, as I was about to find out...

*

Ellie and I had to move out of Moss Hall Crescent at short notice to make way for someone who had offered to take Mrs Curwood's ground-floor bedsit on a long lease. With only a few weeks to go before Ellie was 'due', and the band about to hit the road again, it looked as if a temporary move back to Scotland was on the cards for the mum-to-be. My folks had already offered to put her up – along with the new arrival – until I could find a suitable abode in London. But Ellie, doggedly independent as ever, had other ideas.

'I've found a wee place to tide us over,' she told me when I got back from an all-nighter at Oxford University one morning. 'OK, it *is* a bit cramped, but the landlord says he won't mind having a baby about for a while ... if push comes to shove.'

She took me to see her find right away. It wasn't far – just along the road near Finchley Central tube station. The flat was owned by a Ghanaian doctor, very dark-skinned and extremely cordial, who welcomed us like long-lost friends. He told me I could call him Bobo (I wouldn't be able to pronounce his native name) and led us into a tiny bedroom, with bunk beds against one wall.

'Mmm, this would do fine as a nursery,' I said, and gave Dr Bobo an apologetic smile. '*If* push comes to shove, that is.'

He smiled back, nodding, then looked at Ellie.

She coughed, then looked at me, shaking her head. 'No, ehm, you don't understand. *This* is it.'

I was speechless.

'Don't worry, my friend,' grinned Dr Bobo. 'The beds are very comfortable … *and* you have room for guests on the top one.'

'We'll take the room,' Ellie informed him, shepherding me out before I had a chance to object. 'We'll move in tomorrow. Really looking forward to it.'

She wasn't quite so chirpy when I came back after my first couple of days away. Although Dr Bobo hadn't mentioned it previously, his flat had only one bathroom, a detail which Ellie discovered the hard way.

'Honestly, Peter, I nearly died.' She was speaking furtively, as though she thought Dr Bobo might be eavesdropping through the wall. 'There I was, first night here, going for a bedtime pee, and I flicked the light switch outside the bathroom door. But when I opened it, it was pitch black in there. So, I'm thinking to myself the bulb must have blown. Anyway, I went in and shut the door behind me, ready to grope my way towards the loo. I mean, I knew roughly where it was, all right?'

As Ellie paused to draw breath, all sorts of nasty possibilities began to enter my mind. What terrors had I exposed my young wife to, leaving her alone in a crummy little hole like this? And her great with child and everything. A feeling of failure and impending doom swept over me.

Ellie hadn't noticed. 'Anyway,' she continued, totally absorbed in her story now, 'I'm just getting ready to drop my pyjama bottoms, see, when I hears this strange shuffly, hissing sort of noise.' She gripped my arm. 'And that's when I nearly died!'

Visions of a pet Ghanaian python, or even a panther, appeared befor me. I'd never lived in an African household before, so I was prepared to believe anything. 'Wh-what was it, Ellie?'

'Not it – *him*!'

'Y-you mean … Doctor *Bobo*?'

'Honest, Peter, if he hadn't smiled, I'd never have seen him. Sitting there in the dark with his trousers at his ankles and not even bothering to lock the door!'

Silence reigned while consternation gradually gave way to an overwhelming sense of relief. Ellie was the first to start laughing.

'Now that I think about it, the poor man probably got a bigger fright than I did.' She patted her bump. 'Probably thought I was gonna ask him to do a midwife turn right there and then!'

I was laughing now too. 'Yeah, just when he was busy hissing and shuffling with his pants down!'

Not for the first time, I counted myself lucky that Ellie shared my inclination to look on the funny side of such situations, but resolved to get her out of this one, pronto. How I would manage to pay for appropriate accommodation was as big a problem as ever, of course, and one that wasn't unique to me.

*

'I'm sorry, Pete, but I'm packin' it in.' Bill Bain had been with the Clydes longer than any of us and, as a married man with a young family, had sacrificed more than most in supporting the band's interests. 'Emily and the kids want me with them, and if I can't afford to bring them down here when the band's doin' this well, I never will. So,' he shrugged, 'I'm goin' home – back to Glasgow.'

We were sitting in the Joiners Arms, the Finchley pub where we usually gathered before rehearsals in the church hall along the street. Robbie Winter had joined us just before Bill dropped his bombshell.

'I've come to the same decision,' Robbie told me. 'I never thought I'd ever quit the Stompers, but I'm callin' it a day as well. I'm plannin' to get married back in Glasgow soon, ye see, and … well, ye know how it is.'

I did indeed. Not every new bride would be willing to come to London and put up with the 'disruptive' living conditions Ellie had. And I couldn't blame them.

Tellingly, we had only recently returned from a concert tour of Scotland, playing to full houses in some of the country's biggest venues, most notably the 4,500-capacity St Andrew's Halls in Glasgow. It was here, seven years previously, that the fledgling Clyde Valley Stompers won the Scottish Jazz Band Championships, prompting their decision to turn professional and triggering the start of a high-speed, roller coaster journey which, though having brought them undreamed-of success, had almost hit the buffers just twelve months earlier.

This was the band's first appearance in its native city's most prestigious place of entertainment with a personnel that wasn't totally 'west-coast', and under a leader other than Ian Menzies. I was physically sick with nerves before going on stage. But I needn't have worried; the reception we received was as warm as only Glaswegian audiences can give, and the band responded with a suitably inspired performance. It was an unforgettable experience, and particularly so for the Glasgow lads, whose families had come in numbers to offer their encouragement.

Glasgow folk are as steadfastly supportive of their own as they are proud of their city, and there really is something special about the 'I belong to Glasgow and Glasgow belongs to me' feeling that Glaswegians share. I'd noticed it most vividly on this tour when dropping the boys off outside their homes in the wee, small hours. Those looks of cheery contentment had never been on their faces when arriving back at their digs in London. In this respect, I suppose it should have come as no great surprise when Bill and Robbie decided to 'go home' at this point in time. In any event, we were suddenly faced with the problem of finding a new bass player and drummer.

Ill winds were blowing in with uncomfortable regularity now. And, within the month, trombonist John McGuff also tendered his resignation. We had just recorded a BBC *Jazz Club* broadcast, compèred by the irrepressible George Melly, in London's Paris Theatre, and were enjoying a wind-down drink in the pub around the corner. The band had been in excellent form, stimulated by the arch-enthusiasts who habitually comprised the audience of British radio's flagship jazz programme. And we were spurred on by the peerless drumming of Danny 'Old Dundonian' Craig, covering for the absent Robbie Winter. Danny had been the driving force behind just about every noteworthy British band of the past twenty years, from Oscar Rabin to Harry Roy and Bert Ambrose to Sandy Brown. As a result, the boys in our rhythm section swung their socks off, and the 'fireworks' displays of our two brass men, trombonist John and trumpeter Malky, had never sparkled more brightly. Terry Henebery, the show's producer and one of the most respected jazz buffs around, even made a point of congratulating me on the Clydes having undergone a spectacular change for the better since Ian Menzies' relinquishment of the trombone 'chair'. This made John's decision to leave all the more disappointing.

His reason was, he said, 'just to sort out a few things back home', and he hoped he'd be back with us fairly soon. I had a hunch, however, that John simply wasn't prepared to live away from his wife and young son any longer. He had come to the same conclusion as others before him that the odds were against his ever being able to provide a decent home for his dependents in London.

Automatically, my thoughts were drawn again to how Ian Menzies had lived comfortably with his own family in a pleasant London suburb before retiring, and how, even now, he took a slice of the band's earnings to help maintain what I presumed was an even more comfortable lifestyle in Jersey. Although none of the boys had ever brought up this peculiarity of the Clydes' financial structure, and how it might be affecting their own earnings, I decided the time was rapidly approaching for me to have that long delayed tête-à-tête with Lyn Dutton.

But for the moment, there was the essential business of finding replacement musicians to focus on.

* * * * *

CHAPTER THIRTY-FIVE

'A TRAD DAD'

Trombonist Pete Hodge was, like Joe McIntyre, a highly-rated musician, who had worked for such famous London bandleaders as Harry and Laurie Gold, Freddy Randall and, most recently, Sid Phillips. Having the opportunity to give free flow to his jazz juices was his main reason for agreeing to join the Clydes. The most easy-going and unassuming of characters, Pete admitted that being expected to play 'improvised' solos exactly the same, time after time, had made life with the Sid Phillips Band a touch too humdrum for his liking of late. He was relishing the prospect of having more musical 'freedom', but, I guessed, also looked forward to enjoying a share of the prosperity that the Clydes' new-found commercial success was likely to bring.

Sandy Malcolm, long-serving drummer with the Royal Mile Jazz Band in Edinburgh, offered to help out with most of our 'on-the-road' commitments, while we'd borrow the Alex Welsh Band's uber-ebullient Lennie Hastings for whatever studio dates might come our way. Not having a regular drummer was far from ideal, but the guys fulfilling the role on an ad hoc basis were experienced jazzmen and did a great job.

One unexpected bonus to emerge from the situation came via Sandy Malcolm, who told us about an amazing young bassist he had played with recently in Edinburgh. Purely on Sandy's recommendation, we invited seventeen-year-old Ron Mathewson from the remote Shetland Isles to join the Clydes. And what a stir he created on the London scene! Gangly Ron was as worldly naive as he was musically talented. His wide-eyed wonder at the everyday sights he saw on his first trip along the highways of industrial England would spawn a plethora of comic anecdotes, as would his obsession with breaching the sexual-intercourse barrier for the first time. In the interim, his bass-playing placed him squarely in the 'genius' category by everyone who heard him. This was a gift of which Ron was as delightfully unaware as were the things in the line of vision of his one glass eye – a physical peculiarity which itself would spawn an entirely separate plethora of comic anecdotes.

That was for the future. For now, the band was more or less back to a full complement of musicians. One mission had been accomplished. My next was to get Ellie out of that tiny, bunk-bedded room and into accommodation fit for a new mum and baby, though how I was going to afford it on my current earnings still had me scratching my head.

There was a week of reasonably local engagements to fulfil before we set off on a tour of northern England, during which Ellie was scheduled to 'deliver'. More immediately, however, there were familiarising rehearsals to fit in for the new boys. Although band obligations were getting more exacting by the day, my personal predicament demanded an immediate solution, so I made time to go and tap Lyn Dutton for a rise. And, while I was at it, I thought I might as well ask for a long-overdue review of the boys' wages too.

Lyn responded by apologising for having to rush off to a meeting, then assured me, as he ushered me towards the door, that our wages were always under review. 'But don't worry, Pete,' he smiled through wisps of cigar smoke, 'we'll talk about it some more next time you're in the office, hmm?'

*

Ossulton Way is a tree-shaded avenue flanked by smart villas and neat, low-rise apartment blocks in the typical art deco style of the 1920s. Located in East Finchley, just beyond the edge of Hampstead Garden Suburb (one of the most desirable residential areas in northern London), properties here commanded rental prices way beyond what I could *sensibly* pay. Ellie and I had both been brought up to be careful with whatever money we had and, whenever possible, to squirrel some away for a rainy day. This policy had to be abandoned now; the rent of the 'babies-permitted' flat I agreed to lease would leave only enough in my pocket every week to cover our living expenses, and with some difficulty at that.

But what alternative did we have? If Ellie went back home to stay with my parents now, there would be a chance, no matter how positive our intentions, that we'd end up like the band's other married couples, who had tried, and failed, to live hundreds of miles apart. Anyway, looking on the bright side as usual, I told myself we would soon be benefitting financially from the current upward trajectory of the Clydes' fortunes. It would be simply a case of pursuing that postponed talk with Lyn Dutton 'the next time I was in the office'.

And so, after depositing Ellie in our new nest, I set off with the boys for the north of England. Ellie had been noticing what she told me were the early signs of going into labour on the morning I left. But as my mother had travelled down from Scotland to be there 'when her time came', I was as satisfied as I could be that I had accomplished mission number two – or at least my part of it. The other part would now be down to Ellie.

Weighing in at 6lbs and 11oz, wee Sandy entered the fray, via the Victoria Maternity Hospital in Barnet, at 4.30 p.m. on 12th October 1962; the same day on which I'd left for the band's latest tour. He was bawling like a banshee. I was 150 miles away in the Nottinghamshire town of Worksop, grinning and dishing out cigars to the boys. If Ellie could have got her hands on me, she would have committed murder – or so she said when I arrived in the ward four days later to be introduced to our family's new addition.

'Honestly,' she gasped, 'you've no idea the tortures I went through!'

'It looks like a skinned rabbit,' I said, peering into the cot beside her bed.

'*He* looks like *you*!' Ellie came back, dudgeon rising rapidly.

Just then, the little fellow looked up at me and smiled one of those disarming, toothless smiles that only the very young and very old can smile.

'You're right,' I said, 'it – I mean *he* does look like me, *and* he obviously has a good sense of humour as well.'

'He'll need it!' Ellie muttered.

Even if that hadn't been a leg-pull (and I allowed myself to think it was), Ellie would have been entitled to feel more than a little aggrieved by events of late – if not from the very first day of our marriage. All the hassles and discomforts of being shunted around from one 'home' to another had hardly constituted the ideal conditions in which to prepare for having a baby. But I knew her well enough by now to predict, with a fair degree of confidence, that all would be well once she had settled properly into our flat in elegant Ossulton Way.

And I wasn't wrong. With a sunny sitting room, comfy double bedroom, compact but nicely kitted-out bathroom, a well-equipped kitchenette that led directly out to a grassy back garden, and a boxroom amply big enough to serve as a nursery, this was a place Ellie really *could* turn into a home.

There was a selection of shops nearby, and a couple of public parks, where she could take a stroll with wee Sandy in his pram. We even had a telephone of our very own in the flat. And so what if we'd be pushed to afford the rent? In that regard, we were no different from most young couples, and with the prospect of increased earnings on the horizon, better placed than many.

Yet again, I counted myself extremely lucky, and looked forward to the future with redoubled optimism. Besides, I was a daddy now, so couldn't afford *not* to prosper. Buoyed up by this new-found sense of purpose, I paid my next visit to Lyn Dutton's office, essentially to hand over the takings from the Clydes' latest tour, but with the added intention of holding him to his promise of discussing a review of our wages.

*

'George Martin wants you back in the recording studios,' Lyn said the moment I walked in.

I couldn't have been more delighted. All thoughts of talking about earnings were put on hold while I started to tell him about the handful of potential follow-ups to *Peter and the Wolf* we'd been preparing. But Lyn cut me off.

'No, no, it's a movie theme he wants you to record – title music for the latest Norman Wisdom film – a spoof police thing called *On the Beat*. It's scheduled for release in December, so you'll have to get a move on!'

Love him or loathe him, comedian Norman Wisdom was currently the biggest box-office draw in Britain, so being associated with his new flick would help expose the Clyde Valley Stompers' name to millions who had never heard of the band before. I was all for it, and I told Lyn so.

'OK,' he said, handing me a large envelope, 'here's the music – an original by Philip Green – one of the UK's top movie composers, in case you didn't know. All the parts are in there.

So go to it, and let me know when you've got the boys ready to record.'

I was already half way out the door.

'Make it yesterday!' Lyn called after me.

I got the message, and had the band assembled in the Finchley church hall the very next morning.

George Martin had put a note in with the score, instructing us to play it strictly as Philip Green had intended: that's to say as hell-for-leather, cops-and-robbers 'chase' music in the Keystone style. A tongue-in-cheek element in our interpretation was allowable, but any hint of a send-up was out.

'Rooty-tooty, Mickey Mouse, pie-in-the-face shite!' was how Bert Murray described it after the first run-through.

None of us disagreed. However, I pointed out that if we wanted to reap the commercial benefits offered by this opportunity, we would have to do as instructed. And no-one, including Bert, made any objection to that. Anybody passing the church hall during the ensuing rehearsal would have been forgiven for assuming that a meeting of the musical branch of the local Laurel and Hardy fan club was taking place inside.

A couple of days later, we were back in EMI's Abbey Road studios.

'Perfect!' was George Martin's reaction to our rendition of Norman Wisdom's new title music. 'Just how Philip Green would want it played, I'm sure!'

We also realised it was just how any bunch of session musicians would have played it: note-for-note as written, with not a jot of improvisation involved. But that was the deal, and we had come up with exactly what had been asked of us, even although it had meant swallowing our jazzers' pride as part of the bargain.

Our feelings of guilt at having yielded to such mercenary temptation must have been sensed by George Martin. 'Tell you what, boys,' he said at the end of the session, 'why don't you do your magic on this number? You know, slow it down a bit, give it the same easy-on-the-ear jazzy treatment you gave *Peter and the Wolf*?' He nodded his head, thinking. 'Yes, I reckon *On the Beat* could well turn out to be your next A-side.'

Before I could pipe up that we already had a few potential A-sides in the *Peter and the Wolf* mould ready to record, George confided that featuring a Philip Green composition on our next single could create valuable spin-offs. Philip was, as we might be aware, Musical Director of the Rank Organisation, Britain's foremost film-production company, *and* he also wielded considerable influence within EMI Records. Yes, George concluded, playing a Philip Green card right now could prove to be very beneficial indeed – for all of us.

Who was I to argue?

At our next rehearsal we went to work on what would one day become a much-used accompaniment to cartoons like *The Wacky Races*, and we turned it into a vehicle capable of doing justice to a jazz band that took its output seriously, even when bowing to commercial pressures. It would be unfair to use the terms 'silk purse' and 'sow's ear', since *On the Beat* was originally intended to be nothing other than background music for a slapstick movie. All the same, it would be no exaggeration to say we managed to make the most, jazz-wise, out of a piece of fairly unlikely material.

With Lennie Hastings guesting on drums, the band sounded sharp, spirited and swinging when, early in November, we recorded our next single. A reconstituted *On the Beat*, coupled with another EMI recommendation called *Marching Dixielanders*, turned out to be a very good record, though never likely to emulate the success of *Peter and the Wolf*. Still, if its release helped us benefit from whatever game of politics we might be getting drawn into, all well and good. That's the way I saw things anyway.

But Bert Murray had already waited too many tomorrows for his spoonful of jam. The way *he* saw things was that he had compromised his commitment to playing 'unadulterated' jazz by making an important contribution to the band's commercial status, for which it was becoming increasingly clear the Clyde Valley Stompers' 'company' had no intention of rewarding him – even with some sort of ex gratia backhander. That being the case, he would be accepting an offer to replace pianist Fred Hunt in the Alex Welsh Band. While no-one questioned Bert's musical motives, it was unlikely he would benefit financially from the move. I mentioned this to him on his final night with the band.

'Yeah, but it's the principle, man,' he replied. 'Alex runs his outfit on a co-operative basis. All the guys know what the take is, and everybody gets an equal share.' He looked at me and shook his head. 'Sorry, Pete – you can work your balls off for some guy sittin' on his arse in Jersey if you want, but not me.' He grabbed my hand and shook it. 'Hope you live long enough to get that medal Joe McIntyre mentioned!'

I was accustomed to Bert not mincing his words, so wasn't unduly fazed by his parting shot. He'd made it with the best of intentions, and I was savvy enough to know what he was getting at. But I had made a commitment when accepting leadership of the Clydes, and I wasn't prepared to renege on it just because there were still 'corporate' issues to resolve.

Although only Jim now remained of the personnel in place when I picked up the pieces after Malky's brief time in charge, I felt as responsible as ever for the welfare of the band, both as a business concern and as a team of musicians. OK, nobody had to tell me my position with the Clydes was regarded by many of my peers as one that only a sucker for punishment would have taken on. But I hadn't forgotten how thankful I'd been when asked to join the band in the first place, and I'd regarded being offered the leadership as much an opportunity as a challenge. The perpetual changes to the line-up (made inevitable, according to those same peers, by the band having an albatross round its neck) would have caused most to chuck the towel in long before now. But I'd put too much into this job. It had come with obvious problems attached, and I'd get down to solving them when I thought the time was right. That would be when a suitably strong platform on which to bargain had been built. For 'platform' read 'success', and we were already well on the way to achieving more of that than our albatross might ever have expected.

* * * * *

CHAPTER THIRTY-SIX

'IN VINO VERITAS'

Ronnie 'Bix' Duff succeeded to the Clydes' piano stool in November 1962. In his early thirties, Bix was about the same age as Bert Murray and, like Bert, was a native of Fife in Scotland. With the physique of a flyweight boxer (albeit a round-shouldered, hollow-chested one who chain-smoked), Bix had a darkly-impish sense of humour and a wheezy little laugh, which combined to lend him an almost goblin-like demeanour. We liked him, both as a character and musician. He'd been around the London scene for years and was a survivor of the notoriously hard-drinking, tirelessly-raving Mick Mulligan Band. George Melly had been a contemporary of his in that delightfully degenerate group, as had trombonist Frank Parr, a plain-speaking Liverpudlian who now worked as the Lyn Dutton Agency's 'band liaison associate' (aka nocturnal habitué of jazz musicians' watering holes) and had made the Bix Duff connection for us.

No sooner had our new pianist become familiar with our working repertoire than he found himself playing on our next recording session. Just as George Martin had speculated, another composition by Philip Green had been put our way. Green had written this one, along with several others, for a new Tommy Steele film being shot at Shepperton Studios in Surrey. *It's All Happening* was basically a showcase for some of the current 'names' in British pop. Starring one of the most movie-marketable young rockers of the day, the film had a storyline which didn't pretend to be anything but glue to stick the musical fragments together: a record company's talent spotter, played by Tommy Steele, plans to produce a show to raise money for the orphanage where he was brought up. Predictably, it all eventually happens, with the various guest 'acts' making cameo appearances to help things along.

Tommy Steele's co-starring actors were Angela Douglas, Michael Medwin and Bernard Bresslaw, while the long list of 'names' from the music world included the ubiquitous Russ Conway and Danny Williams, Shane Fenton (later to be reborn as Alvin Stardust), John 'James Bond Theme' Barry, Geoff 'Manuel and his Music of the Mountains' Love, Marion 'Spot the Tune' Ryan and ourselves. The tune Philip Green had written for our spot was called *Casbah*, which, as the title suggests, was created to blend with the steamy, north-African atmosphere of the night club we were supposed to be playing in. Despite the fact that the atmosphere *and* temperature inside a hangar-like Shepperton sound stage in December could hardly have been less steamy, the effect looked authentic enough, with Tommy and his chick jiving up a head of steam in front of the band.

Casbah was what it was: a piece of quasi-jazz, written specifically for consumption by the mainly non-jazz-minded audiences who would flock to see a Tommy Steele film. In that respect, Philip Green knew what he was about. However, instead of allowing the band to put its own stamp on the music, his arrangement left no scope for any collective improvisation at all. So, as with *On the Beat* in its original state, it might just as well have been played by a group of studio musicians. But I suppose that's the modus operandi essential to someone writing diverse styles of music to a strict brief. Although it might have been more to our own potential advantage to have played one of the tunes we considered an appropriate follow-up to *Peter and the Wolf*, this would have precluded Philip Green from earning any composer's royalties, and I assumed that our agreeing to perform one of his own pieces was why we had been slotted into this movie in the first place. Anyhow, if we were being used as pawns in some sort of political game, I was happy enough for us to be shuffled around in exchange for the valuable exposure the band would gain when the movie went on general release in a few months time.

Perhaps inevitably, we were starting to take some flak from self-styled 'jazz purists' for selling out to commercialism. We paid such criticism as much heed as we felt it deserved, which wasn't a lot. There was no danger of our abandoning jazz for pop; we were much too devoted to our chosen music for that. Also, in practical terms, we had all taken a gamble in life by attempting to make a living from playing jazz, and for me, helping the Clyde Valley Stompers stay in business had turned out to be a crucial factor in keeping that aspiration alive. Exploiting current commercial opportunities was, at least in my case, essential to having a chance of remaining a professional jazz musician in the longer term, and if armchair paragons of jazz virtue couldn't reconcile themselves to that, then tough. I'd paid my dues.

*

In an odd way, it was actually the presence of *Peter and the Wolf* in the pop charts that prompted Max Jones, the *Melody Maker* newspaper's widely respected jazz writer, to do an in-depth interview with me, based on why Scotland seemed to have consistently produced more jazzmen per head of population than England. A notably serious man, Max probably wasn't sure if I was joking when I offered the suggestion that he could find the answer by listening to the top pipe bands and Scottish Country Dance combos.

'No kidding, Max,' I said, 'they all *swing*, which is the essence of jazz. And that doesn't necessarily apply to guys who play for morris dancers cavorting round a maypole with hankies on their wrists and bells on their ankles.'

I doubted that Max would ever put my theory to the test, but I'd given him a good angle for his piece and, as he said himself, it was likely to stimulate some contentious feedback from the purists among his readers. It takes all kinds.

Around the same time, the Clydes were photographed in party mode for the front page of the *Melody Maker*'s Christmas issue. Streamers, paper hats, balloons and glasses of wine were afforded due prominence, and some of the boys even managed to fake cheery expressions, in spite of discovering the 'wine' to be only diluted blackcurrant juice. That's the thing about jazz musicians: they're only genuinely happy when they're playing jazz, or when chewing a rag with kindred spirits. A request to give the appearance of enjoying themselves for publicity purposes is like being asked to pull their own teeth.

Travelling with the same bunch of guys for lengthy periods can be a real test of camaraderie, but I'd always found life on the road to be surprisingly feud-free – allowances being made for occasional niggles caused by hangovers, exhaustion, bad map-reading and empty pockets, of course. The Clydes' current combination of youth and experience was proving to be one of the most harmonious of recent times. Bix would regale us with yarns about the shamelessly outrageous capers the Mick Mulligan Band had got up to on tour, while Pete Hodge's unflappable approach to the job, honed by years of playing for so many top bands, served as a valuable example to us younger guys. Pete was a consummate professional: dependable, a master of his craft, yet modest and always great company. Although he had probably forgotten more about being a musician than I had learned, he returned the respect I showed him and never once made me feel inferior to any of the abundantly more experienced bandleaders he had worked with over the years

Pete had proved to be a great asset, so we were all truly sorry when, after only a couple of months, he said he was leaving the band before we set out on the customary Scottish tour the Dutton office arranged to allow the lads to spend the festive season 'at home'. But Pete was a Londoner, and he didn't relish the thought of being away from *his* home and family at Christmas. This, at any rate, was the reason he gave, but I fancied that two months of being subjected to the hurly-burly life of a Clyde Valley Stomper had probably flushed the yen for 'freedom' well and truly out of his system. What's more, as a seasoned pro who had been around the block a few times, he had doubtless seen enough of how the band was managed to guess that any hope he might have had of profiting from its growing popularity was likely to be a forlorn one.

That old elephant in Lyn Dutton's room had trumpeted yet again.

Fortunately for me, the growing pressure to resolve the matter was relieved, at least temporarily, by John McGuff agreeing to resume trombone duties for our upcoming engagements north of the border.

Big venues, such as Dundee's Caird Hall, the City Hall in Perth, Hamilton Town Hall, the Aberdeen Music Hall and Leith's Eldorado Ballroom, predominated again on this trip, the dates scheduled to fit round a *Come Thursday* broadcast for BBC Radio Scotland and a couple of TV appearances.

The first of those was on Scottish ITV's *Roundup*, a weekly magazine show catering for a young audience and introduced by Morag Hood and Paul Young. A regular feature involved a panel of invited teenagers assessing a few of the latest pop records. As one of the panellists hadn't turned up, I was roped in to deputise, being introduced by Paul as 'Britain's oldest teenager'. All good fun. Until, that is, I said Frank Ifield's new single stood a better chance of being a hit than one by the Beatles, a group I admitted to knowing little about. I'd probably have been sentenced to death by the two girls on the jury, if one of them hadn't given me a reprieve because, in her own words, 'He's got nice dimples'. A narrow escape, and so much for my twenty-two-year-old's knowledge of the way youthful tastes in popular music were heading.

The other TV spot was on the BBC's current affairs programme *A Quick Look Round*. We had been invited to give a live performance of *Loch Lomond* (the B-side of *Peter and the Wolf*), as it had been adopted as signature music for the show, which was transmitted at peak early-evening viewing time five days a week. *Loch Lomond*, as mentioned earlier, is a traditional tune 'in the public domain', so the equivalent of composer's royalties would be payable to the arranger, noted on the record label as 'Valley' (Clyde Valley Stompers), but paid in this case, not to those of us in the band who had done the arrangement, but to 'the company'. Since this anomaly applied to royalties on record sales (mechanical rights) as well as to performing rights (radio and TV airings), the boys and I would surely be entitled to expect a full accounting at regular intervals. This was particularly relevant considering the composer of the B-side of a single earns exactly the same royalties from the record's sales as the composer of the A-side. Here was yet another wrinkle for me to iron out with Lyn Dutton at the appropriate time.

Meanwhile, this festive season tour had been a success on several fronts: the live dates had helped assuage many of the Stompers' longer-established fans, who thought they'd been deserted when the band emigrated to London; the radio and TV appearances had won us, we hoped, a wider and younger following than before; on a personal level, Ellie and I had enjoyed introducing our new baby to family and friends;

and lastly, the band itself had been given a most welcome Christmas present by John McGuff when he announced he'd be staying with us on our return 'down south'.

I didn't doubt that John's desire to be at home with his wife and son had encountered stiff competition from his love of playing jazz on a full-time basis. But I also suspected that spending two months laying bricks on a bitterly cold Scottish building site had made the prospect of touring England in the cosiness of a fug-filled bandwagon seem overwhelmingly attractive. Time, and the changing seasons, would tell.

*

Our arrival back in London had coincided with being given a regular Tuesday-night spot in Jazzshows at 100 Oxford Street, one of the best-known jazz addresses in the world. As part of the club's recent refurbishment, an entire wall opposite the entrance had been adorned with a montage of blown-up photographs of the country's leading bandleaders. Mug shots of Humphrey Lyttelton, Chris Barber, Kenny Ball, Sandy Brown, Alex Welsh and Acker Bilk were there. As was mine, and I was genuinely perturbed when I saw it.

'I don't think that's a good idea at all,' I said to Frank Parr, the Dutton Agency's all-seeing night owl, who had downed a few eye-openers in the Blue Posts before popping into the club to wish us well on our first night.

Frank hunched his shoulders. 'The Clyde Valley Stompers are up among the top bands, and you're the leader, so...'

'Yeah, but I'm not Clyde Valley. OK, *no*body is, but there's one person who probably *believes* he is, and he's not gonna be happy when he finds out my face is up on that wall.'

Frank shrugged again. 'Shouldn't have jacked in the band and buggered off to Jersey then, should he?'

The subject was duly dropped by Frank, who, aptly enough, had been a pro wicket keeper for Lancashire County Cricket Club in his pre-Mick Mulligan days. But my concerns lingered. I had never tried to catch the limelight while fronting the Clydes, being content to delegate the more extrovert tasks, like taking vocals, to Jim and Malky, or any of the other lads who could actually sing a bit. I knew my limitations as a showman and was happy to remain within them. I also knew that Lyn Dutton had held a position of some influence at Jazzshows since its earlier guise as the Humphrey Lyttelton Club, so it was quite likely he'd been responsible for having a picture of me pasted on the wall. And for the soundest of business reasons, no doubt. But I still worried.

What mattered more at present, however, was that our latest tour of Scotland had delivered John McGuff back into the fold. Yet it would soon become apparent that it had had the opposite effect on Malky Higgins. That old tug of war between the family man and wandering minstrel in him had been triggered again, and this time it looked as though the pull of a normal life with his wife and children would win – permanently.

Things came to a head late one afternoon in Cambridge, where we had arrived after crossing the country from a college job in Loughborough the previous night. We were a couple of hours early for the start of our gig in the Rex Ballroom, so repaired to a pub nearby for a pint and a game of darts. Malky waited, puffing his pipe, while we ordered our lagers, bitters, shandies or whatever, then stepped forward to draw the barman's attention to one of the draught taps on the counter.

'Ah'll have a pint o' that *Merrydown* beer, pal.'

The barman responded with a little chuckle. 'Er, it's not actually beer, sir. It's what the *Merrydown* cider company call their "Vintage Cider Wine".'

'Aye, fair enough. First time fur everything. Geeza pint, like Ah say.'

The barman shook his head. 'No, you don't understand, sir. It's wine – quite potent, and sold by the glass. *Wine* glass, that is.'

Now, Malky had never been short on bravado, so wasn't about to be relegated to a sipper of small measures of anything – especially when his mates were looking on.

'Naw, Ah fancy a pint, so just geez wan, OK?'

The barman's chuckle was tinged with anxiety now. 'Are you *sure*, sir? I mean, even in a university town like this, we've never been asked before for a *pint* of –'

Malky held up one hand and slapped the other on the bar. 'A pint! Aye, an' geeza coupla sets o' darts once ye've pulled it, eh!'

An hour later, Malky had quaffed three pints of the stuff. Then, to the barman's obvious amazement, he departed the pub with the rest of us – walking upright and unaided. I recalled my father's adage: 'It's when the fresh air hits them that the piss artists go doolally.' But Malky showed no sign of being even slightly tipsy on the walk round to the ballroom. And he was still in the same state of composure when we took to the bandstand. It seemed the barman had been exaggerating the strength of the *Merrydown* cider company's best.

'Fuckin' gnat's-piss apple squeezins fur pansified poofter students!' Malky muttered, putting mouthpiece to lips as I stomped in the opening number of the evening. But instead of the first blast of *St Louis Blues* coming out of his trumpet, the force of Malky's blowing propelled him backwards to land on his butt in front of the drum kit. Wide-eyed and unblinking, he was mumbling the words of *I Ain't Gonna Give Nobody None of My Jellyroll*. Malky was out of it, solid gone and sent – literally.

'A virus,' I told the anxious ballroom manager, who had helped drag Malky from the stage and into the band room. 'It's left him prone to sudden fainting attacks like this.'

We deposited Malky on a couch, where he curled up in the foetal position and went to sleep. It turned out to be a long and unconventional evening, with John and I having to take turns at playing the lead. Hard going, but we got away with it – just. When we finally came off the stand, the ballroom manager was waiting outside the band room. He was holding a glass of water.

'I thought your friend might be glad of this,' he said, 'but I didn't want to disturb him earlier.'

He needn't have worried. Malky was sitting up and, apparently, wide awake. The only unusual thing was that his eyes still looked as if they were glued open.

'I've brought you this to sip,' said the manager, handing Malky the glass of water. 'Might make you feel better.'

Slowly, Malky raised his eyes to meet the manager's, then, his top lip curling menacingly, he snarled, 'If ye don't get the fuck oot ma face, Ah'll break yer fuckin' neck!'

I had never seen Malky in a foul mood like this before. As a rule, he was the most jovial, inoffensive character you'd be ever likely to meet.

'Beat it!' he barked at the manager. 'Piss aff, or Ah'll melt ye!'

Prudently, the manager did as requested.

While the rest of the boys busied themselves loading the bandwagon, I sat down beside Malky and, gingerly, put an arm round his shoulder. 'Everything OK, man? Anything bothering you at all?'

Malky didn't reply, but continued to stare blindly across the room.

'Don't worry about tonight,' I said. 'Everybody deserves a wee rest occasionally.'

A few more moments of silence passed, then Malky finally blinked, a tear appearing at the corner of his eye, to dribble down and fall like a raindrop from the end of his nose.

'Ah cannae take it any more, son,' he sniffed. 'Ah want tae stay wi' the band, but ... Nancy and the kids...'

I patted his back. 'It's all right, Malky, I understand. You have to do what's best for you and your family. Nothing's more important than that.'

* * * * *

CHAPTER THIRTY-SEVEN

'THE ALBATROSS GOES CUCKOO'

'Be careful when ye're feedin' beasts, boy – there's always one that'll butt ye in the arse!'
(My grandfather, Thomas Muir – in his cattle shed, winter 1954)

*

'Ulcerated colitis. That's what you've got, young man.'

So said the doctor Ellie had browbeaten me into seeing about a persistent stomach upset that had started a few weeks earlier.

'A fairly mild form at present,' the doc continued, 'but it isn't a condition you want to aggravate by over-work, irregular and unhealthy meals, lack of sleep, insufficient fresh air, prolonged stress – that sort of thing.'

I told him he had just recited textbook terms of reference for anyone who aspired to lead a touring jazz band.

'Maybe so,' he frowned, scribbling out a prescription, 'but you'll have to take better care of yourself. Take a couple of weeks off. Go home, relax and enjoy that new baby of yours.'

Two hours later, I was bound for Manchester, where we were booked to play the Bodega Club that same night. The medicine I'd picked up earlier from the chemist tasted awful, but was already having a soothing effect on my innards – or so I told myself.

*

Malky Higgins' departure put us right back in the old position of having to use stand-in trumpeters until a lasting replacement could be found. Not an ideal situation for someone trying to kick a stress habit, but I persevered. There was nothing else for it. As before, the Dutton office did a good job of finding horn players who were available at short notice, even if only for limited periods at a time.

The Clansmen, a fine band led by Forrie Cairns, the clarinettist I had replaced in the Clydes, were preparing to return to Glasgow after being based in London for a couple of years. Forrie, putting aside his past frictions with Ian Menzies, was happy to allow his trumpeter Alex Dalgleish to guest for us whenever possible.

Dean Kerr, another former sideman and adversary of Menzies, was an especially interesting 'dep', as he had been in the Clydes' line-up the first time I saw them live, about five years earlier in Haddington's Corn Exchange. By now, Dean was a manager with the Selmer Musical Instrument Company in London, but his 'lip was still in' and his unfussy, gutsy trumpet lead was a treat to follow. He had been on the losing side in the well-publicized debacle that ended in the auctioning of the Clyde Valley Stompers' name, so I was itching to get his side of the story. To his credit, he avoided being drawn into discussing bygone differences with Ian Menzies, but he did say something at the end of his last job with us which I guessed could have had some relevance: 'The band's done really well during your watch, Pete, so just look out for the cuckoo in the nest. It's got green feathers!'

In the midst of all this disruption to the front line, our rhythm section was given a massive boost by the long-awaited recruitment of a new drummer. It was Ron Mathewson, our 'boy genius' bass player, who tipped us off about Edinburgh's Billy Law, with whom Ron had gigged a year or so earlier. Since then, Billy had been playing on the Continent with a Danish band, but had recently returned home and was available. Coming from anyone of a lesser musical talent, the build-up Ron gave Billy would have seemed over-the-top. But Ron's word was good enough for me. Billy arrived at King's Cross railway station just two days after I phoned to ask if he'd like to join the Clydes. At twenty-two, he was the same age as me, single, as sociable as they come, blessed with outstanding technical ability and seriously committed to being a professional musician – based, preferably, in London. Hallelujah!

It was ironic that a drummer of Billy Law's prowess could only *appear* to be playing on his first engagement with the band. *Thank Your Lucky Stars* was an ITV network programme focussing exclusively on pop singles. A forerunner of the BBC's *Top of the Pops*, it blazed a trail by featuring recording artists performing their latest releases live. Yet the performances were no more live than those of the showband we had witnessed in Northern Ireland a while back. The producers of *Lucky Stars*, leaving nothing to chance, insisted on everyone miming to their records.

Setting another trend, the show was pre-recorded, allowing for re-takes of anything that went drastically wrong. Perhaps not surprisingly, the adrenalin flow of a truly live TV performance was missing, and the hours of hanging about during rehearsals even more tedious. The edition we were appearing in was taped before an audience of mainly teenage girls in the ABC Studio Centre at Teddington, south-west London, on Sunday 17th February 1963.

Introduced by Brian Matthew, our old 'mate' from the *Saturday Club* and *Easybeat* radio programmes, the show was headlined by Billy Fury, regarded by many as the most authentic of the UK's several Elvis clones, and also featured Jet Harris and Tony Meehan (late of Cliff Richard's Shadows), Carol Deene, Duffy Power, Billie Davis and the Beatles. But if anyone doubted that Billy Fury was the star attraction, those teenage girls in the audience were ready to convince them otherwise.

'Mark my words,' a middle-aged studio hand said to me just before the videotaping got under way, 'them silly young bints is gonna wet themselves when Fury comes on. No kiddin', cock, I seen it all before, like, and it ain't pleasant 'avin' to mop the piss offa the seats afterwards!'

Billy Fury's fans certainly did plenty of squealing every time he flicked his pelvis during his rendition of *Like I've Never Been Gone*, which was in marked contrast to the relative indifference shown to the Beatles' performance of *Please Please Me*.

'I recognise that song from somewhere,' I remarked to Jim from our vantage point behind the cameras.

'Yeah, it's the one ye said was a no-hoper on that *Roundup* telly show in Glasgow, remember?'

'I do, now you mention it. Yup, and I still don't think it'll be a hit.' (Little did I know how quickly I'd be made to eat those words!)

We hadn't really noticed the Beatles all that much during rehearsals. They had kept themselves to themselves, lounging in a corner looking slightly jaded. What I did spot, though, was that they seemed to blank Billy Fury any time he came near them.

Our in-the-know studio hand wasn't slow to tell me why. 'They've took the hump 'cause he knocked 'em back when they done a try-out to be his backin' band.' He shook his head. 'Nah, loada crap, the lotta them – flashes in the pan – Fury included! Yeah, gimme David Whitfield, Joan Regan, Pearl Carr an' Teddy Johnson. Them's *real* stars for ya!'

If the soon-to-be Fab Four weren't already miffed by being upstaged by Billy Fury during the show, they certainly would have been by the situation in the car park after it. While Billy's limo was being mobbed by dozens of screaming female fans (and a fair few male ones, too, as it happened!) the Beatles, unnoticed and alone, were loading their gear into a little Ford Thames delivery van.

'No wonder the poor buggers looked cheesed-off all day,' John said as he climbed into our comparatively opulent minibus. 'Imagine havin' to travel all the way back to Liverpool cooped up in a windowless tin can like that!'

*

I finally got a chance to broach the subject of the band's monetary management with Lyn Dutton a fortnight later. Shortly before that, Frank Parr had delivered a package to me in the Blue Posts, following one of our regular Tuesday-night spots at Jazzshows. It was another musical arrangement that Lyn had commissioned (without our knowledge) from Kenny Graham.

'*In a Monastery Garden* – your next A-side, according to Lyn,' said Frank, with the disdainful air of a true hater of anything that smacked of commercialism. 'Pretentious bollocks, according to me!'

I could see why Lyn, or someone, had selected this particular tune. Jazzed-up versions of *In a Persian Market*, another of Albert Ketèlbey's popular light-classical compositions, had long been standard fare on the menu of many trad bands, including the Clydes under Ian Menzies. The difference, however, was that while *Persian Market* lent itself to such radical treatment, *Monastery Garden* didn't, and wouldn't, no matter how clever the arrangement. Paying anyone to do the impossible was, therefore, a waste of money – our money.

I was about to say this to Lyn, as an introduction to discussing how the band's general finances were being handled, but I wasn't quick enough.

'Oh, by the way, Pete,' he said while I took a seat at the opposite side of his desk, 'the publishers of *In a Monastery Garden* have killed any chance of recording it the way we thought. They say they regard it as almost sacred, and would pull out every legal stop to prevent it being mucked about.'

I was pleased to hear it, and decided not to bother asking who the 'we' were who had been doing the thinking. Perhaps it had been a piece of communal input from the Dutton office staff, and I wouldn't have wanted to show ingratitude for their interest; I got on extremely well with all of them. At the same time, it would make no sense to have the band's recording repertoire decided 'by committee', while the material already prepared by us hadn't even been heard by Lyn – or, more importantly, by our producer George Martin. This was another issue I'd have to get sorted out without further delay. But first things first...

Lyn listened intently while I suggested that all the musicians who had left the band since Ian Menzies' retirement shared a feeling, justified or not, that the band's income wasn't being distributed fairly.

'They told you that, did they, Pete?'

'Not all of them, but it would be a real bozo of a bandleader who wasn't wise to that sort of vibe.'

'So, you're saying there's discontent within the ranks?'

'Absolutely not. Keeping morale up has never been a problem, which makes it all the more frustrating to lose guys for reasons beyond my control.'

Lyn was quick to counter that one. 'Ah, but their wages are guaranteed, and the guys must surely realise there may be occasions when what they're paid isn't covered by what the band pulls in.'

I couldn't resist a wry smile. 'I remember you saying, on the day Big Ming told us he was giving up, that our wages would be guaranteed, but only if the band continued earning enough to justify it.'

'So?'

'So, it follows that the band *has* continued to earn enough.'

Lyn contemplated his cigar for a few seconds, then looked me in the eye. 'OK, Pete, say your piece.'

I took a deep breath and began by stating that Ian had first put the future of the Clydes at risk by foisting the leadership on Malky, then left the band to sink or swim in the choppy waters his own suspect judgement had created. I swiftly acknowledged that the Dutton Agency had helped our initial survival by keeping an already-full date sheet intact. But that would have counted for nothing if the patched-up remnants of the band hadn't managed to win the continued support of promoters and fans alike. *And*, I stressed, we'd done all of that without the assistance, or cost to the company, of a featured vocalist or PR manager.

'Point taken,' Lyn said with a shrug, 'but I *did* agree to let you have a piano player.'

'OK, but there were still two less on the payroll than before the Clydes moved down here to London. And if we hadn't hired that piano player, the band wouldn't be reaping the benefits of its first hit record right now. I'm talking about benefits as in film work, appearances on top TV shows and more lucrative live engagements.'

'But what makes you think the Clydes' income isn't being distributed fairly? After all, *you* collect the gig money every night and you know what the band members earn, so...'

I couldn't tell if Lyn had said that with tongue-in-cheek just to see what my reaction would be, or whether he was being serious and therefore taking me for a soft touch.

Either way, he had given me the incentive to cut straight to the chase.

The crux of the matter, as he would be aware, was that I only collected the money at the end of bread-and-butter gigs, usually at jazz clubs where the band was on a percentage of the take. In the case of most bigger jobs – concerts, festivals, the 'season' at Blackpool's Empress Ballroom and the like – the band's fees were agreed in advance and invariably paid direct to the agency. In many instances, I wasn't even told what those fees were. I added that I had still been able to glean a fair idea of what they *might* be, simply by talking to the leaders of similarly-rated bands. Likewise, the boys had formed an opinion of what their wages *should* be by chatting to their counterparts in those same outfits.

Lyn had lowered his eyes, rolling his cigar between thumb and fingertips in his usual meditative way.

I didn't wait for him to comment, but continued on the same theme by pointing out that the boys and I were never informed what the band was being paid for radio, TV, film and recording dates – whether it was basic Musician Union rates or more; we weren't told the terms of our contract with EMI Records – what the royalty percentages were and the size of associated advances; we hadn't been given access to the earnings accrued from sales and performing rights relating to *our* arrangement of *Loch Lomond*; nor were we being kept informed of sales figures and related royalty income in respect of both *Peter and the Wolf* and its follow-up.

'You all knew the deal when you joined the Clydes,' Lyn retorted. 'You were offered guaranteed wages, which meant you waived any right to *ancillary* income – session fees, record royalties and so forth. Such moneys had to be paid into the company's pot to help fund those wages, come rain or shine. That's surely easy enough to understand, Pete, isn't it?'

'In a word, Lyn, no.' I proceeded to tell him why...

The whole point was that the Clyde Valley Stompers were a more saleable commodity now than they had ever been. Yet the musicians whose efforts and talents were responsible for this achievement were expected to give away an undisclosed part of their earnings to a person most of them had never met – and, in some cases, had scarcely heard of. In their view, Ian Menzies had contributed nothing to the band's current success, but continued to earn from it, just because he had bought the name for sixty quid back in the Fifties.

'That's one way of putting it,' said Lyn, 'but, like it or not, you can't escape the fact that the use of the Clyde Valley Stompers name has to be paid for.'

'But what we're paying now is really only a *rent*, which increases according to the value *we* add to the property, while the owner chips in zippo. I mean, if we were talking about a house or flat here, the landlord would be on thin ice.'

I had been apprehensive about having this oft-postponed tête-à-tête with Lyn, basically because I expected him to take instant umbrage. But, to my surprise, he seemed almost relieved to have the subject of the Clydes' finances brought up. Could it be that he found the weight of an albatross round his neck just as bothersome as the rest of us?

'Well, I see where you're coming from, Pete,' he said, stroking his chin, 'although I'm not sure what can be done about it. However, if you've any ideas yourself, now's the time to come out with them.'

This was the opportunity I had been waiting for, so I waded right in. I said that transparency was what was lacking in the relationship between Clyde Valley Stompers Ltd and those of us in the band. I pointed out that musicians weren't machines in a sausage factory, but creative, intelligent human beings, who deserve to be treated as such. Admittedly, the Clyde Valley Stompers name was a valuable commodity, but without the musicians who comprised the actual band – and, more recently, had taken it from near collapse to a position of unprecedented success – the name would be worthless.

Lyn arched eyebrows. 'Strong words, but I take your point. Nevertheless, the use of the name still comes at a price.'

'Which is where transparency comes in. The boys and I are entitled to know *precisely* what price we're paying.'

'Oh, you think so, do you?'

'I *know* so. We've earned that right, and if a policy of openness isn't adopted in the band's financial affairs, then we'll never have a settled line-up. In fact, before long it'll be impossible to persuade *any* good musicians to join the Clydes.'

Lyn's expression showed that my last remark had stung. But I was telling the truth, and he knew it.

'Fair enough, you've said your piece, and I appreciate your frankness. However, you'll have to tell me exactly what you mean by transparency. There's a limit to how much any employee needs to know about his employer's business.'

'But a jazz band isn't just a business, or a collection of machines in a sausage factory, as I said before. The employees *are* the business.'

Lyn leaned back in his seat, folded his arms and looked at me poker-faced for a few seconds. 'OK,' he sighed, 'what is it you want, Pete?'

'The boys and I need to know everything about all aspects of the Clydes' earnings – fees for engagements, session payments, record royalties, everything. And we need to know where the money goes. The agency is entitled to the standard percentage off the top – nobody can argue with that – but what's paid in *rent* to Ian Menzies will have to be stipulated, preferably as a percentage of the band's gross earnings as well. Then, most importantly, the musicians will have to receive equal shares of the balance, once all necessary expenses are taken into account.'

'So, in short, you're talking about the Clydes becoming a co-operative band – correct?

'That's it, Lyn – just like so many other bands on your books. Transparency and openness – the only way forward.'

'But your wages wouldn't be guaranteed any more. In a co-operative band, they can fluctuate from week to week, depending on the band's overall income.'

'Which would give us all the more motivation to work hard. The same motivation that's being knocked for six under the present system.'

'OK, Pete, message received and understood.' Lyn stood up and led me towards the door. He hesitated before opening it, frowning slightly. 'We're, uhm, we're not facing some sort of mutiny here, are we?'

I assured him that we certainly were not. 'In fact,' I said, 'the boys don't even know I'm having this powwow with you today.'

'Ah, that's fine. I'll, uh – I'll discuss everything on the phone with Ian and his wife – they have the final word, as you know – and I'll talk to you about it some more after that.'

'Better still, why don't you ask Ian and his wife to come over and have a chat face-to-face? You know, a businesslike but friendly discussion. After all, it's about laying new foundations for the band's future, in which they'll continue to have a financial interest. Besides, we haven't seen or heard from Ian for about eighteen months, so it's about time he paid us a visit.'

Lyn gave me a thin smile. 'Yes, well, I'll see what I can do, Pete. I'll see what I can do.'

I was called into the office the very next day. Lyn's smile was even thinner now, and he seemed unusually ill at ease. He didn't waste time with small talk.

'I had that chat with Ian on the phone after you left yesterday – told him exactly what we had discussed.'

'Thanks. Good of you to get on the case so quickly. Much appreciated.'

'Yes, well, he was pretty quick to come back to me about it as well.'

I'd noticed Lyn was avoiding eye contact, so everything was pointing to confirmation of my hunch that Ian wouldn't have taken kindly to my proposition. But I hadn't anticipated what came next.

'We're letting you go, Pete.'

'Go? Where to?'

'What I'm saying is that your position with the Clydes is being terminated.'

'You mean I'm ... *fired*?'

Lyn nodded his head, but still didn't look directly at me.

I felt poleaxed. It took a few moments for the full gravity of what I'd been told to sink in. All I could say was: 'Why?'

Lyn didn't answer.

'Why?' I said again. What had I done wrong? Hadn't I put my heart and soul into the job? Hadn't I worked for the Clydes' survival as if the band were my own? Hadn't I successfully overseen it's revival, no matter how unfavourable the odds? Hadn't I handled all financial responsibilities with absolute honesty? Hadn't I presented myself to promoters, producers and the public in a way that was a credit to 'the company'?

Lyn raised his hand. 'There's no need to go on, Pete. Nobody can fault anything about your leadership of the Clydes. In fact, I wish *all* the bandleaders I represent were as capable. But the decision has been made – you're services are no longer required, and there's nothing more to say.'

I was seeing red now. 'But, hell's bells, you can't just kick me out without giving a reason!'

Lyn was looking suitably embarrassed. 'There are three directors involved, and the will of the majority has to be upheld.'

'It's all right, I get the picture. The albatross turns into a green-feathered cuckoo, eh?'

'Sorry?'

'Just a passing thought. Anyway, is the spokesman for the majority going to come over from Jersey and tell the chump who's been herding his milch cows for him that he's sacked? Maybe shake the idiot's hand and give him a medal?'

'Pete, there really is nothing more I can say. Except, you don't have to worry about informing the boys in the band. I know they've got tonight off, but I'll contact them myself in the morning and break the news.'

'Don't tell me *they*'re going to be fired as well!'

'Oh, no, not at all – their position won't change, I promise you.'

'Well, thanks a lot, Lyn, that shows real heart, I must say!'

*

Ellie was tucking wee Sandy into his cot for the night when I got home. 'So, did you manage to negotiate a better deal?' she asked without turning round.

'Ehm, no, not really. Not exactly.'

'Oh well, never mind, we'll still manage.' Ellie bent down and gave the little fellow a kiss. 'Goodnight, pet – see you in the morning. *If* not before.' She flashed me a smile brimming with pride. 'I think he's teething – *already*!'

'Quick off the mark, just like me.' I was trying my best to appear upbeat.

But I wasn't fooling Ellie. She tweaked my cheek. 'Come on, cheer up. They'll come round to paying you and the boys more soon enough, you'll see.'

I knew Ellie's gift for always looking on the bright side would be hard pushed to survive what I had to tell her, but there was no point in putting off.

'You're joking!' she gasped. '*Are*n't you?'

'Nope, I've never been more serious. Sacked, fired, dismissed, axed, given the boot. No matter which way I say it, I've been kicked out on my ear.'

'But *why*? You've always said you get on really well with Lyn Dutton.' Ellie was shaking her head in disbelief. 'Why on earth would he do such a thing?'

'I don't think he would have, if it had been up to him. I mean, Frank Parr confirmed that Lyn had arranged for the mug shot of me to be put up on the Jazzshows wall with all the others a couple of weeks ago, and he'd hardly have done that if he was planning to give me the chop.' I gave a little chuckle. 'Oh, and he even offered me a job with the agency on my way out of his office today. Yeah, and I told him what he could do with it – politely, of course.'

We stood and looked down at Sandy until he was asleep, and we knew we were both thinking the same thing: what sort of world had we brought this little mite into?

I followed Ellie through to the kitchen, where she poured herself a coffee. I poured myself a measure of stomach medicine. A double.

We sat lost in our own thoughts for a while, then Ellie said, 'Why don't you phone Ian Menzies in Jersey – ask him why he's messing up your life like this?'

It was only then that I realised I had never been given his phone number. Never been given the name of his boarding house, or even what town it was in. I told Ellie, then said she could make what she wanted of that.

'Well, it certainly says a lot about the sort of person you've been working yourself sick for.'

I poured myself another spoonful of anti-colitis potion. 'Seems like it. But I wouldn't phone him even if I did have his number. Why should I make it easy for him? Come to that, it's a cert he wouldn't have the nerve to speak to me anyway.'

Silence settled around us once more. After a while, I noticed Ellie looking round the walls of the kitchen, at the shelves, the cupboards, the pots and pans. 'We'll have to move out of this flat, won't we?'

I nodded my head. ''Fraid so. And pretty quick too. Clyde Valley Stompers Ltd won't be coughing up any severance money – you can be sure of that.'

Ellie gave me one of her stoical little smiles. 'Never mind, something will turn up, you'll see.'

I patted her hand. 'Yeah, course it will. Always does, doesn't it? But right now, it's all about maintaining our dignity, putting this rotten experience behind us, rising above it, moving on.'

Ellie's smile faded. 'So, ehm, what will we be moving on *to*? And *where*?'

'Well, I'll – I'll maybe have to sleep on that one.'

I hardly slept at all that night. Neither of us did. But wee Sandy managed to. Right through till dawn without a murmur.

'The sleep of the innocent,' I smiled, peeping into his cot.

'Hmm, if only he knew,' Ellie said. 'If only he knew...'

* * * * *

CHAPTER THIRTY-EIGHT

'A GOOD NAME IS SOONER LOST THAN WON'

It was early afternoon when Jim phoned. 'The boys and me are havin' a pint here in the Blue Posts. Just came from a meetin' wi' Dutton. We thought you'd be there as well, though.'

'Sorry about that, Jim. I would've been in touch to explain, but Lyn said he'd –'

'It's all right, Pete, he told us he'd decided to do that himself. He also told us you'd been fired.'

'And did he tell you why, by any chance?'

'All he said was it had been a *company* decision – couldn't see eye-to-eye wi' you about a demand you'd made for the band to go co-operative.'

'Hence foot-to-arse instead of eye-to-eye. Yeah, Big Ming and his missus would have flipped because I insisted on seeing the books from now on.'

'No surprises there, then. Anyhow, we told Dutton he'd only shot the messenger.'

'How do you mean?'

'Simple – if we'd known you were about to open *that* can of worms, we'd have gone with you yesterday. Lend a bit o' support, you know?'

'I appreciate that, Jim, I really do. But it's all over for me now. I'm absolutely gutted, believe me, but all I can do is wish you and the boys well.'

I heard Jim tutting, and I could visualise that same look of controlled exasperation he'd displayed when I'd mistakenly thought he was offering to supply washboard players for the school pipe band.

'Nah, nah, you've missed the point here, man. What I'm sayin' on the shoot-the-messenger front is that Ian Menzies no longer has his Clyde Valley Stompers. Well, correction – he's still got his precious sixty-quid name, and he's welcome to it.'

'And so say all of us!' came a concerted background shout, followed by the clinking of glasses.

For the second time in twenty-four hours, I found myself pausing to allow the gravity of what I'd just heard to sink in.

Jim came back on before I could say anything. 'Of course, when we said, "If Pete's out, we're all out," Dutton just about swallowed his cigar. Tried to make us see sense, by his way of it. Said we'd regret leavin' the Clydes. Anyway, he was wastin' his breath.'

'You – you surely don't mean you've handed in your notice, do you?'

'*Notice?* How much notice did he give you?'

'Well ... none.'

'And that's just what we gave him.'

I was stuck for words, yet again.

Jim's staccato laugh rattled down the line. 'So, daddy, you've still got a band. All you've gotta do now is find us some work!'

*

The Pete Kerr's All-Stars' bandwagon hit the road in mid-March, 1963. Its first journey was from a south-east London used-car lot, which specialised in selling 'retired' police vehicles. Just three weeks earlier, we'd appeared as the Clyde Valley Stompers, dubbed the most televised jazz band in Britain, on ITV's *Thank Your Lucky Stars*. That was the day we had felt sorry for the Beatles having to travel in a little windowless Ford van. I suppose the Morris LD thirty-hundredweight Black Maria I had just purchased was a *slight* step up from that. At least it had side windows. It would be just a matter of removing the bars and no-one would guess our new means of getting around had spent the best years of its life ferrying lags between the Old Bailey and Wormwood Scrubs Prison. In any case, it was all I could afford. What little remained of my rainy-day savings had been spent on band uniforms: faux shot silk suits from the 'clearance' rail in Cecil Gee's Oxford Street store. Again, they were all I could afford, and even if the material looked a bit poncy in daylight, I reckoned it'd show up well on stage – if we ever managed to get on one again.

For this was the ludicrous situation which now existed: while Ian Menzies had a band's name but no band, and the Dutton Agency had a full diary of engagements for that non-existent band, I had the band that so recently bore that name, but now had no work. What's more, it would soon become apparent that finding *any* work was going to be a tough task, and for the most bizarre of reasons.

As much as I had been touched by the boys putting loyalty before self-interest – the exact opposite of the way in which I had been treated by someone I had once looked upon as a big-brother figure – there was no escaping the stark reality of what I was now faced with. I had not only my own two dependents to provide for, but also six professional musicians, each with the inescapable cost of living in London to meet. Cards had to be put on the table and hard decisions made – but fast.

With the best will in the world on the part of Bix and John, it would have been unfair of me to expect the two oldest members of the band to compromise their domestic responsibilities in favour of sticking around waiting for a pay day that would be a long time coming. The advent of spring and the chance of a lucrative building contract back home in Scotland was an opportunity John would have been foolish to reject. And I told him so. Likewise, it made sense for Bix to accept an offer of a solo residency in a club only a short tube ride from his London home. I told him so as well.

Now, in addition to looking for a trumpet player (Malky Higgins had never been permanently replaced), I was short of a pianist and trombone player too. I also had to make provision for the welfare of Ellie and wee Sandy; financial facts dictated that vacating our Ossulton Way flat would have to be undertaken with utmost haste. So, the first test of our 'new' bandwagon's mettle was to haul my little family four hundred miles north to Haddington, where the haven of a room in my parents' house awaited them. I was driving south again a few hours later, conflicting priorities battling it out in my head, the contents of my anti-colitis bottle diminishing rapidly. With every passing mile it became more clear that my old friend Lady Luck would have to blow damned hard to keep the gathering clouds of despondency at bay.

But blow she did, and with sufficient gusto to allow a glimmer of sunshine to light the way ahead. It was evening when I arrived back in London, having arranged to meet the remaining members of the band, guitarist/banjoist Jim Douglas, bass player Ron Mathewson and drummer Billy Law, in the Blue Posts pub. They were standing at the bar having a drink with three equally young guys, whom they introduced as Mike Scott, a fresh-faced trumpet player from Devon; Mike Oliver, a laconic Londoner who sported an Abraham Lincoln beard, played piano and smoked roll-up fags; and bespectacled Eddie Lorkin, a trombonist who'd just graduated from the Royal Scottish Academy of Music in Glasgow.

'The boys are lookin' for work,' said Jim, 'and you're lookin' for musicians, so…'

'Are you also happy to eat ozone sandwiches for a while?' I asked the three job-seekers.

'If you supply the bread, we'll bring the ozone,' quipped Eddie Lorkin.

'Well, you'll maybe have to *bake* your own bread, but I can just about stretch to the flour.'

Handshakes and laughs all round indicated that Pete Kerr's All-Stars were once again a seven-piece band. And if describing all (or any) of us as stars would be regarded as a tad presumptuous by the jazz cognoscenti, I think we all accepted that this might prove to be the least of our immediate worries. However, with an average age of less than twenty-one, we had youth on our side and shared an irresistible urge to play jazz for a living – or at least the occasional round of ozone sandwiches.

The very next day, Lady Luck got her second wind and blew us Mike Scott's father, who, it would transpire, had the rare distinction of being both a successful lawyer and a man of selfless compassion. Mike had arranged for us to meet him in Chandos Road, one of the most tranquil and exclusive locations in East Finchley. He was standing outside a particularly handsome Victorian villa when we trundled up in the old Black Maria. Mr Scott didn't bat an eyelid at the incongruous sight of our ex-paddy wagon edging between the two gleaming Jags that were typical of the cars skirting the pavement. Presumably, he had seen enough criminal transporters in the execution of his professional duties not to be fazed by the appearance of another one, even here. Similarly, he would have been sufficiently familiar with the typical villain's looks to be able to assess pretty quickly whether or not his son's new companions were upright citizens – or as near so as could be expected for young jazz musicians. His smiles as we piled out suggested we had passed the test.

After pleasantries had been exchanged, he informed us that the house belonged to one of his clients, who had gone overseas on business for a few months and required his property to be looked after by live-in caretakers. Would we be interested in taking on the responsibility? Unfortunately, we wouldn't be rewarded financially for our troubles, but neither would we have to pay for electricity, gas or any maintenance costs that might crop up.

Instead of kissing Mr Scott's hand, I grabbed it before he had time to turn into a frog. Done deal!

Up to then, Jim, Ron and Billy had been sharing a room in the house of an inebriate Irish doctor, who was in the habit of waiting up for them when they were returning from gigs, booze at the ready, his mood indicator set to party mode. It was a situation that had more disadvantages than attractions for the boys: even itinerant jazz musicians have to sleep occasionally. In any event, it wouldn't have been long before they'd have been unable to pay the doc his rent, and as much as he loved the boys' after-hours company, their rent money was needed to pay for the booze. Catch 22. They'd eventually have been evicted.

As pianist Mike Oliver was married with a flat of his own, the other five boys and I fitted comfortably into the spacious interior of the Chandos Road house, and with a level of comfort unknown in any of the London pads we had previously lived in. Now, as Jim had said, *all* I had to do was find the band some work.

*

The first thing I did was to phone round the promoters of engagements already on the now-defunct Clydes' date sheet. I thought it worth a try, despite expecting Lyn Dutton to have started making arrangements for such gigs to be played by other bands in his stable. However, I was taken completely by surprise to be told by all the promoters I spoke to that no such substitutions had been made. As far as they were concerned, the Clyde Valley Stompers remained booked to appear as per contract on the appointed dates.

A mystery. And no better way to have it solved than by paying another visit to the Blue Posts. There, the drums of the jazz scene's jungle telegraph were about to start beating out a message that beggared belief. A virtually unknown English band, the Leathertown Jazzmen, had been brought back from their base in Germany to assume the guise of the Clyde Valley Stompers. That none of the musicians had had any previous connection with the Clydes – nor, indeed, Scotland – appeared to matter not a whit to 'the company'. A goose to replace the one that had been laying all those golden eggs of late had been conveniently conjured up. After a few glasses of Blue Posts tongue-loosener, a 'usually reliable' Lyn Dutton Agency source divulged that, in addition to showing such contempt for fans and promoters, a revised level of avarice had been arrived at by paying the members of the 'new' Clydes considerably less in wages than the old line-up.

Not that it mattered. The assumption that such a clumsy ploy would fool either the public or band bookers was doomed to fail, as it duly did. The good will associated with the Clyde Valley Stompers name, built up over so many years, had been squandered at a stroke – or, as one particularly eloquent observer put it, had landed in the gutter after being prostituted by the pomposity of a seriously misguided egotist. This frank summing-up heralded the ignominious end of the mighty Clyde Valley Stompers.

In years to come, jazz historians would suggest that the Clydes had been the first and most prominent band to have fallen victim to the demise of the 'Trad Boom'. In fact, what the Clydes had fallen victim to was the short-sighted arrogance of one man. Rather than accept an invitation to sit down and discuss an equitable and transparent basis for the band's future, he had given way to a side of his nature which seemed to lack any sense of fairness. The result? Instead of everyone involved being apportioned his slice of a cake that had been painstakingly baked to ensure a long shelf life, no-one got even a crumb.

* * * * *

CHAPTER THIRTY-NINE

'HEAD NORTH, YOUNG MEN!'

Our association with a once respected name, so cynically tarnished, made it even more difficult to secure engagements for Pete Kerr's All-Stars than it might otherwise have been. Many clubs were already switching their allegiance from jazz bands to beat groups, idols of the latest fad to invade the fickle world of popular music. Even promoters who had stood by the Clydes through thick and thin – and in all likelihood would have still have done – gave my approaches a polite, but firm, brush-off. Once bitten, twice shy.

The irony was that the band now comprised a group of young lads whose commitment to their music was such that they were prepared to accept whatever hardships might lie in the way of realising their aspirations. Also, we got on really well together – most of the time. We had to, living under the same roof, with more time on our hands than money in our pockets. But keeping everyone busy was the trick, and when we weren't rehearsing, we addressed envelopes for a mailshot advertising agency. It was Mike Scott's father who put us wise to this way of earning a few bob in our spare time. The snag was that, try as we might, we still ended up with more spare time than money. And with our worsening financial state came the prospect of starving – literally.

From the first day of our moving into the Chandos Road house, I had made a habit of writing to every source we could think of that might hire a jazz band occasionally: sports clubs, military bases, holiday camps, cruise lines, schools and even prisons. But it was university and college students who proved to be our best source of work, albeit sporadic, usually at short notice and inevitably modestly paid. With the Clydes, it had been a relatively easy task getting to and from distant campuses like Durham in the north-east of England, Exeter in the south-west of the country, or Bangor in north-west Wales, since the dates were always part of a tour, involving other engagements en route. But we now found ourselves compelled to accept one-stop trips to such far-flung venues, and as the fees were never sufficient to cover the cost of overnight accommodation, the long drive back to London always loomed large at the end of each gig.

Yet, no matter how frugal our ways, the length of time between pay days forced us to penny-pinch ever more severely. When we first took up residence in Chandos Road, some pears, unpicked the previous autumn, still hung on trees in the small orchard behind the house. Their skins were like leather and their insides mushy, but we ate them gladly. Cornflakes became a welcome change from the ozone sandwiches we had recently joked about. And when we ran out of milk, we doused the cereal in sauce made from a jar of curry powder we found in a cupboard. The era of make do and mend had made a comeback. Eventually, however, the craving for something more wholesome became so great that we pooled our pennies one evening and trudged en masse to the local butcher's shop just before it closed. Drooling, we gazed at the juicy steaks, chunky joints and succulent chops displayed in the window. Everything was beyond our budget, except for the contents of one tray: gristly morsels of meat-mottled bone, labelled *Scrag End of Mutton – Scraps – 1/6d to Clear*. Bingo! Manna within our means!

'Got a dog, 'ave ya, boys?' smiled the butcher as he handed us the bundle.

'Nah, we used to have,' said drummer Billy, deadpan, 'but we ate him last week!'

*

The impending return of the house's owner coincided with a rare occurrence for the band: four gigs in a row. Great news, but for one detail. The Clyde Valley Stompers may have been tagged the most-travelled band in the UK, but even they had never tackled a trip like the one we were now faced with. Southampton, on the south coast of England, is 700 miles from Thurso, on the northern tip of Scotland – almost as far as a crow can fly between any two points on mainland Britain. We broke the journey half way for a dance gig in the Scottish Borders, drove over to Glasgow to record a *Come Thursday* broadcast for BBC producer Ben Lyons, a staunch supporter of music and musicians he believed in, then completed the marathon with a 280-mile haul to Thurso.

Again, there wasn't much money to divvy up once travelling expenses had been accounted for, but at least we were back in Scotland, and I personally couldn't have been more relieved. It had been some months since I had last seen Ellie and wee Sandy, during which time I had come to appreciate how living far away from their families had been so painful for my earlier married colleagues. To make ends meet in the absence of any money from me, Ellie had returned to nursing – on permanent night duty, so that she could look after Sandy during the day. Somehow, she managed to find time to sleep as well, thanks in no small measure to my mother's help. Meanwhile, there had never been a single night in the Chandos Road house that I hadn't gone to sleep worrying about Ellie cycling five miles to her work along twisty country roads in the dark. And the knowledge that I wasn't contributing anything to support my wife and child tugged continually at my conscience.

We had made a couple of fleeting forays into Scotland before this one, and the two English boys in the band had really enjoyed the experience. Just as well, because the possibility of more engagements than we had been accustomed to 'down south', plus the fact that we no longer had access to freebie lodgings in London, meant we'd be basing ourselves up here for the immediate future. Which, we guessed, would be until the burgeoning craze for beat music had peaked and started to subside.

While I joined Ellie and Sandy in a room at my folks' place, Jim's mother Nancy Douglas opened her almost-identical house to the rest of the boys. Ah, the priceless gift of considerate, selfless parents! It must have been trying enough for mine to have a young married couple with a boisterous infant disturbing the well-earned serenity of their middle-age; but how Nancy Douglas managed to cope with having six extra bodies crammed into a three-bedroom house that she already shared with two of Jim's younger siblings, their granny and an old collie dog defies comprehension. Yet, quintessential earth mother that she was, Nancy not only *insisted* on 'fitting the laddies in until they got themselves sorted out', but managed to produce nourishing meals for them every day on the meagre pittance they were able to pay for 'bed and board'.

So, every mean act that had been experienced not so long ago was being offset many times over by the kindness and support of understanding families. It engendered the same one-for-all-and-all-for-one spirit in this band that had been enjoyed way back in the earliest days of the Hidden Town Dixielanders, when a bunch of lads had committed themselves to playing jazz just for the fun of it. Money had never been the prime motivator then, nor was it now. A welcome breath of fresh air after the covetous atmosphere that had blighted and eventually killed off the Clyde Valley Stompers.

Still, this was a full-time professional band, and enough money had to be generated to keep it that way. As had been the case in the early days of the Hidden Town Dixielanders, we needed a shop window in which to advertise our wares to potential customers. BBC Radio's *Come Thursday* programme went some way to providing that. So would two EPs to be released by the same record company that had issued the singles which triggered my resignation from the civil service by providing me with an opportunity to take my first band to Germany in December 1960. Bryce Laing, the principal of Waverley Records, had a lot to answer for – and I could never thank him enough.

On these EPs, entitled *Jazz at the Capital* (released 1963) and *More Jazz at the Capital* (1964), Bryce allowed us free rein to showcase the new band's strengths, both commercially and in a 'straight' jazz context unconstrained by category. Included were a couple of numbers, *The Ugly Duckling* and *Who's Afraid of the Big Bad Wolf?*, that had been intended as possible follow-ups to the Clydes' hit version of *Peter and the Wolf*, but, for reasons known only to the band's management, had never even been heard by producer George Martin. At the other end of the spectrum was a funky *Night Train*, and *Drum Break for Billy*, a hard-driving original concocted in the studio as a feature for the dazzling dexterity of Bill Law.

Slowly but surely the engagements started to come in, though usually far-scattered and not yet in sufficient numbers to earn us any more than a bare living wage. But it was a marked improvement on our previous plight. After a while, pianist Mike Oliver was confident enough about the situation to persuade his wife to give up her job in London and join him in a little flat he had found in Edinburgh; the rent for which, significantly, would be paid mainly from the salary his wife earned from a job she had swiftly found in Edinburgh! Around the same time, the other Mike, Ron, Eddie and Billy risked combining their resources to rent a couple of rooms in a terraced house just off Leith Walk in Edinburgh.

Once again, there would be space in the big-hearted Nancy Douglas's home to swing a cat, or at least the old collie dog. I owed her a debt I would never be able to repay – not that she expected or would have accepted recompense in any case.

The next parent to give us a leg up was Ron's father, Rognvald Mathewson Sr., Town Clerk of Lerwick, the capital of the Shetland Isles, Britain's most northerly outpost. As the head of one of the most talented musical families in a small and fairly remote community renowned for the plethora of fine musicians it produced, Mr Mathewson was justly proud of the reputation young Ron had already started to earn nationally, even if he wasn't yet earning much financially. So, using his municipal influence, he arranged for us to be the first jazz band ever to set foot in Shetland, thereby giving the local population a chance to see and hear just how much his own *peerie* boy had developed as a musician since moving *doon sooth*.

Ron didn't disappoint the Shetland folk, nor they us. Our week of appearances was actually limited to Lerwick, by far the most sizeable town in the archipelago, with a population then of about 6,000. The 'tour' consisted of playing for dancing in three venues, the Town Hall, Territorial Army Hall and the Planets Ballroom, night about. Packed houses (but only after the pubs closed), the Shetlanders' inherent love of music and natural inclination to let their hair down, plus their unstinting hospitality combined to make our stay a truly memorable one. That said, none of us remembered too much of our only night off, the Sunday, when a conglomerate of local musicians and prominent townsfolk entertained us to a party. This took place in the Planets Ballroom, and we soon realised why the building's original use as headquarters of the Shetland Temperance Society had long since been abandoned. Inevitably, the evening's jollifications degenerated into a mass jam session, with 'traditional' fiddlers, accordionists and even a couple of pipers grooving along with us jazzers. My last recollection is of trombonist Eddie Lorkin taking a nosedive off the stage in mid-chorus, to be grabbed by local pharmacist-cum-pianist 'Spew' Campbell just before the end of his trombone slide hit the floor. For once, a spew was responsible for a set of teeth being *saved*.

By rights, our departure for Aberdeen on the ferry St Clair early the following morning should have been accompanied by self-inflicted miseries, but the looming clouds of our hangovers were quickly dispersed by a crowd of new-won friends who had assembled on the quayside to see us off. At their insistence, we set ourselves up on the top deck and played the ship out of port, feeling as much like musicians on the Mississippi paddle steamers of old as we were ever likely to. If only the Shetland Isles had been populous enough to support just one professional jazz band, I'm sure we would happily have stayed. However, harsh realities awaited us on the mainland, and they had to be faced.

* * * * *

CHAPTER FORTY

'BYE BYE BLUES'

There's an old Scots saying that 'you can't take the breeks off a Highlandman', and although we had persevered for the best part of a year to find sufficient work in Scotland to provide us with a reasonable living, the fact of the matter was that the work just didn't exist. What little there once was had been steadily lost to what Bert Murray, our grumpy pianist in the Clydes, had dismissed after a gig in Liverpool's Cavern Club as guitar-toting, here-today-gone-tomorrow 'electric skiffle groups'. It was two of those, in their own distinctive styles and under totally different circumstances, that finally forced us to admit that the horse we'd been trying to flog hadn't just paused to draw breath, but had actually breathed its last.

Mid-February 1964 found us booked to play in The Place, an Edinburgh club run by Paul and Brian Waldman, brothers from London who had pioneered the establishment of night spots in the Scottish capital catering for an increasingly liberated younger generation. The teenagers of Edinburgh, like their counterparts everywhere, knew what they wanted in the way of live entertainment, and shrewd entrepreneurs like the Waldmans were only too pleased to provide it. The Place, originally a tea warehouse, or rather a warren of upstairs-downstairs storerooms, was a bit like a double-decker Cavern Club, being cramped, dimly-lit and steamy – just the way the young folk of the early Sixties liked it.

We had played The Place before, but always sharing the bill with another jazz band. This time, though, the group appearing opposite us turned out to be the guitar-thrashing Alex Harvey Soul Band, fronted by a singer who had once won a competition to find Scotland's Tommy Steele. What a mismatch! If Tommy was pop music's typical boy next door, Alex struck you as a neighbour from hell who would beat you up sooner than say good morning. It was all part of his stage persona, of course: loud, menacing and rebellious, with the accent on *LOUD*! He exuded an energy that had certainly sprouted from roots planted by 'old-time' American blues shouters, but had been developed into the raw, aggressive style for which British R&B artists were already establishing a demand. The Alex Harvey Soul Band were the first blues rockers I had encountered, and the reaction of the kids in The Place that night left me in no doubt that they symbolised a new force capable of leaving other pedlars of popular music, including jazz bands, floundering in its wake.

A week or so later, the boys and I were sitting one afternoon in the Waterloo Bar just beyond the east end of Edinburgh's Princes Street. We had been using the first-floor function room to rehearse in for some time, and were in the habit of retiring to the bar afterwards to discuss upcoming dates. There were precious few to discuss on this occasion, but that hadn't diminished anyone's commitment to building a future for the band, recent reality check at The Place notwithstanding. Then the national news came on the TV set perched on a shelf behind the bar.

The headline item showed the Beatles' arrival a fortnight earlier at New York's John F. Kennedy Airport for the start of their first US tour. There were long-shots and close-ups of the four thousand screaming fans who had been there to greet them, before the camera panned to a motorcade of four limos (one for each Beatle) heading for the city centre.

'No sign of their wee Ford Thames van now,' said Jim, dryly.

He was referring back to the decidedly miserable image of the four mop-heads we had witnessed in the car park of Teddington TV studios after recording *Thank Your Lucky Stars* in Billy Fury's shadow almost exactly a year earlier. Their fortunes and ours had taken diametrically opposite routes since then. But if the start of the present newsreel footage had opened a wound, salt was about to be rubbed in.

The TV newscast cut to the present, to London's Heathrow Airport, where the Beatles had just landed following their all-conquering invasion of the USA. According to the commentary, the number of hysterical British fans waiting for them here exceeded *ten* thousand.

'This is phenomenal,' the reporter gasped as the Fab Four descended the plane's steps, 'quite unprecedented. No wonder they're saying in America that the Beatles are bigger than anything that's happened in the history of popular music. Bigger than Crosby, bigger than Sinatra, bigger than Elvis. The Beatles' John Lennon goes further – claiming the Fab Four are even bigger than Jesus Christ!'

We sat gaping at the TV screen, slack-jawed and utterly bamboozled.

'Why *them*?' said pianist Mike.

'Fuck knows,' said Eddie.

'Could've happened to anybody,' said Billy. 'Like chickenpox.'

'Take me to a chicken,' said the other Mike.

'It's the end of the world,' said Ron.

'As we know it,' said Jim. 'Yeah, as we know it, daddy.'

I didn't say anything. The boys had said it all.

The world didn't end, of course, but a large part of mine did when I finally said goodbye to the boys for the last time. Although there was no dramatic parting scene (the only emotion jazz musicians show is when they're playing), I knew the boys were as sorry as I was about having to call it a day. We had been through a lot in those twelve months together, and had survived even the most difficult times without losing belief in what we were trying to achieve. My grandmother's old maxim of 'sticking in and doing your best' had been followed by us all, so we had no reason to feel guilty about yielding to unforeseen and, as it transpired, insurmountable odds. Hard work and dedication had paid rich dividends in the way the band sounded. And we'd had fun. We'd spent a happy year together, without earning much money, but also without anyone entertaining a thought of quitting. In that there was a moral I would never forget.

*

Ellie and I were looking out over the rolling East Lothian fields one spring morning a few weeks later. We were standing outside a little cottage we had been lucky enough to rent, thanks to my father, who for many years now had been employed as sales rep for an oil company supplying fuel to the local farming and fishing communities. He had brokered a deal on our behalf with the farmer who owned this particular cottage, its condition reflecting the rent agreed, which in turn reflected my parlous financial state.

Dad, supportive as ever, had managed to wangle me a temporary job driving one of his employer's little delivery tankers, until (echoing Nancy Douglas's words of some months earlier) 'I managed to get myself sorted out'. Actually, I was as happy as could be driving that truck from farm to farm along the pretty country lanes, but the pressure was on me to find a *proper* career that would provide a secure future for Ellie and our son.

For the present, though, this cottage needed loads of tender love and care to make it fit for purpose. With all my life's savings 'invested' in the band long ago, there would be nothing else for it now but to get stuck in and do the work myself – with a little help from Ellie, naturally!

'It's going to be a pleasant change having a place of our own again,' she said. 'Hmm, and it's nice having you home every night too. I mean, it was like being married to a sailor, these past two years or so.'

I chuckled quietly to myself, thinking about what she'd said. 'But at least I avoided the clap and cirrhosis of the liver.'

'I *beg* your pardon!'

'Oh, it's a long story. Yeah, I could write a book about it, believe me.'

Ellie thought about *that* for a moment. 'Maybe you should.'

'Nah, too off-the-wall. Nobody would read it.'

'*I* would – if it had a happy ending.'

I allowed my eyes to wander over the countryside surrounding us. 'I've a hunch it would,' I nodded. 'In fact, I *know* it would.'

Ellie gave a little giggle.

Pretending I hadn't noticed, I put an arm round her shoulder and turned towards the cottage door. 'Come on – there's stripping to do – wallpaper, that is.'

'I'm game,' she chirped, 'if the wallpaper is.'

'I like your attitude,' I grinned. 'You'll go far.'

It was the rolling of Ellie's eyes I pretended not to notice this time.

'I don't doubt it,' she said, smiling sweetly, 'but not for a *long* time … I hope!'

THE END

AFTERWORD

What became of the members of Pete Kerr's All-Stars after going their separate ways in 1964?

Mike Oliver (piano) returned to London and continued playing jazz, mainly as a soloist but also in small groups, often with a 'modernist' slant.

Mike Scott (trumpet) went back home to Devon, forming a dance band, which soon built a loyal following for its innovative mix of pop and jazz.

Eddie Lorkin (trombone) joined the legendary BBC Big Band in London, remaining a key member of its brass section throughout his long career. The list of world-famous names he played for and accompanied goes on forever, but prominent among them are Ray Charles, Tony Bennet, Mel Torme, Manhatten Transfer, Buddy Greco, Billy May, Robert Farnon and Les Brown.

Billy Law (drums) freelanced briefly in London, then joined the Terry Lightfoot Band. A few months later in 1964 he was drafted into the ranks of R&B star Long John Baldry's Hoochie Coochie Men. Other members of the Baldry crew were up-and-coming singer Rod Stewart and keyboard player

Reg Dwight, one day to metamorphose as Elton John. Billy then had a spell with, ironically, the Alex Harvey Soul Band, and remained active on the London scene throughout the decade, before returning to Edinburgh to concentrate on session and theatre work.

Ron Mathewson (bass) was soon snapped up by Alex Welsh, London-based leader of what was universally regarded as the best Dixieland band outside America. Alex was also a shrewd judge of instrumental talent! Ron's technical prowess would eventually attract the attention of the top exponents of modern jazz in Britain, and in 1966 he began a long association with tenor sax whizz-kid Tubby Hayes. This led to an even longer alliance with another tenor ace, Ronnie Scott, host of London's eponymous modern jazz mecca. Ron's reputation as a bass-playing phenomenon resulted in his performing with many of the foremost 'modernists' on both sides of the Atlantic, including Oscar Peterson, Stan Getz, Ben Webster, Ray Nance and Kenny Clarke. As a mark of his adaptability, he even played in a big band led by none other than Rolling Stones drummer Charlie Watts!

Jim Douglas (guitar/banjo) was, like Ron Mathewson, swiftly recruited by Alex Welsh. Ever the loyal team man, Jim remained in the Welsh band for eighteen years, during which time he won awards, appeared at the celebrated Newport Jazz Festival in America, and toured Britain with such all-time jazz greats as Earl 'Fatha' Hines, Wild Bill Davison, Henry 'Red' Allen, Ruby Braff, Bud Freeman and Peanuts Hucko. In later years, his reputation made him an automatic choice for the rhythm sections of even more legends visiting Europe from across the pond: Yank Lawson, Bob Haggart, Vic Dickenson, Nick Fatool and Matty Matlock, to name but a few. However, as a devotee of Django Reinhardt, the incomparable maestro of jazz guitar, Jim had no greater thrill than to play alongside the late Django's one-time partner, virtuoso swing fiddler Stephane Grappelli. Jim has written of his extraordinary career in a book called *Tunes, Tours and Travelitis*. He came a long way from Long Yester!

Peter 'Pete' Kerr (clarinet) accepted an invitation, shortly after his All-Stars disbanded, to help with record production at the Edinburgh studios of Waverley Records, the company that had helped launch his career as a professional jazz musician. Eventually working as a freelance for major UK and American labels, he would go on to produce upwards of two hundred albums, mainly featuring international Scottish stars like Andy Stewart and Jimmy Shand, but including three memorable jazz LPs by the Alex Welsh Band. From 1970, he managed to combine his recording work with running his own 50-acre farm in East Lothian. He hit the jackpot in 1972 when he produced *Amazing Grace* with the Royal Scots Dragoon Guards, a worldwide hit which sold some thirteen million records to become the biggest-selling instrumental single ever. When the recession of the early Eighties hit, Peter threw in the towel as a farmer of beef and barley and moved his family to the Spanish island of Mallorca to try his hand at growing oranges for a living – something he knew absolutely nothing about! This ultimately led to his writing humorous accounts of their adventures (and misadventures!) in the *Snowball Oranges* series of best-selling books which have been translated into twelve languages to date. *Thistle Soup*, a set-in-Scotland prequel, tells of his life from boyhood in East Lothian, and serves as a companion book to his latest, *Don't Call Me Clyde!* With several fiction books also to his credit, Peter has been a full-time author since 2000 and regularly appears at book festivals throughout Britain and beyond.

Visit Peter's website: www.peter-kerr.co.uk.

* * * * *

If you enjoyed this book, you may be interested in its
companion title:

'THISTLE SOUP'

by

- PETER KERR -

(Paperback ISBN 978-0-9573062-2-6)

(Kindle E-book ISBN 978-0-9574963-0-9)

"Funny and emotional ... touching and highly enjoyable."
(Goodreads.com)

"Beautifully written, gently humorous ... a real gem
of a book."
(Amazon.uk)

"Kerr draws the reader into his vivid and fondly
remembered past."
(Library Journal USA)

www.peter-kerr.co.uk